ALBERT "PRODIGY" JOHNSON

with Laura Checkoway

A TOUCHSTONE BOOK
PUBLISHED BY SIMON & SCHUSTER
NEW YORK   LONDON   TORONTO   SYDNEY   NEW DELHI

MY
INFAMOUS
LIFE

THE AUTOBIOGRAPHY OF
MOBB DEEP'S PRODIGY

Touchstone
An Imprint of Simon & Schuster, Inc.
1230 Avenue of the Americas
New York, NY 10020

First Touchstone trade paperback edition February 2012

TOUCHSTONE and colophon are registered trademarks of Simon & Schuster, Inc.

For information about special discounts for bulk purchases,
please contact Simon & Schuster Special Sales at 1-866-506-1949
or business@simonandschuster.com.

The Simon & Schuster Speakers Bureau can bring authors to your live event.
For more information or to book an event contact the Simon & Schuster Speakers Bureau
at 1-866-248-3049 or visit our website at www.simonspeakers.com.

Designed by Ruth Lee-Mui

Manufactured in the United States of America

20 19 18 17 16 15 14 13 12 11

The Library of Congress has cataloged the hardcover edition as follows:

Prodigy (Musician)
    My infamous life : the autobiography of Mobb Deep's Prodigy / Albert "Prodigy" Johnson
with Laura Checkoway.
        p. cm.
1. Prodigy (Musician) 2. Rap musicians—United States—Biography. 3. Mobb Deep (Musical
group) I. Checkoway, Laura. II. Title.
    ML420.P97527A3 2011
    782.421649092—dc22
    [B]

2010044439

ISBN 978-1-4391-0318-0
ISBN 978-1-4391-0319-7 (pbk)
ISBN 978-1-4391-4933-1 (ebook)

I dedicate this book
to my entire family tree.
KiKi, Kiejzonna,
T'Shaka, and Fahtasia,
I love you.

CONTENTS

June 28, 2008
Mid-State Correctional Facility
Marcy, New York
2:30 P.M.

Sitting alone at my table in the visiting room, I had to wait until three P.M. when visiting hours were over before I could go back to my dorm. I wished I could have gotten up and walked out of the prison with Alchemist when he left. But I had more than two years to spend in that eight-by-ten box before I would be a free man again. This was the second time my friend and producer Alchemist had taken the four-hour ride up from Manhattan to visit me. He looked good. Healthy and focused. The visiting room was packed, around sixty other inmates, their families and friends. During our visit, a few inmates shouted, "Mobb Deep!" "What up Alchemist!" "What up Prodigy!" I told Al how the inmates and correctional officers had been showing me love and asking for autographs. But after Al left I sat there observing everyone around me, and I was reminded that I was just another inmate like anybody else. DIN #08A1481. My Department Identification Number represents the year I got locked up, '08; the facility code A for Downstate, the prison I was initially in; and then 1,481 indicates that I was the 1,481st inmate to get locked up in that prison that year. We were all the same while stuck inside.

Even though I didn't want to be in this prison, I deserved to be here. I would hear inmates complain and bitch all day and night about how uncomfortable they were, how unfair the officers and rules were, and how stressful being locked up was. *Stop crying and do ya time,* I'd say to myself. I've done plenty of damage in my days. I've done some wicked, evil, terrible things to people in my past. *Shiiiit* . . . the three and a half years I got was just a slap on the wrist when I think back on all the things I've gotten away with. So I just accepted my circumstances and made the best out of it, putting my time to good use.

Prison has given me time to reflect, look deep inside, realize where I've been, where I am, and where I'm going. I used to be cold and emotionless. I believe the disease I was born with, sickle-cell anemia, made me that way. Factor in my environment and the people I surrounded myself with, and yeah, you got the makings of a sinful person. I'm different now, only 'cause I choose to be. I know now that good is the correct way to be. I'd been straddling the fence for a number of years, thinking it was okay to do a little bit of evil if I was doing a lot of good. But life doesn't work like that. You have to choose a side. My mind, body, and soul are in excellent condition now. I've never felt so invigorated.

I've been in the music industry since I was sixteen years old, touring the world, selling millions of albums—groupies, drugs, alcohol, sex, radio, TV, magazines, videos, money, jewelry, cars, fashion, rap verses, beats, and studios at my disposal nonstop for seventeen years straight. Nonstop. Seventeen years. Do the math. I came to prison when I turned thirty-three. The truth is, I never took the time to stop and mature mentally until now, to step outside my little fast-paced world and see what needed to be adjusted. It's like I was suspended in time. Like I was sixteen years old for seventeen years. I never grew up. Do you follow what I'm saying? I am a man now. My hardheaded ass took the long rocky road to get to this point, but at least I've finally made it.

CHAPTER 1

GENESIS

Here's a brief family history, because these are the pieces of my puzzle that are the most important.

Both of my grandparents on my pops's side were half black, half Cherokee Indian from the dirty South—Grandpops from Dallas, Texas, and Grandmoms from Richmond, Virginia. Budd and Bernice Johnson were big-time in their day. Grandmoms, who had the rare combination of dark brown skin and very soft, straight hair, was one of the first Cotton Club dancers at the world-famous nightclub in Harlem. Singer-actress Lena Horne, who also danced at the Cotton Club before her rise to fame, was one of her close friends coming up. In order to be a black person inside that club, your complexion had to be lighter than a brown paper bag or you had to be part of the entertainment or the help, and that's where my grandparents met

My grandmother told me that my grandfather, who played in the club's band every night, wanted her to stop dancing there, but I don't think she stopped until she was ready.

Grandpops was a world-famous jazz musician, now in the Big Band and Jazz Hall of Fame, who played the saxophone and clarinet and was friends with the major jazz players of that time. Billy Eckstine, Dizzy Gillespie, Gary Bartz, and Frank Foster would come over to the crib to chill.

My grandfather wrote his own sheet music and released many albums. He helped teach Quincy Jones to read and write music and toured the world as a member of one of Quincy's first big bands. On weekends as a kid, late at night, Grandpops—or Big Budd, as they called him—would sit me on his lap and try to teach me all these funny-looking music notes while he puffed away on his tobacco pipe. It was a foreign language, and I was too young.

Soon after the Cotton Club gig, Grandmoms opened her own dance school in Jamaica, Queens—the Bernice Johnson Dance School. She started the business in the basement of her house with only a handful of students but it grew so big that she became the first black woman to own a building on Merrick Boulevard and dubbed herself the H.N.I.C., Head Nigga In Charge. In the seventies and eighties, movies like *Saturday Night Fever, Fame, Flashdance, Beat Street*, and *Footloose*, plus the Michael Jackson, breakdancing, and rap-music craze, made people really want to dance. Her school was a huge success.

But don't let the good fortune, showbiz, and spotlights fool you: My grandparents and parents came up during the 1940s, '50s, and '60s during major segregation, racism, lynching, and pure hatred for black people. When they gave birth to my father, Budd Johnson Jr., they were very well-off moneywise, so growing up my pops was known as the rich kid in South Jamaica. He got into a lot of fights to prove himself in the streets, extra-wild shit to show people he wasn't no punk.

This was my pops's side of the family—Moms's side was different.

On Moms's side, my great-great-great-grandpops William Jefferson White and great-great-great-grandmoms Josephine White were 5 percent black and 95 percent Irish. Her entire side of the family could pass for Caucasian.

Great-great-great Grandpops wasn't a joke. He was a minister who founded and built Morehouse College in the basement of his Baptist church in Augusta, Georgia, in 1867. When I found that out, I had to pick my jaw up from the floor. So many famous black men graduated from Morehouse, including Dr. Martin Luther King Jr., Samuel L. Jackson, and Spike Lee.

William's grandson, my great-grandfather William J. Shaw, was secretary of the Republican Central Committee of Georgia from 1926 to 1961, the only black member to hold a political position in Georgia at that time. In 1950, he established the first post office for blacks in Atlanta. Black people had to travel outside of Atlanta for postal service before that.

Finding out about my family tree blew my mind. At first, I was disgusted that I had white blood in me. All I could think about was some white slave master raping my black ancestors. But then I learned to accept it.

My father, Budd Johnson Jr., was born September 14, 1942, and raised in my grandparents' Jamaica, Queens, house right behind Guy Brewer Boulevard. My moms, Fatima Frances Johnson, was born July 29, 1944, and raised in Harlem until age six, when her family moved to South Jamaica projects right next to my pops. Her mother's name was Bernie Johnson, similar to my pops's mother, Bernice Johnson.

Moms and Pops met at Grandmoms's dance school. Pops was eleven and he loved playing the drums. My moms was nine, a girl with a sweet heart who loved to sing and dance. She took every class there was.

Their puppy love was short-lived. Pops thought he was a player, and Moms left him when she found out that he had a handful of girlfriends. At fifteen, Pops was in a doo-wop group called the Chanters. They had a couple of lukewarm records. Moms's music career, on the other hand, must have had Pops wishing he never messed up with her.

In 1962, six years after my pops's short run in the music biz, Moms was asked to join a group called the Crystals. Moms was a dime—a nineteen-year-old light-skinned sista with hazel-green eyes who happened to be in the right place at the right time. She had a young son, my older brother, Greg (we have different fathers), and she left him with family so she could hit the road.

Moms was big-time. The Crystals had a bunch of hit records, including "He's a Rebel," "Da Doo Ron Ron," "Then He Kissed Me," "Uptown," and "There's No Other Like My Baby." They went on world tours with Diana Ross and the Supremes, Dick Clark, and the like. At one point she was engaged to Charlie Thomas from the Drifters, but that didn't last. That was just some on-the-road-too-long-and-feeling-lonely thing.

After being on tour for three years straight, Moms and Pops got back together soon after she came back to New York. I guess he really loved her, but he was a wild boy. I know that she loved him. They finally stopped bullshittin' and got married.

I was born on November 2, 1974, at approximately nine thirty-two P.M. at Nassau Medical Center in Hempstead, Long Island. By the time I popped out, Hempstead had become almost all black because of what was called white flight. That means black people started buying property in white neighborhoods and the whites moved out. My grandmother owned two houses at the time, one in Hempstead and another in Lakeview, the next town over. Moms, Pops, my brother Greg, and I moved into my grandmoms's crib in Lakeview.

At less than one year old, I was admitted to the hospital for the first time. Bright lights; doctors poking, stabbing, pushing, and pulling all over my pain. My mother. My father. Relatives' faces bending down, looking at me. Wires connected to my arm with bags of fluid dripping through them. All these foggy memories—I guess the trauma I went through forced me to remember.

I wanted to crawl back into my mother's stomach the same way I came out, back to the warm, dark place where I was safe. *Who said I wanted to come out anyway? I was fine where I was.* But the witch and wizard doctors cut my mother open and pulled me out like they were conducting some twisted ritual that forced me to take part in this crazy world. There was nothing I could do but be confused and wait.

I was diagnosed with sickle-cell anemia SS type, the worst form of sickle-cell, a painful hereditary blood disorder that affects mostly blacks and

Latinos. There was very limited info about sickle-cell when my parents were planning to have a child, so they were just as confused as me.

When I got out of the hospital, my parents brought me to Grand-moms's dance studio in Jamaica, Queens. I went from being a science experiment screaming in a cold dark hospital alone to laughing while doing the baby bounce to the sound of African drums, stomping feet, girls joltin' and gyratin' their bodies to the beat with hundreds of smiling black faces surrounding me. My father was a master African drummer and my mother was a dancer. I'd sit in my stroller on the sidelines or someone would hold me in their lap for a better view, bopping my head to the beat so intensely that my father called me Bop Head.

Extreme pain to extreme pleasure has been the story of my entire life. That tremendous joy then pain then joy then pain again turned me into one moody li'l muthafucker.

My grandmother's dance business was making a lot of money and she enrolled me in a private preschool at age four. During winter, waiting for the school bus in the morning, my ankles would start to ache. I hated cold winter mornings. A sickle-cell attack would creep up slowly in my ankles, legs, arms, back, stomach, and chest. Sometimes my lips and tongue turned numb and I knew I was going into a crisis. Crazy, right?

When the bus came, I would walk slowly to avoid the pain bum-rushing my whole body while the other kids stared through the bus windows wondering if I was crazy or retarded. But I learned to stay calm and not be embarrassed. *I'd rather move slow and look crazy than take a trip to the emergency room.* If I moved my body parts fast, it would agitate my sickled cells and cause my pain to increase, but if I moved slowly and was lucky enough, the pain would remain minimal and sometimes go away.

One chilly autumn morning, after walking extra slowly to the bus because the pain was sneaking up, I sat in a seat where the sun was beaming hot. The sun shined in that spot the entire ride. I sat very still without moving a muscle. Fifteen minutes later, I got off the bus and the pain was gone. I learned a new trick! The sun's heat actually killed the sickled cells. So every cold morning, I sat in the sun, and I cursed Mother Nature on cloudy, rainy days.

I was a very serious child who never got to enjoy life to the fullest like a normal, healthy kid because of my sickle-cell. All my boys were into sports and physical fitness. But as bad as I wanted to, I couldn't join in because overworking my body would trigger my pain. Sometimes I'd wake up with severe pain in my stomach and back, a constant throbbing like my bones were broken. Pain and I got real close in those early years. Ever since I was born, I was in the hospital at least four to six times a year with sickle-cell. *Every year.* Sometimes for a week, sometimes up to a month.

There's no conventional medical cure for sickle-cell. The only treatment was high doses of strong pain medication like Tylenol with codeine as a child and Demerol or morphine as I got older, the stuff they give soldiers when their limbs are blown off in war. Hospitals only allow doses every four hours, but I had a high tolerance for the medication because my pain was greater than most people's. After an hour, I was screaming again.

As a child, I'd be in the emergency room screaming and squirming on the stretcher like I was about to die. Some evil nurses and doctors would try to shut me up. When they couldn't, they called security, wheeled me into a back room, and closed the door to muffle my screams. Finally the meds would settle me down. My family would rub the painful spots, trying to soothe me. But after visiting hours were over, it was just me and my comrade pain.

I saw a lot of death and disease in those hospitals. I shared rooms with white kids with leukemia whose parents bought them everything they could wish for because they were on their deathbeds, and it had a profound effect on my mentality. It turned me into a very no-nonsense little kid.

As I got older, people always asked, "Are you tired? What's wrong with you? You look angry. Why are you so quiet? Are you upset?" I always hated that. *No,* I'm not tired! *No,* I'm not angry! (Well, maybe a little angry.) I'm just not a happy-go-lucky muthafucker. I'm a serious dude because I grew up with a lot of pain, death, and madness. It's rare for me to be smiling, in a good mood.

At age four, I got into a fight with a white kid in the schoolyard for calling me a name I can't remember. I hopped off the swings and threw a toy teapot at him and missed. He threw it back and I tried ducking by bending over to the front, but I ended up using the top of my forehead as a bat for his wild pitch. *Bing!* A big cartoon lump rose on my forehead. Head bleeding, I saw the scared look on the white boy's face. He didn't mean to hit me in the head.

The teacher called my father. After I told Pops the story in the car, he told me to stop crying. "Don't ever duck down if somebody throws something at you," he said. Pops was also a karate sensei, a natural-born fighter, and had his own karate school for a few years before I was born. "Just move to the side."

After my forehead lump went down, Pops started teaching me karate moves. He enrolled me in a karate class on Jamaica Avenue and 169th Street. My mother didn't like it because of the full-body contact, though contact didn't come until second- and third-degree white belt. My sensei had me cleaning the wood floor with a wet rag while barefoot in my uniform. This was for balance and stamina like in the movie *Karate Kid*—strength training. After two months, I got frustrated because I wasn't learning to fight yet. I caught a sickle-cell crisis from that cold wet floor, and Moms said my karate lessons were over. Pops was pissed. "You're turning him into a punk!" he barked.

Chest pain overwhelmed me and I was admitted to Jamaica Hospital, definitely not the best hospital in Queens. My mother's friend Dr. Francis worked there, a black female sickle-cell specialist. After Dr. Francis got us in, the doctors informed my mother that I had acute chest syndrome, the sickle-cell form of pneumonia.

On that visit, I learned to make my presence felt in the emergency room. The squeaky wheel got the oil. My parents had been trying to coach me on how to conduct myself, but I didn't catch on. *Make noise!* Hospital ERs didn't give a good goddamn about people with sickle-cell. By the time I hit my teens, going to the ER was like going to war.

A sickle-cell crisis gets gradually worse as time passes. Normal red blood cells are small round circles that resemble a round piece of candy like a Certs mint or a Lifesaver without the hole in the middle. When going into a sickle-cell crisis, normal round red blood cells change to a crescent or sickle shape. Those sickle-shaped blood cells create a domino effect, interlocking throughout the body, creating clotting and blocking oxygen from flowing through the bloodstream. Loss of oxygen combined with loss of blood flow creates tremendous pain, risk of stroke, bone damage, and other life-threatening consequences. It also causes the immune system to weaken and makes it easy to get infections.

Acute chest syndrome was no joke for a four-year-old, and they put me in a big plastic bubble in the intensive-care unit. My mother worked during the day, so my grandmother stayed all day and Moms came at night. One afternoon when Grandmoms came to see me, I was sleeping hard for a few hours, and when she tried waking me I wouldn't open my eyes. She called the doctors to check on me and they said I was just sleeping. She called their superiors, and they said the same.

But my grandmother, a Southern, strong-willed female from the old school, knew better. She told them that the next person she'd call was her lawyer if they didn't wake me up immediately. They went into a frenzy, finding that all my vital signs were deadly low and I was slipping in and out of a coma. Grandmoms saved my life.

Moms and Grandmoms had a meeting with Dr. Francis to get me out of Jamaica Hospital. Dr. Francis had her own sickle-cell clinic in a house on Farmers Boulevard in Jamaica where I hated going because it meant I was getting a penicillin shot in my butt, one of her remedies for sickle-cell. She told Moms and Grandmoms that Long Island Jewish Hospital was more prestigious than Jamaica Hospital, so I was transferred there for at least a month.

The pediatrics unit at Long Island Jewish Hospital had air hockey, foosball, toys, and movies. Jamaica Hospital didn't have a single game or activity. As soon as I felt well enough, I'd drag my IV pole down the hallway to the playroom. I was in sick-kid heaven. The food was like home cooking. They had name-brand cereals—Corn Pops, Sugar Smacks, and Frosted Flakes. But no matter how much good stuff they had, it was still just a nasty hospital with people dying and infectious disease all around.

When I got out the following month, it was back to the cold mornings, walking slowly to the school bus. I started getting used to this routine, landing in the hospital at least six times between ages four and five.

My parents realized I had another serious problem around that age. Pissing in the bed. Most men, let alone rappers, wouldn't dare admit this, but a side effect from drinking tons of water to keep my blood hydrated was waking up with a flood in my bed.

"Why didn't you just get up and use the bathroom?" my pops used to yell. I tried to explain that I was sleeping when it happened, so how could I get up? Pops wasn't trying to hear it. He'd whip my ass with the belt, thinking I was just scared of the dark and didn't want to walk to the bathroom at night.

Grandmoms bought this crazy gadget that's supposed to put an end to bedwetting—a pair of padded underpants with a sensor in the crotch attached to a wire that attached to my pointer finger, powered by a nine-volt battery. As soon as you started pissing, the sensor made the finger attachment vibrate to wake you up: basically a pair of high-tech diapers. I felt like an idiot, but it was worth a try.

The first night I slept through the vibrating and woke up with the usual flood in my bed, my finger still vibrating when I woke up. We tried a few more nights to no avail. The gadget went into the garbage.

In 1980, when I was six, my grandmoms paid for me to go to Woodmere Academy, a private elementary school five minutes from West Hempstead in a town called Malverne. The school was 99 percent white. The only other black kids were my friend Darren and his sister Michele. Darren smelled like he stepped in shit all the time. It had to be his breath.

I never had any racial problems at Woodmere except one day in the locker room after gym class. A kid named Max had forty dollars stolen from his locker and tried to blame me. Max was the first person I'd ever seen with his own credit card. Most people I knew had never even heard of credit cards, but this seven-year-old kid in my school had one. It was American Express.

"Did you take my money?" Max looked in my direction.

"No!" Max and I had a body-blow fight in the locker room, punching each other in the stomach, ribs, and chest, and the teachers broke it up. He found his money later and apologized. Why would he accuse me? The only reason I could think of was because I was black. The white kids were cool, though, and a few of the girls had crushes on me.

In my first-grade class there was a pretty white girl named Michelle with long brownish-blond hair. After graham crackers and apple juice during snack time one day, the whole class went outside for recess. Michelle and I were the last two to leave the classroom. She told me she liked me and put her leg around my waist and placed my hand on her ass. I was a scared punk. My mind wasn't as advanced yet because I was absent from school so often and didn't hang out in Lakeview Park like the other kids my age due to my sickle-cell. Being hospitalized for weeks and months caused me to miss out on the birds-and-the-bees activities.

I wasn't ready for Michelle's advances, but she was all over me. I think it had a lot to do with my grandmother's car. Sometimes Grandmoms would drop me off at school in her brand-spankin'-new black Cadillac with a burgundy pinstripe on the side and burgundy leather seats. "Those white kids' parents drop them off in Mercedes-Benzes and Rolls-Royces, so we gotta show them that your family has money too," she said. Michelle saw me getting out of the car one morning and stared, starry-eyed.

Grandmoms knew how to make a grand entrance. She lived, breathed, ate, slept, and shit show business. The world was her stage, and I learned a lot from her flashy actions. She would tell me about how she came from Southside Jamaica to become the first black woman with her own building on Merrick Boulevard; then hers was the first black family in Hempstead, Long Island, to build their own house. "T'Chaka, you have to own your home," she said firmly, using my family's nickname for me, after the Zulu king. "Black people must own their things." She bought her cars with cash, brand-new out of the showroom. "You should see the look on those white people's faces when they ask me how do I plan to pay. I say, 'Cash,' pull out a bagful of money, and they start treating me very differently."

"Never put all of your money in one bank," Grandmoms said, showing me bank-deposit booklets, each from a different bank and adding up to a couple million dollars. She taught me not to touch my money once I had millions like she did. "Do you see all this money I have in these little books? I get thousands of dollars in interest payments every month," she explained. "I can either deposit the interest and increase my accounts every month, or I can live off the interest and use it to pay my bills. But I'll never go broke." Grandmoms was very rich at that time; she wasn't supporting my mother and father finan- cially. We were struggling to survive, but she did make sure her only grandson, me, was well educated.

At Woodmere Academy, I got the best education that part of Long Island had to offer. On the bus ride after school, I was the last one dropped off, so I'd stare at the spacious mansions that the white kids went home to, watching the neighborhood become worse and worse the closer we got to my house. And I'd go home to Lakeview, back to all the blackness.

I learned a couple of things at that school. I found out white girls were real aggressive when they liked you, and little white boys had credit cards.

On weekends at my grandparents' house in Hempstead, my grandfather Big Budd worked on sheet music in his room while watching baseball on his small TV. The walls of his room were covered with posters from his tours in Russia, Japan, and all over the world. Besides baseball and jazz, Grandpops had a passion for golf. He bought me a mini plastic Playskool golf set and tried teaching me on the lawn. He also bought me a small saxophone and signed me up for the Woodmere Academy band. But as hard as Grandpops and I tried, I couldn't even handle "Mary Had a Little Lamb."

That year, my whole family came to see me play at a band concert in the school auditorium. There were five saxophonists onstage including myself. "You were so good!" my folks encouraged me after the show. "You sounded great!" *If they only knew I was only pretending to play*, I thought, keeping it to myself. *My horn wasn't blowing a damn thing.* But I played it off because my grandfather was proud.

My two best friends were Carey, who lived on the same corner as my grandmother's Hempstead house, and Stobo, who was like a brother. We were two months apart in age and had known each other since birth. We called each other cousins, even cut our hands and rubbed our palms together to become blood brothers. When Carey and Stobo slept over, Grandpops always came home drunk from his shows and took out his false teeth, smiling and chasing us around the house. It was a scary sight for a kid. Grandmoms would get pissed at him for being so drunk and loud. "Go to hell, you jack- ass!" she'd yell after him as we scampered by.

My father took me to see my grandfather perform at the Blue Note in Manhattan. I was the only little kid in the bar, but it was nothing new because Pops was a heavy drinker and liked taking me along. As always, I ordered my favorite drink, 7UP with cherry syrup and a couple of cherries on the rocks. And my pops would order his, peach schnapps. People would stare as if to say, "How you got this little kid in a bar?" But nobody messed with my pops.

Grandpops played the sax like a madman and the Blue Note crowd loved it. After Grandpops's shows or Grandmoms's dance concerts, our tradition was to eat a big meal at a swanky restaurant and for me to order the same dish: lobster tails. It was usually the most expensive thing on the menu and I never actually ate it, just dipped my bread in the butter. But Grandmoms got a kick out of me ordering it.

My grandparents usually brought one of their famous friends to dine with us, like Ben Vereen, the dancer-actor from the movie *Roots*. He was Grandmoms's student when he was a kid. Or Grandpops would bring Dizzy Gillespie and other jazz friends, and they all enjoyed watching the look on the white waiter's face when I ordered first and chose the lobster tail with melted butter. My grandparents were from an era of vicious racism and poverty, so my grandmother especially loved to show off and let white people know she had money.

One dreary winter evening, my mother, father, and I were at home watching *Buck Rogers* on TV when we got a call from the Nassau County emergency room. Grandmoms had been hit by a car while crossing Hempstead Turnpike leaving the A&S department store. A hit-and-run! We rushed to the hospital. The doctor said that she was paralyzed from the waist down and would never walk again. Ms. Bernice Johnson, the Queen of Dance, paralyzed?

Grandmoms came home in a wheelchair a few weeks later. I didn't see her down or depressed one time. "Doctors don't know shit. I can walk if I try hard enough," she said. She came from a family of tough Southern women. "I don't believe in *can't*."

After about a year, Grandmoms was walking on crutches, and the following year she was teaching classes, moving and kicking without assistance. Grandmoms's annual concert at Lincoln Center was a major event that year—her big comeback.

Stobo and I ran around Lincoln Center every year like it was our personal amusement park, sneaking into the balcony and box seats. Cousin Craig dared us to climb up the catwalk to the lights in the rafters. We loved peeking at the women and girls changing costumes backstage. Our favorite was Tina Douglas, R&B singer Ashanti's mother. Ashanti, who wasn't born yet, would soon grow up in Grandmoms's school too. Tina was fine as hell—dark brown skin with a fat ass, big breasts, and green eyes, decked out in Gucci boots and bags. She made us want to grow up fast. A few of the ladies would bend over and stretch, secretly knowing that Stobo and I were watching.

At the end of the show, my grandmother came out to thank the Lincoln Center crowd while Ben Vereen clapped onstage behind her. The audience gave her a standing ovation. After the show, you already know what it was . . . lobster tails with hot butter, of course!

When I was six years old, Moms and Grandmoms enrolled me in dance school classes. They decided it was a good way to keep me healthy because with sickle-cell, the body needs light exercise to allow the blood to properly circulate. I enjoyed the classes but I never understood why Moms, Grandmoms, and everyone else there was so passionate about that type of dancing. To me, it was boring and corny. The only things I liked about it was that my boy Stobo was there too, and being around all those girls.

Tap dancing was my favorite class. One of Grandmoms's close friends was an old-school tap dancer named Sandman Sims. He had this routine in which he'd sprinkle some sand on the floor, and when he tap-danced on it, it made a unique crunching sound under his shoes, like the sand was part of the beat. I was amazed.

What I loved most about the dance school was that my grandmother owned it. Stobo and I ran amok in that place. It was our clubhouse. Plus Jamaica Avenue, the major Queens shopping area, was right outside. What more could a young devious mind ask for?

On my seventh birthday, my pops pulled out a shiny, nickel-plated .380 in my uncle Eddie's basement. Pops always told me that Eddie was a punk because he didn't bust his gun when they had beef with somebody over Eddie's sister.

"I'm gonna teach you how to shoot a gun," Pops said. I was shook, but I did what he told me.

Pops put a small tin garbage can across the room to use as a target. He put the gun in my hand, showing me how to aim, warning that the gunshot was going to be very loud when I squeezed the trigger. I calmed myself down. Finally, I fired my first shot.

The first shot was stupid loud and scared me so bad I jumped way back. For the second shot, I held the gun with my right hand, tilted my head covering my right ear with my right shoulder, put my left hand over my left ear, and shot at the can again.

Pops was really crazy. I think he just had me shooting to scare Eddie. We shot at that can for a couple of hours, then we went home.

Around that same time, Pops came home with a big BB rifle. We'd practice shooting birds up in the trees in our yard and at the park across the street from our house in Lakeview. After a week, the whole park was full of dead birds. *Gross.*

I guess Pops was trying to make sure his son wasn't no punk because of sickle-cell. That's why Pops was teaching me all this stuff. He was very intelligent, but as smart as he was, he must've had a criminal gene in his DNA. He was a very wild boy who got into a lot of fights with the hands and the guns. Pops was one gun-happy muthafucka.

Moms got a job working for the New York City Housing Authority helping people get apartments in the projects. Every two years she was transferred to work in a different project. During the summer, she brought me to work with her and I played in the playground of whatever hood she was working in—Harlem, Brooklyn, Queens. But the best was when they transferred Moms to Queensbridge projects. She worked there for six years.

It was the summer of 1982, I was eight, and Moms enrolled me in Reese Day Camp. Moms's office was on the infamous hill in Queensbridge and the camp was across the street. Almost all the kids from QB went to Reese because it was right in the projects. I loved it because of the girls. QB had some real pretty girls.

But when five P.M. hit we would be back on the Long Island Rail Road to Lakeview. Even though Moms toured the world with hit records, you know the music biz—after all the filet mignon, champagne, caviar, and limo rides, she never got the money she was owed.

We were on welfare and food stamps until Moms got the Housing Authority job. But no matter what, Moms always kept a positive attitude and a kind heart. Maybe that's why Pops thought he could get away with murder.

One evening when we came back from QB, Moms found Pops's heroin works hidden in a cosmetics bag—needles, syringes, spoons, cotton balls, tourniquet. They argued back and forth. He left and didn't come home for months. When he did come back, Moms made him sleep on the couch.

When I was eight, Pops took me for a ride and told me about how he'd been addicted to heroin since he was fourteen and that he and Moms might split up. No kid wants to see his parents split up, but Pops explained it in a way that made sense. Then we pulled up to a jewelry store.

"Wait in the car," Pops told me. "I'll be right back."

Five minutes later, he came running out with a big brown shopping bag full of gold and all types of jewels. *This fool just robbed the spot!* We got four blocks away and the Nassau County police were immediately on our ass. After a high-speed chase through Hempstead, Pops finally came to his senses and stopped the car. They put me in the backseat with him. Pops had the cuffs on behind his back and I held his hand all the way to the police station.

The cops gave me chips and soda while I waited for Moms to pick me up. She went buck stupid on Pops after that, screaming and yelling. "How could you do this? That's our son! Our little boy!" My grandmoms bailed him out seven hours later, and he and Moms separated permanently.

When he came home later that night, though, we finished our conversation from earlier in the car. My pops was a cool, calm nigga, chillin' like what happened earlier was nothing. I loved that muthafucka.

The next day, Moms and I were back in QB. She dropped me off at camp and went to work. Reese was empty that morning; only the counselor and three other kids were there. Two of them were girls. The best-looking girl walked over to me and asked if I was new to the hood. We walked away to talk by the card tables right outside the door. She made it real easy for a li'l eight-year-old without much game because she did all the talking.

Meanwhile, the girl's boyfriend and seven of his friends walked up behind me. She was quiet all of a sudden. Just as I started getting into the conversation, a hand grabbed my neck from behind and turned me around.

"What you think you doin'?" her boyfriend barked. He grabbed my face and pushed me up against a wall to let me know I was talking to his girlfriend.

"I'm new here! I ain't know that was your girl!" I told him.

"You better watch yourself!" the kid warned as he and his boys walked off. I went back in the building. *I was really about to start kickin' it to shorty!* I thought, embarrassed and mad as hell. *But I'm happy I ain't get jumped.* It's funny how life works, because I ended up being cool with that kid, Diki, like ten years later, and he never remembered that day when I brought it up.

Later that day, they took us to free lunch at a school on Twenty-first Street. Free lunch was disgusting. I found maggots at the bottom of my salad on a cardboard tray the first day and I never ate there again, but they still made me go. Sometimes we got on a yellow bus for free lunch at another school in Astoria, Queens. I carried a pocketknife that came in handy one afternoon.

On the bus to Astoria free lunch, a big fight with four-by-fours and bottles broke out with kids from another hood. The kids tried to run inside our bus and beat people up. I started swinging my pocketknife. I had them niggas shook. It was rough for a little kid, man; something was bound to go down at free lunch in QB or the locker room at Astoria Pool. *I ain't never telling Moms 'cause I know she won't let me go anymore.* I kept all the crazy stuff to myself.

A popular thing with the kids in Queensbridge was making rock shooters out of quarter-water bottle tops. When I first came around, I would see kids shooting rocks out of them shits, and if one of those rocks hit you it felt worse than getting shot with a CO_2-powered BB gun. I quickly learned how to make one because all the kids were carrying them around like guns.

First, you buy a quarter water and a pack of balloons. Drink the juice. After it's empty, take a knife or razor and cut the top of the bottle off, put the balloon over the top part that you drink from. After that, all you need is a pocket full of small rocks or pennies. Drop a rock or penny in, pull the balloon back, let go. Man, that shit will go through a windshield if you do it right! We used to have ill shoot-outs, twenty kids against twenty kids.

Queensbridge didn't have concrete pavement back then, it was all dirt paths and hills. The projects were being rebuilt with basketball courts, fences, and playgrounds.

On the block after day camp, I'd listen to the older dudes freestyling back and forth. I wrote my first song, "You's a Crack Head," when I was nine. I heard one of the older dudes rapping about a crackhead, so I made my own version. My moms, brother, and friends in QB told me it was good and gassed me up. That was the beginning of my road to riches, the moment I first started rapping.

A Broadway show, *The Tap Dance Kid*, needed a little boy to play the starring role. Since Grandmoms had major connections in that world, she gave the producers photographs of me and they called saying they wanted me to be the new tap-dancing kid. Grandmoms explained that the casting people were on the phone and they wanted me to be the star. She told me I'd be famous and make a lot of money but that it would be very hard work and I'd have to perform two shows every night. I was stuck. I was scared, plus I wasn't really into dancing. I thought about it for five minutes and told her, "No, thank you." For the next ten years, Grandmoms kept telling everybody how I turned down a starring role in a Broadway musical.

The kid who wound up getting the part was Alfonso Ribeiro. He appeared in a Pepsi commercial with Michael Jackson after that and became a TV star on *The Fresh Prince of Bel-Air*. Hey, I guess Alfonso owes me. I did him a huge favor. Ha! Sometimes I think, *What if . . . Nah.*

In 1983, near to when the movie *Breakin'* came out, Grandmoms talked me into performing at her annual concert at Lincoln Center. I'd been taking her classes since I was six. But at age nine, breakdancing and rap music were my new thing and I wanted to stop the other dance stuff. I was at the age where I wanted to be cool. Stobo and I would be outside the crib in Hempstead with a flattened cardboard box and a radio battling two other kids on my block. We wore gray nylon windbreaker outfits, white gloves, and trucker hats with Playboy bunnies, and thought we were breakdance masters.

I asked my grandmother to let us do a breakdance routine at her next concert. "Only if you both perform the regular dance classes at the show," she told me. We agreed. It was a small price to pay and was the first time Grandmoms incorporated a hip hop routine in her concert. We killed it along with the tap, African, ballet, and all that! She thought it was cute to have her little grandson dancing in her school. But Stobo and I were quickly growing out of it.

I can't front, dance school was fun when I was younger. An older girl named Kerri hooked Stobo and I up with these twins Renee and Michelle—two fly-ass light-skinned West Indian shorties—they were in all of our classes. Stobo had Michelle; I had Renee. We all had fun.

Grandmoms was cool with singer-actress Diana Ross, who enrolled her daughter Chudney at the school. My grandmother told Diana that Chudney couldn't pull up in limos or Bentleys because it would make too much of a scene. They agreed it would be better for her to arrive in a regular car. Chudney was real cute. She was the same age and in class with Stobo and me. When the word got around that Diana Ross's daughter was taking a class, Kerri pulled me into the hallway, offering all kinds of ways that I should approach her and get her to be my girlfriend.

"T'Chaka, I'm telling you, you gotta get her!" Kerri said. "Forget about Renee, Chudney's rich!" Kerri tried her best, but it never happened. Chudney was there for six months, then she got tired of all the attention.

Diana Ross was doing a huge concert at Central Park in Manhattan on July 21, 1983. My grandmother provided her with backup dancers and my father helped with stage-set production. Diana asked me to join her onstage because she thought I was cute. "I want you to walk out with me at the end and say good night," she told me during rehearsal. "Do you want to do it?"

"Yes."

On the night of the show, there was lightning and thunder then buckets of rain. The lawn was a blanket of deep muddy patches, but it was summertime in Central Park, so the crowd wasn't concerned. They came to see Diana Ross. It was packed. She performed, soaked, and you know black women and their hair in the rain don't mix. But Diana didn't care.

The production people told me to get ready to go onstage. I was petrified and changed my mind. My moms, pops, and grandmoms tried to convince me, but I said no. That was the first and last time I caught a case of stage fright.

Our feet got stuck in the mud on the way out of the park. My sneaker came off in the sludge and so did my mother's shoes. No lobster tails that night, just our tails in the shower.

On October 20, 1984, Moms got a phone call from my grandmother saying that my grandfather had a heart attack and died in his sleep in a hotel room in Kansas City while on tour. He was seventy-three.

The entire jazz community came out for his wake five days later at St. Peter's Church on Fifty-fourth Street and Lexington Avenue in Manhattan. Minister Reverend Gensel, who's also a jazz musician, helped make it all possible. My father was on the run from his jewelry-store case, laying low, so he couldn't make it. I know that hurt him.

The service was like a party with a lot of sad faces. I walked up to Grandpops's open casket and stared at him. My boy Stobo was with me. I leaned over and kissed Grandpops's forehead. It was ice-cold. That was the first and last time I touched a dead body.

While Stobo and I were staring at him, it felt like Grandpops might sit up and do the scary face with his false teeth in hand. After the service, his body was cremated and his ashes spread out into the ocean.

Pops kidnapped me that same year and took me to Detroit, where he'd been staying since he and Moms split. I went over to my grandmoms's in Hempstead and Pops was waiting for me. He didn't take me by force, he just didn't tell Moms where we were going. I guess he missed me and decided to take his son.

I think Pops also wanted to show me how he was living now, because his cousin Beverly had that nigga ballin'! She had her own investment firm in

Detroit and gave Pops a high-paying position. Pops was wearing fly three-piece suits without the necktie. He was open off his new whip, a five-speed Renault he had shipped from France.

Beverly was richer than a muthafucker. In downtown Detroit, there was a skyscraper with her name on it. We lived in the finished part of a mansion she was having built. Beverly's son Eric was around eighteen and her daughter Cecily was twelve, two years older than me. Their backyard had a river where we went fishing for crawfish.

We were in Detroit living the life. I think Pops waited almost four months before he called Moms and told her where we were. She knew Pops had me, she just didn't know where. She threatened to call the cops, but I lived in Detroit for more than a year. Moms probably didn't want to upset me because I was happy to be with Pops's crazy ass anyway.

Plus, Cecily and I had a crush on each other. The term "kissing cousins" comes to mind. I found out Pops and Beverly had a li'l something going on themselves. No wonder he was an overnight success!

We went to Detroit Tigers baseball games a lot. I enjoyed the popcorn and hot dogs more than the baseball. Pops took me to see *Scarface* starring Al Pacino on opening night. Now *that* was a fuckin' movie! Those three-piece suits without the necktie that Pops was wearing looked almost exactly like the ones Tony Montana had on. I guess that was the style.

Cousin Cecily was a very pretty dark-brown-skinned girl. She grew up with a lot of money but was a down-to-earth tomboy. She made her own experimental facial-cream products out of mud, perfume, and all types of weird stuff, using me as the guinea pig, putting crap all over my face. She was like a white girl compared to the black girls I was used to back home—she spoke like a white girl and introduced me to rock 'n' roll music.

The J. Geils Band's "Centerfold"—Cecily's favorite song—constantly played on her little 45 portable record player. She taught me how to eat artichokes, watch WWF wrestling, and speak Detroit. Instead of saying *soda*, they said *pop.*

Then all of a sudden the ride was over. Moms's threats of calling the police worked, and Pops agreed to send me home. I was back in New York, except we weren't in Lakeview anymore. Moms had moved to LeFrak City, Queens.

Pops wound up coming back to New York too, got caught by the police, and ended up doing a year in Nassau County jail for the jewelry-store thing. Once his bid was over, he moved back into the house in Lakeview with his new woman, Rita, and her teenage kids, Leon and Loretta. I wanted to be with my pops, so Moms allowed me to stay with him and go to school over there for a while.

I walked to Howard T. Herber middle school, cutting through the woods and crossing a construction landfill, with my next-door neighbors Angel and Raynoldo. In Lakeview, I had only a handful of friends—Angel and Ray, Todd, and my man Shameek.

Shameek had all the cool shit—gazelle glasses, shell-toe Adidas, and a giant boom-box radio. When I saw his shell toes I told my moms and pops I wanted a pair, but they bought me Olympians instead. At school the next day, Sha said, "Nigga, them shits got five stripes! Adidas only got three." But Sha was my nigga. He didn't make fun of my shoes, at least not to my face.

One afternoon, on the walk home from school, a crew of brothers—the Charlestons—were beating everybody up who cut through the woods. As I walked out of the woods onto their street, I saw one of the brothers hitting people with a wooden Louisville Slugger bat on their legs, arms, and back-packs. Pops had taught me how to snatch a bat or stick from somebody if they were about to swing at you, practicing with a broomstick in slow motion.

"Never duck or try to move out of the way if somebody is about to swing at you with a bat," Pops told me. "Rush them and get in close, then use your arm to grab the arm that they're swinging with and hyperextend their elbow."

But it's not the same in a real-life situation. The kid was about to take a swing at me, so I rushed him, but he was too big and hit me in the mouth with the Slugger. *Yo! This nigga made my bottom teeth go through my bottom lip!* I was leaking blood in a daze.

The expression on my friends' faces as they walked me home made me think my face had been destroyed. In my bathroom mirror, I saw a little vein hanging out of a hole right under my bottom lip. Uncle Lenny came by, and when he saw my face he took me to the hospital to get stitches. I've still got that scar to this day.

Uncle Lenny was always very elusive. He'd be missing in action for long periods of time and then suddenly show up at our house. Lenny wasn't my real uncle, but I was raised to call him Uncle Lenny. He always took care of me when he was around.

My mother made me move back with her after about a year because I was sleeping in the cold, damp basement in Lakeview and kept getting sick. Moms's move to LeFrak in 1985, the hood right between Jamaica and Queensbridge, was a major turning point in my life. I turned eleven and she let me hang outside until the streetlights came on. The apartment complex was co-ops, not projects, but with all the drug activity there wasn't much of a difference. Crack had come out a few years earlier and almost every kid my age was selling it for the older dudes.

My first week in LeFrak, I was walking to the store, and who was sitting on a short wall by the parking lot but my friend Shameek, who lived around the corner from me in Lakeview! Sha and his family had just moved to LeFrak, what a fuckin' coincidence!

Sha was obviously doing his thing slinging drugs. You could usually tell if someone was slinging drugs by looking at their jewelry and clothes. Shameek had all the new sneakers before they even came out, fresh jeans, and snorkel coats.

I enrolled in Halsey Junior High School right across the Long Island Expressway from LeFrak. On the first day of school, I saw kids with big rope chains, rings, and all the latest fashions. LeFrak was a cash cow for drug dealers.

Everybody sold drugs. It made me stop caring about school and start caring about how I looked—jewelry, clothes, and sneakers, Nike Air Maxes, Louis Vuitton, Triple F.A.T. Goose bubble jackets. When the school bell rang at three P.M., everyone from LeFrak walked home together.

Within the first two weeks, I got into it with this Indian kid who thought he was tough because he was taller than me. Everybody called me

Pee Wee because I was so small. I don't recall exactly how the fight started, but I know for sure how it finished. A bunch of people from my block whipped the cowboy shit out of the kid.

After that day, we beat people up on our way home just for fun. This African kid named Abunda didn't like me and wanted to fight. I was shook. In the crib on the couch, I'd be daydreaming of ways to sneak-attack the mutha-fucker.

One of my ideas was to walk up to him:

"I don't want no beef with you, man," I'd say, reaching my hand out to shake. While I had his hand, I'd try to break his nose or something. I prac-ticed my punches beating up my moms's flowery forest-green couch pillows. I had another idea of carrying a D battery in my pocket to make my fist more solid. Abunda and I never got around to fighting and became cool a year later.

The first year of school was wild, and it only got wilder.

Every building in LeFrak was named after a foreign country. I lived on the fifth floor of Peru. I made friends with two Puerto Rican brothers, Eric and Boobie, on the opposite end of the hallway. The Peru building's lobby was at-tached to Colombia, where a dude called E and his brother Pop and my boys Justice and Zion lived. We all went to school together. I was closest with Boo-bie. I used to be across the hall at their crib every day. We ate dinner together and stayed up all night watching TV. I tried learning some Spanish from them, but I only picked up on the curse words.

Boobie was a DJ and had all the new rap albums. We wrote down entire songs to learn every lyric word for word. The Jungle Brothers' "Jim-browski" was our jam. They shouted out, *"Jimbrowski in LeFrak!"* It made us proud to be from LeFrak.

Nineteen eighty-six was the year of Mike Tyson. I saw my first Tyson fight at Boobie's crib. It lasted about thirty seconds. After the fight, Boobie and I went outside. Rakim, Biz Markie, Slick Rick, the Jungle Brothers, and Big Daddy Kane blasted from boom boxes, and everybody was drinking and smoking. It was almost dark, so my time was limited. We drank our first tall can of malt liquor, Schlitz with the blue bull on the label, 'cause the curiosity was killing us. My brother Greg gave me sips of his beer when I was five or six and even let me take a pull of his weed. One toke and I was choking. After we tried a few swigs from the tall cans, I didn't drink again for a long time—it was nasty.

By the time I turned eleven and was living in LeFrak, my attitude about dance class changed. *I can't do that shit no more.* But I was still there every Saturday because that was my family's business and became the hangout spot. I got my first piece of pussy in that place when I was eleven.

One Saturday evening, my Spanish homie Shawn from Roosevelt, Long Island, took a girl to the basement and told her if she wanted to have sex with him then she had to let me hit it first. "Go ahead, have sex with him," he told the girl, nodding toward me. She agreed. I kept my boxers on. Afterward, I went upstairs to wash up in the bathroom and there was blood all over my boxers. I looked down like, *Yo, what the fuck is this?!* She had her period. Disgusting. I must have washed my pole thirty to forty times in a row. It was traumatic. And that was my first time having sex.

My moms took dance classes at Grandmoms's school in Jamaica ever since she was a little girl and was still doing it faithfully every weekend. My grandmother had a group of female friends who helped her run the dance studio, including one of her best friends, Ms. Barbra Brooks. Her grandson was Stobo and he was still there every Saturday just like me.

No longer confined to classes, we ran wild in the school and on Jamaica Avenue along with Stobo's real cousin Craig. Grandmoms's other best friend, Joyce Gresham, had a grandson John-Michael. We called him JM. He was only six but he always wanted to hang out with Stobo and me.

It seemed like every girl in Queens went to my grandmoms's dance school. A lady named Ms. Beverly Edge had three daughters: Donna, Wendy, and Kerri. The youngest, Kerri, who'd tried to set me up with Chudney Ross, was around seven years older than us and taught Stobo and me all the secrets about what girls wanted and liked.

Sitting on the floor in the dance studio one afternoon, Kerri was stretching while schooling Stobo and me about what women want. "T'Chaka, you're always quiet and laid-back," Kerri told me. "That's good, 'cause girls don't like guys that act foolish like little boys."

Kerri tried to play matchmaker, hooking Stobo and me up with the pretty girls. We used to stare at the older girls in their tight dance uniforms, and Lord, there were some real thick bodies.

Stobo and I had a crew called the Jungle Brothers, named after the rap group. The crew consisted of me, Stobo, our friend Roger (who became a professional dancer), and my homie Shawn. The sole purpose of our crew was to run trains on the girls in the dance school. I'd find a girl and take her into an empty room at the school, trying to convince her that if she wanted me then she had to show my brothers love too. Some girls went for it and some didn't. At least eight of the girls who went for it were snitched on by other girls. When parents started pulling their daughters out of the school, we got in trouble. But we kept right on doing our thing on the low.

Roger was serious about making dance his career. He was West Indian and lived across the street from the USA Diner on Merrick Boulevard in Rosedale, Queens, a popular hangout for girls and hustlers. There was loads of action by Roger's house. His mother was strict, and he had a sister Sandra and an older brother known as Call Me Al. Roger explained that they called his brother Call Me Al because when they first moved to Rosedale, the dudes in his neighborhood tried to test his heart. When they asked his name, Roger's brother replied, "Just call me Al." A fight broke out and his brother whipped everyone's asses. From that point on, they gave him respect and the name Call Me Al stuck.

Kool Rock-Ski from the '80s rap group the Fat Boys lived down the block by Rosedale Lanes bowling alley. His bandmate Buffy aka the Human Beat Box always drove up and down Merrick Boulevard in different Mercedes-Benz 190's with two-tone colors and curtains on the windows. Kool Rock's brother Blaze, who I was real close with, often hung out at Roger's crib.

There was endless mischief to get into at Roger's crib. Green Acres Mall and Sunrise Multiplex were within walking distance. The 9th Posse, a well-known street gang in that part of Queens, threw a lot of parties. Kerri dated one of the gang members, so she invited us. There were also a lot of reggae-music parties because that side of Queens had a huge West Indian population. Roger, Stobo, Shawn, Stobo's cousin Craig, and I bought forty ounces of beer from Pop & Kim's convenience store on Merrick Boulevard, ice-cold with frost on 'em, and hit all the parties. Beer was still nasty to me but we all drank it on those party nights.

Late one night, Craig came up with a plan to break into a school a few blocks away in Rosedale. Craig had just come home from jail the year before and was already looking for trouble. He was seven years older than us, around eighteen, and was the ringleader of all our early rebellion. We climbed up the side of the school and through an open window. We stole phones, copy machines, and other electronics. Craig sold it all for petty cash.

Craig always had some kind of scheme. He took Stobo and me on missions all over Queens, daring us to cross the Long Island Rail Road tracks by Linden and Farmers Boulevard and to run across the Belt Parkway for thrills. After Craig turned us out with all the crazy shit he had us doing, we started doing a lot of wild pranks on our own.

One summer morning around two A.M., Roger and I saw a McDonald's sixteen-wheeler delivery truck pull up into the McDonald's parking lot across from the USA Diner. From Roger's backyard we saw that the back of the truck was open, so we ran over and took what we could—crates of eggs, boxes of hash browns, burgers, buns, cheese, biscuits, pancakes, syrup, ketchup . . . Roger's refrigerator and freezer were filled with food. I don't remember what he told his moms, but the next morning she cooked us a big breakfast.

Stobo and I were chillin' at my grandmother's house in Hempstead one day when Grandmoms told us the TV star Emmanuel Lewis, aka Webster, and his brother were coming over. A girl from dance school had started dating Webster's brother. Even though Webster was a dwarf or midget, his brother wasn't. I called Carey down the block to tell him the news. "Webster's coming to my house!" I said. "Come over if you wanna meet him."

A few hours later, Webster, Carey, Stobo, and I were in the living room when Webster started showing us his breakdance moves—back spins, wind-mills, even head spins. *Oh shit! Webster can breakdance! He's good too!*

I remembered seeing pictures of him and Michael Jackson together with Mike holding him up, carrying him like a baby. That didn't look right to me. "What's up with you and Michael Jackson?" I asked Webster straight up. "What do ya'll talk about when you're together?" Webster got quiet and changed the subject. So I asked again. "Is Michael gay? What's up with him for real?" Webster acted as if he didn't hear my questions and walked into the room where my grandmoms was talking to his brother. I know that Webster later denied it, but Carey, Stobo, and I laughed about it for a long time, saying that Michael was a fruit cup and Webster was his little boy toy.

I wanted my twelfth birthday to be an event. Since Craig had just come home from doing a bid, Grandmoms had given him a job cleaning and locking up the studio at night so his parole officer would get off his back. I told Craig to get some weed and I'd buy the forties. We were all going to get high for the first time late that night after everybody left—Stobo, Craig, Roger, Shawn, and a tap-dance teacher named Derrick. Craig and Derrick were the oldest; they'd both been high and drunk before. But it was the first time for the rest of us.

We got so high and pissy drunk in my grandmoms's office. Stobo stumbled out of the building crying and screaming, "I'm blind! I can't see!" We walked from Jamaica Avenue up Merrick Boulevard all the way to Rosedale and crashed at Roger's crib. Stobo threw up in the toilet and passed out with his pants around his ankles on the bathroom floor. He had us all cracking up.

That night was a pivotal point. I was about to become a teenager and thought I was becoming a man. I guess all the criminal juvenile-delinquent mischief I was getting into was my way of having fun, since sickle-cell didn't allow me to do sports and stuff other kids were into. *I'm becoming a man*, I thought. *I have to make my own decisions and take control of my destiny.*

At twelve, I started seriously getting into rap music. Rap exhibited the aggressiveness that had been in my heart and mind all of my life. The first albums I bought were LL Cool J's *Radio* and Run-D.M.C.'s self-titled debut "Sucker M.C.'s." I repeated the verses to my moms acting as if I wrote them. Rap music made me feel good for a change.

One day after school, Boobie came over and spit a verse for me. "Whose verse is that?" I asked. He looked at me like I was crazy. "You don't know about 'The Symphony'?"

We walked to Boobie's crib and he played the record for me. The song was from Marley Marl's *In Control Volume 1* album. The verse Boobie spit was by Kool G Rap: *"You can't replace me, ice me or ace me, bass me, face me, slice me or race me, bite me or taste me, I'll show you that I got force, my rap burns your mouth like hot sauce. . . ."* After I heard that, there was no turning back. I was going to be a rap star.

September came around again. It was time for back-to-school shopping, and Moms couldn't afford the black construction Timberlands I wanted. She put a pair of discount nineteen-dollar motorcycle boots that looked like they were from *Mad Max* on layaway. I hated them. I wanted what was popular in the hood. So I decided to try my hand at crack.

The biggest dealers in LeFrak went to my school. Two of them were my man Steve and my other man Jassen, both of whom wore jewelry, suede jackets in every color, and different sneakers every day. They had to be making 10K a week, no lie. Those kids had other kids our age moving G-packs for them—a G-pack was a thousand dollars' worth of crack. There was an older dude in his mid-twenties, B, who everyone worked for.

After the first day of the new school year, I went to Jassen's crib, where they cooked and bagged up the stuff. I told Steve and Jassen that I wanted to get down. They gave me a test pack, about a hundred dollars' worth of crack in ten-dollar vials. I walked around the hood, sold it, and brought them the money. *This is easy*, I thought.

Jassen gave me one more test pack. I walked around and made three sales in the multilevel parking lot where people sold because it was shielded from the outside view. Two white plainclothes cops came toward me. I tried to walk away. "Hey, kid, come here! Stop!" They ran up and found the crack in my pocket. "What the hell is this little kid doing selling crack?" one undercover asked the other, then turned to me. "Why is somebody your age selling drugs?" I was twelve but looked eight. They took the vials and sent me on my way. Still shook, I hopped a fence and took a shortcut home.

The next day, when I told Jassen what happened, he didn't believe me. He wanted the money but I didn't have it to give. The following morning, Jassen was waiting for me outside of school. He wanted to fight. "A'ight cool," I said. "We can fight."

While I was taking off my jean jacket and backpack he snuffed me, knocking me down. He kicked me in my stomach and groin. All I could do was ball into the fetal position until some girls from my building pulled Jassen off of me. People watching the fight said Jassen didn't score points by not letting me take my backpack off. He didn't leave any bruises on my body, just my ego.

Shameek, my boy from Long Island who also moved to LeFrak, and his homeboys asked if I wanted to get Jassen back, but I let it go and stopped selling drugs for a while.

I bought a switchblade and BB gun and brought them to school every day. A gang called Boom Bash from Jamaica would beat people up, like fifty of them waiting after school. A couple of the gang members, Bam Bam and K-Love, used to sit at my lunch table. I got cool with them so I didn't have to worry about getting jumped, but I kept weapons on me just in case. You never know.

One day, I left my mini black elephant-skin Jansport backpack in class by mistake and the teacher brought it to the principal's office. "*Albert Johnson!*" I was called to his office over the loudspeaker. "*Albert Johnson! Please report to the principal's office immediately!*" When I got there, he pulled the switchblade and BB gun from the bag. "I'm supposed to call the cops and have you arrested and expelled," the principal said. "But I'm going to give you a break this time." He called my moms instead to tell her I was suspended for two weeks.

Moms had to leave work to get me and yelled the whole walk home. I was on punishment for a month. I had to be home by four P.M. instead of when the streetlights came on. Lying in bed with my window halfway open, I could hear the whistle from the beginning of Rakim's "My Melody" blasting from a boom box, laughter, and loud chatter from everybody on the block chilling on the benches in the spring air. I was fienin' to be back outside.

After I got off punishment, I started spending weekends at my grandmother's house again. My grandmother had a VHS camcorder and tripod to record her classes and concerts. Carey and I made a video to Slick Rick's "Teenage Love" from his new album *Adventures of Slick Rick* in my grandmother's living room along with at least ten other videos. Carey and I watched them just to make fun of ourselves.

One night I passed out on a foldout cushion seat in Carey's basement bedroom. In the morning, I woke up soaking wet. *I pissed on the nigga's cushion seat. Foul.* Carey gave me dry clothes and a towel to clean up. I was too damn old to be pissing in the bed.

The night after that embarrassing episode, Carey stayed at my grandmother's crib along with Stobo. Grandmoms had just bought an Isuzu Impulse. She bragged about the car because it talked when you left the door open, didn't wear your seat belt, or left the lights on. And it was fast.

Two A.M. rolled around and I stole the keys from my grandmoms's nightstand while she was sleeping. Carey, Stobo, and I snuck outside and got in the car. *"The left door is ajar!"* Goddamn talking car almost got us busted. We quietly shut the doors, started the engine, and we were gone. I'd never driven before except when Pops would sit me on his lap and let me steer when I was six or seven.

Hempstead was like a ghost town at night. No police. After an hour circling blocks and practicing parking, we snuck back inside. There's nothing like the thrill of stealing your grandmother's car for a late-night joy ride. Stobo and I borrowed the car until we had driving down pat. We never got caught.

Back in LeFrak, I finally got off suspension and went back to school, back to the drama. After school one day, the Boom Bash crew was outside deep. My boys Bam Bam and K-Love told me some white boy had called a girl a nigger. When the white boy came out of the school, he had no idea what was waiting for him. Fifty black gang members alongside the girl. *Ouch, this is gonna hurt,* I thought.

The girl screamed and spit a lungy in his face. One by one, all fifty gang members spit on the white kid. When they were done, the white boy went home with his entire body covered in yellow slime. They could've beaten the life out of him but decided to humiliate him instead. We walked back to the hood laughing our heads off.

That weekend, Stobo stayed at my crib in LeFrak. We saw a large shadow drop past my fifth-floor bedroom window and heard a loud thump. A man had jumped or been thrown off the sixteenth story of the Peru building and landed on a park bench, cracking it in half, blood pouring from his face. Stobo and I ran outside. "Oh, wow!" we both exclaimed, staring at his splattered brains. *Cool. . . .* We passed by the man's dead body, gazing in amazement, before the cops came and covered him up.

We walked to a store on Fifty-seventh Avenue, the drug strip in Le-Frak. We went straight to the toy aisle and filled our pockets with bendable WWF wrestling figures. Suddenly I felt a hand on my shoulder.

Store security escorted Stobo and me into a back room and threatened to call the cops but called our parents instead. *Here we go again.* Stobo started crying. My mother's sister, Aunt Charlotte, who was watching us that day, came to get us. Aunt Charlotte's gangsta like a muthafucker. She was a bartender at a bar in Long Island City, Queens, back in the day, and one night a man with a gun walked in, taking everybody to the roof one by one and shooting them dead. Aunt Charlotte was last. The gunman led her to the roof and shot her in the back of the head. She was the only one lucky enough to live. The bullet was lodged in the base of her head by her spine and still caused her severe migraines.

"Why did you have to pull this while I'm watching you?" Aunt Charlotte said. When my moms got home she held my right arm in the air and whipped me like a slave with a plastic laundry line, the same cord girls used to jump rope. *Yow!* I hopped around trying to block the hits. When she finished, welts burned all over my legs and ass. I didn't shoplift again for a long time.

That Easter, my moms, brother, and I went to Nana's crib in Ravenswood projects. Nana, my mother's mother, Ms. Bernie Johnson, was a heavyset high-yellow woman with hazel-green eyes like my mother's. Nana chain-smoked cigarettes and worked as a token-booth clerk at the train station on Jackson Avenue in Long Island City, a sweet lady who spoke with a classic nasal New York accent. Her apartment in Ravenswood looked like a souvenir store because Nana traveled the world collecting trinkets. Her favorite possessions were her *Jet* magazines, every issue stacked on the coffee table. My favorite thing to do at Nana's was climb on the big Central Park–looking rocks in front of her building. Nana and I would toss shelled peanuts down to the squirrels on those rocks and watch them pounce.

Besides her token-booth job, Nana had a side hustle selling bottles of imitation perfume and cologne at beauty salons in Long Island City. The boxes for the bottles would read, *If you like Ralph Lauren then you'll love Rudolph Laurenté*. But the knockoff smelled just like the real thing. My favorites were the fake Drakkar and Grey Flannel. Nana had me smelling good in school.

Uncle Charlie, my mother's brother who came back from the Vietnam War mentally messed up, traveled from the VA hospital upstate to Nana's for the holidays and always brought me a black garbage bag full of model army tanks, planes, and trucks. There were ninety pieces to glue together, put stickers on, and paint, and I was too young and impatient, so I never completed one of those things.

The highlight of going to Nana's crib was her fried chicken wings, the best in black history. Salty like a muthafucker but amazingly good.

The summer of 1986 was a wild one. A lot of older dudes were getting murdered in LeFrak over drug wars. Guns were easier to get than ever. The hoods became more violent and the streets of New York began to change.

The following September, my moms transferred me to a Lutheran school on Queens Boulevard near LeFrak. She realized that I was being influenced by my environment after seeing that bag of weapons I'd been bringing to school. We had to wear uniforms—a white button-down shirt, clip-on tie, blazer, shoes, and slacks. I was embarrassed to walk home in my uniform while the public-school kids wore regular clothes. I started acting up even more after school to prove to my friends in the hood that I was still cool.

When Halloween came around, fifteen of us ran around LeFrak wildin' after dark, egging and breaking car windows and slapping innocent people with socks filled with baby powder. A cop rolled by inside a three-wheel scooter car. We egged him and ran across the bridge that crossed the Long Island Expressway while the cop chased us in his little scooter. We got to the top of the bridge and all looked at each other like, *Why we running*? We turned around, surrounded the scooter, shook it back and forth until it tipped over, then jetted back to LeFrak. I wasn't trying to be on punishment again, so I ran home fast without looking back.

My birthday was major that November because I turned thirteen. Moms and Grandmoms gave me a Genesis turntable, headphones, a speaker, and cash to buy records. A month later, I got another turntable, mic, and a mixer for Christmas. I started making my own mix tapes, rapping and blending records like Too Short's "Freaky Tales" and Biz Markie's "Nobody Beats the Biz."

Two years flew by at the Lutheran school. The classes were small so the work was easier to learn, but the uniforms sucked. I couldn't wait for it to be over.

The summer after junior high school graduation, I wanted to get a tattoo like the flying parachute my father had on his left forearm, an airborne tatt from his paratrooper days. Before I was born, he was a Special Forces Green Beret in the army who went on several POW rescue missions. I brought my fake ID to a tattoo shop in Long Island right across from Belmont racetrack. The heavyset gray-bearded guy behind the counter who looked like Jerry Garcia from the Grateful Dead laughed and told me to come back when I turned eighteen.

During a trip to Virginia to visit my cousins on Pops's side of the family a few months later, I found a tattoo shop that didn't care that I was thirteen and gave me my first tattoo for thirty bucks—the Tasmanian Devil on my right shoulder. Back in New York, I was one of the only kids my age with a tattoo, so I rolled up my T-shirt on the right side for everybody to see.

My second tattoo was a skeleton swinging from barbed wire on my right biceps. I only wanted tattoos because Pops had 'em. When I showed Moms, she almost had a heart attack. She worried they would affect my sickle-cell, but they didn't. I got three tatts that summer. The third one was a dragon that I saw on the tattoo-parlor wall and thought would look cool on my right hand.

I was a crazy little kid. I blame sickle-cell and my father.

A month later, I had to go to the hospital for two days. Back home, depressed and fed up with the pain, God, the world, and myself, I wanted to commit suicide because of my sickle-cell.

I tied a rope to my closet pole and tried hanging myself, but it didn't feel too good. I wanted to end pain, not create more, so I scrapped that plan. My next idea was to slit my wrists. The sharpest knife in the house was a steak knife with a brown wooden handle. I took it to my room and started cutting my wrist but that hurt, too. Suicide was too damn painful.

Moms walked into my room while I was on the closet floor looking crazy with a steak knife in my hand and a noose on my closet pole. "What the hell are you doing?" she asked. I told her I wanted to kill myself because I was tired of sickle-cell. She spoke to me for a few hours trying to make me feel better.

Moms brought me to a psychiatrist, Dr. Z, on Queens Boulevard the next day. I didn't want to talk to no damn shrink, but Moms insisted. My first day, I didn't speak much. I ran through his glass bowl of candy at every appointment. We spoke about my sickle-cell pain and he tried to convince me that all would be well. *Yeah, whatever.* I tried four appointments and told my moms it wasn't worth the money. I wasn't planning on following through with the suicide anyway. I'd rather live.

I was glad that I didn't have to go back to that shrink's office because I didn't like people in my business. Never did, never will. This book is a damn miracle. I never thought I would be writing my life story, but once I started getting it all down, I realized that it could help inspire others to do great things with their own lives. So here it is, I'm sharing, dammit.

Toward the end of that summer, a bunch of friends from my block were talking about what high school they wanted to go to in September. Most of them were saying the High School of Art and Design, some were saying John Bowne. Art and Design was a prestigious art school in Manhattan. They said in order to get in we had to take an art test and bring a portfolio showcasing our own artwork. I bought white T-shirts and airbrush paint and made my own version of the graffitti crew the Shirt Kings' airbrushed T-shirts with Louis Vuitton and Gucci logos for my portfolio. I figured that the white people at the school had never seen anything like that before and would be impressed. It was worth a try.

I really didn't give a fuck about school; I'd already made up my mind to be a rapper. I just wanted to be with my homies from LeFrak. Little did I know that I wouldn't be hanging with them anymore—I was about to meet a whole new set of friends with whom I would change the course of the world.

POETICAL PROPHETS

The first day of high school is one of the most important days of a teenager's life. I spent the entire summer of 1989 getting prepared. *I'm fifteen years old now so I have to step it up.* The hottest gear out was Fila, Nautica, Polo, Benetton, and Banana Republic, plus Guess and Girbaud jeans. I did a jux (robbery) with my boy Stobo to get the money. I had it all.

My idea for the imitation Shirt Kings' T-shirts worked and I was accepted into Art and Design. The school had students from every borough. I thought Grandmoms's school had some bad girls—ha! Art and Design was a gold mine of dimes.

The first few days I didn't see anybody from Le-Frak but I made a new friend, Derrick from the Bronx, in photography class. His mother worked for the radio station WBLS and he had a lot of information about the music industry. We sat at the same lunch table every day.

Lunch was where it all went down. People at one table in a rap cipher, a kid Terrence giving five-dollar haircuts, drugs and guns being sold in the bathroom, and random robberies taking place all over. Lunch was like the yard in prison.

Around that time, I was shopping my first demo for a record deal. My mother was my manager since she knew the ropes of the business. I was going by the name Lord-T (The Golden Child) after Eddie Murphy's movie *The Golden Child*.

After shopping at a few companies throughout the summer, we inked a demo deal with Jive Records just as school started in September. Jive agreed to pay for my studio time. If I came up with good songs, they'd offer me a real contract. It was like a trial. Even though it was almost nothing, it felt like something to me. It was a start.

I flirted with the women at Jive and one of them, Kim, a good-looking heavyset black woman, got me on the sound track for a movie coming out that summer called *Boyz 'N the Hood*. They let me open the song "Too Young" by R&B group Hi-Five with sixteen bars. After that first big break, Jive wanted to sign me up for a real contract.

At school the next day, I told Derrick about the deal. "You should meet my man Havoc," he said as we dipped photos in solution in the darkroom during photography class. "He's a rapper too. You should partner up because you're both the same height and have a similar style."

After school, I waited outside for Derrick to introduce me to Havoc. A crowd of people came running out of the front door. A short kid about my height was getting ready to fight a taller dude. Derrick walked up. "That's Havoc right there, about to fight," he said. The tall kid pulled out a knife and tried stabbing Havoc in the stomach, missing by inches. A few people from the crowd rushed over and took the knife. Havoc proceeded to beat the shit out of the dude.

"*Kiwi! Kiwi! Kiwi!*" The crowd chanted Havoc's nickname, lifting him into the air and carrying him all the way to the train station. "*Kiwi! Kiwi! Kiwi!*"

I followed Derrick and Havoc onto the train and Derrick introduced us. "Nice fighting," I told Havoc.

"Did you see when he tried to stab me?" Hav asked. We rode to Queens Plaza making small talk about Queensbridge and the music industry. We spit some verses back and forth as we walked to Ravenswood, where Hav's grandmother lived. I told him how ironic it was that my Nana lived in Ravenswood, too. He told me how this rapper from Queensbridge named Tragedy was his mentor and gave him the name Havoc. I told him about my situation with Jive and that I was going to try to include him in the deal.

The next day at school, Havoc snuck his way into our lunch period. "Hav and I are going to Jive after school," I told Derrick. "You should come."

Before my next class, I went to the bathroom wearing a bunch of new bracelets and rings, looking like Slick Rick. A dude followed me into the bathroom. *This nigga's scheming*, I sensed right away. He had some big rings himself. One with a Scorpio symbol stood out because that's my birth sign. I felt his eyes on my jewelry. Nothing happened, but after that, I bought a .22 Dillinger with a pearl handle and a bunch of bullets from this kid selling guns in the school cafeteria.

I admired Slick Rick for his jewelry and how he'd shot his cousin who tried to rob him. I thought to myself, *I'm goin' out like Slick Rick!*

Later that day, I arrived at Jive before Havoc. I was really feeling the idea of us being partners and decided that if they wanted to sign me, they were going to have to sign Hav too. I sat down with the A&R. "Look, I've got a partner now and things have changed," I told him. He responded that Jive just wanted to sign me—they weren't interested in my partner. Hav showed up and spit for the A&R but the guy didn't change his mind. So I turned down the deal and never came back. My moms was upset but ultimately let me do what I wanted. They kept me on the *Boyz 'N the Hood* sound track, so it wasn't a total loss.

Havoc, Derrick, and I hung together every day. Hav had his lunch period switched so we could kick it even more. I started going to Ravenswood with Hav after school to work on song ideas. I met his younger brother T.J. and their cousin Todd.

Todd was a real smart kid when it came to school; he was also into photography, so he told Hav and me that he'd take our demo pictures. Hav started bringing me three blocks over to Queensbridge projects to hang out with his friends. He bugged out when I told him I used to be in QB every day because my moms worked for Housing. It had been years since I'd been to QB, and who's the first person I saw? The kid who had me up against the wall for talking to his girl: His name was Diki, aka Nice, and he's one of Hav's boys. He didn't even remember me. I also saw some of my old friends from Reese Day Camp. They remembered me right away. Havoc, his boys, my old friends, and I sat on the benches on Hav's block and reminisced about old times while drinking forty-ounces. There was a party going down later that night in the projects.

The energy at the block party behind Reese Center that night was intense—ice grills, screw faces, weed smoke, and hard liquor. The party was in a park enclosed by a tall black steel gate with sharp tips on it, with only one way in and out. Everybody was standing around trying to look tough, smoking, drinking, bopping our heads to the music. Something was going to pop off at any moment. About an hour into the party, it did.

This rapper from QB who was unknown at the time named Nasty Nas had a younger brother named Jungle. Jungle got into an argument with somebody and gunshots started flying. Everybody ran to the exit or hit the deck. Hav and I and the two chicks we were with ran and hopped the gate. My pants hooked on one of the sharp tips. I was hanging upside down yelling for Hav to get me off the gate while shots were flying. Hav and one of the chicks, Jessica, darted back, and by the time they ripped me down my jeans were shredded, torn open like those NBA pants with the buttons down both sides. If Jessica's reading this, I know she's dying laughing right now.

That was my first Queensbridge block party and the first time I had bullets whizzing around me. I guess you could say I was hooked on QB from then on.

Hav and I bonded quickly and decided that music was more important to us than school. We went to school just to check in for homeroom attendance, met in the cafeteria, and cut out after lunch. Most of the time we'd jump out of the lunchroom window since it was on the first floor. Sometimes we'd linger by the front door and run when the security guard wasn't looking. A lot of times we'd go to school just to rob people for their clothes, money, Walkmen, train and bus passes, and anything else worth taking.

One Thursday, Hav and I cut out of school to meet two girls at his grandmother's crib in Ravenswood. When we got there, Hav's brother T.J. and their friends from Queensbridge, the Twins and Ty-Nitty, were already at the crib cutting school as well. The Twins, Nitty, and T.J., who were all a few years younger than Havoc and I, said they were on their way out to catch some juxes. Hav pulled some small fruit-cup snacks out of the freezer. "Check it out, P," he said. "You gotta get 'em nice and cold, then pour a little on shorty's clit and lick it off. They go crazy, son, I'm telling you." Yeah, that nigga Hav's a freak. I'd never given a girl head before but that cold fruit-cup thing had me ready to try it.

The girls came through and we went into different rooms for privacy. Nothing happened with me and the girl I was with. Then T.J. and the Twins came back sweaty and out of breath with a mini color TV and other electronics. The guy they'd robbed had started shooting at them. One of the Twins was shot in the leg and went back to QB for help. When Havoc finished up with his shorty, we walked the girls to the train, then I went home.

I took an instant liking to Havoc and his boys because they were into all the criminal risk-taking that I was into. I was sort of living a double life, taking the bus and train to school during the week to make Moms happy, then on weekends going to parties, having sex, drinking, using all kinds of drugs, and doing stickups. We'd rob anybody who looked flashy and even people who didn't. Most of the time, the nonflashy ones were the ones with all the money. In Queensbridge, we would have knockout contests seeing who could knockout a crackhead with one punch. We hung out in the walkway on the Fifty-ninth Street Bridge and robbed people who walked and rode their bikes across, beat up cab drivers for their money, and whatever wasn't cash we took to the pawn shops on Sutphin Boulevard in Jamaica. When the money ran out, I was back to being broke, robbing people for petty shit.

At school one afternoon, I saw this new kid with a dope gray hooded Polo jacket with POLO in big blue letters across the chest, so Hav, Derrick, and I followed him to the train station after school. I jumped in front of him and threw a wild punch but instead of hitting his jaw, I hit his forehead and broke my hand. It probably hurt me more than the kid I hit. I fell back while Hav and Derrick robbed him.

My uncle Lenny had just gotten his hands on a ten-million-dollar brownstone on Ninety-second Street around Eighth Avenue in Manhattan. Uncle Lenny had a lot of mafia connections and said somebody owed him a favor, so they let him live there for a few years. My grandmother never trusted Lenny. She told me, "If you let Lenny in your house, he'll leave with your TV and you won't realize it."

Lenny taught me a lot of street shit. He knew how to manipulate and use people. He taught me the mental part of the game and my pops taught me the physical. I hope he doesn't get upset with me for sharing this, but my uncle Lenny is gay. He doesn't show it at all. There's no reason you should treat a person foul because they're gay.

After I broke my hand on the kid's forehead, Havoc and I took the train to Uncle Lenny's brownstone. I showed my swollen hand to Lenny and he told me it was broken. One of Lenny's "friends" stopped by while we were there, an older Italian man who was a retired boxer. He looked at my hand and confirmed that it was broken, or what's called a boxer's fracture. I saw a lot of tough mafia guys around Lenny who I knew were his "friends." Uncle Lenny told me that he managed gay bars all over New York City for the mafia. After checking out my hand, Lenny made Hav and me some pasta and we left.

I took the train to Moms's job down by the World Trade Center. She'd become a high-ranking employee of the New York City Housing Authority and no longer had to work in the projects. When I got to her office on Murray Street and Broadway, Moms left early to take me to St. Vincent's Hospital. The doctor told me I had a hairline fracture and my pinky knuckle was out of the socket, a boxer's fracture, just like Uncle Lenny's "friend" had said. The doctor pulled my knuckle back into place, wrapped my hand in a small cast, and told me it would ache later in life.

At school the next day, our boy Taffari from Coney Island took a photo of Havoc and me laughing about the situation in the lunchroom, my arm in a sling. It's a classic.

Taffari knew this kid Silver in Coney Island who had a small studio. Havoc and I cut out of school every day and rode the D train for an hour from Manhattan to Silver's crib. In one month we made like fifty songs at Silver's.

I did a couple robberies and got like twenty thousand dollars. Thinking back, I regret it. In time, I paid for every red cent I stole and for every person who got hurt along the way. Karma is very real.

Anyway, I got the bread. At the Coliseum Mall near Jamaica Avenue, I bought Havoc a big gold link with a Mary Mother of God pendant with a big ruby in it. Hav was happy. I bought myself a thick herringbone chain with the biggest Nefertiti piece they had, plus three gold rings. Hav told me about the Steinway Street shopping area in Astoria so we went on a shopping spree, spending about seven hundred dollars on clothes and sneakers. My fifteenth birthday had just passed, so I decided it was time to start driving.

At a used-car lot on Hillside Avenue in Jamaica, Queens, I bought my first car for nine thousand dollars cash. A Sterling luxury car imported from England. I was fifteen with no license, insurance, nothing. But the used-car dealer was so grimy and happy that I had cash, he gave me a temporary registration and said to come back when it expired and he'd give me a new one. I was the littlest muthafucker with big jewelry, the flyest clothes, and a nice car. Since I didn't have a license and looked so young, I had tints put on the windows and mostly drove it at night or on the weekends I spent at Grandmoms's crib.

Back then, people were still walking around with beepers on their hips and if you were lucky to have a cell phone, which was damn near unheard of, it was big and doofy. Car washes sold fake plastic car phones with antennas to stick on your windshield. I bought one and pretended like I was on the phone when I drove past girls. Don't laugh; I got a lot of girls with that trick.

I'd park a couple blocks away or around the corner from my crib so my moms and grandmoms didn't know I had a car. Nine thousand dollars was stashed, left untouched. Almost all the biggest rappers talk about how they've been getting money since back in the day, but I guarantee that none of them were doing what I was doing at fourteen and fifteen. Anybody who knew me from back then can vouch for me.

•   •   •

One Saturday, Havoc came to Grandmoms's dance school. "Is it like this every Saturday?" Hav asked me. He was open and bagged a few girls from there. "I've got to start coming here more often." That weekend, I found out that cousin Craig got locked up again. Somehow he'd been shot in the foot and they locked him up right after.

Havoc and Stobo spent the weekend at my grandmoms's crib in Hempstead. We drove uptown and bought some weed from the patty shop by the Polo Grounds projects, stopped at Willy Burgers on 145th, and then jetted back to Long Island, where I introduced Hav to Carey, Money No, Dirty Harry, and some other friends.

Later that night we went to White Castle, the after-hours hangout in Hempstead. It had just started raining and Hav asked if he could drive my car around the block. We were drunk and high, so even though I knew Hav had never driven a car before, I let him. This kid Kevin who lived around the corner from me went with him just in case. I watched Hav circle around one time, then another. Then he hit the gas too hard when he tried pulling back into the parking lot and almost drove into White Castle. Luckily, he ran over a fire hydrant instead.

My car was stuck on top of a hydrant! When I snapped out of shock, six of us pushed the car off the hydrant and hurried out of there before the cops came. My brand-new imported Sterling sputtered like a moped.

"I'm sorry, son," Hav kept saying. "I'm a pay for it, don't worry." I didn't care because I didn't work hard to get the car anyway. We laughed it off, although it wasn't funny that I'd had the car for only two weeks and was already back to riding the iron horse. If you don't know, that's the train.

Two weeks later I got my car back from the repair shop but it never really drove the same. And Hav and I came up with a name for our group: the Poetical Prophets. Around that same time, my man Carey called and gave me my new name: Prodigy. As soon as I heard it, I was like, "That's it! That's me! I'm runnin' with that."

Hav's cousin Todd took our photos. My brother Greg had a new camera he was proud of, so he took some pictures of us too. Hav agreed to let my moms be our manager and we were ready. We had pictures, a manager, and a fifty-song demo.

We kept cutting school, except now we were walking to record labels all over Manhattan hoping to be heard. We looked on the back of rap albums, got the office addresses to labels, and stood outside until we saw rappers coming or going. Def Jam was our first pick.

While waiting by the front door, this rap group the Afros walked out. I approached them with my Walkman and asked them to listen to our music. "Ain't got time for that, shorty," they said, and kept walking. *Fuck them niggas.*

One afternoon we saw Q-Tip from A Tribe Called Quest by the office on Elizabeth Street and Houston. He was cool. He stopped, put on our headphones, and gave one or two songs a listen. It was 1989 and there were no young rappers with lyrical content like ours. Hav and I made graphic, reality-based hood music. There was nothing like us at that time.

We had Q-Tip open. "Yo, I'm gonna take you inside and introduce you to some people," he said. He brought us inside Def Jam on the spot and introduced us to the entire office. He was the first person in the industry to recognize our talent and give us a chance. Q-Tip even helped set up a meeting with Russell Simmons and Lyor Cohen, the president and owner of the label. We were excited. We felt like that was our pass. *We coming to Def Jam every day now!*

The next day we went to school and stayed the entire day. We hadn't spent a whole day at school in like four months. There were signs on the bulletin board for a school talent show. You know we signed up!

We only liked school because of the girls and robbing students for their goods. Plus, that's where our friends were at. We got drunk and high right before class mostly every day when we actually stayed. We were terrors in that school. We did a lot of things I can't discuss because it would incriminate us. But we ran through that school like we owned it.

Hav and I were pissy drunk at talent-show practice one day, drinking forties of Ballantine Ale and OE. Hav was more bent than me. He told me how he and our boy from school Derrick were planning to set me up to rob me when Derrick first introduced us, but they ended up feelin' my style so they changed their minds. *Wow, crazy. I guess the truth does come out when you're drunk.*

After the rehearsal, somebody in the crowd of ten people started clapping and making a lot of noise for our song "Ahh Shit!" When I got a good look, to my surprise, it was my pops! I was happy as hell to see him and Hav was too. Pops told me Grandmoms was letting him hide out at her new condo on Roosevelt Island, right across the water from my school. My pops—man! It felt real good to see him.

I was excited about my new career as a rapper and told Pops we had a meeting with Russell Simmons in a couple of days. He was happy for us. We walked around Manhattan for a few hours and rode the tram by the Fifty-ninth Street Bridge to Grandmoms's luxury condo on Roosevelt Island. We talked mostly about music, but he asked me about my health and explained that he was on the run again for guns and drugs. "I gotta be careful about how I move around," he said. Pops told me that since he'd be staying at Grandmoms's spot, he'd see me more often. *Cool.* I was happy to see Pops. I ain't seen him in a long time. I rode back from the Island alone and went home.

A couple of days later, it was meeting time. We changed DJs from Taffari to Hav's man Prince A.D. from Queensbridge. Taffari was like six foot one and Prince A.D. was real little like us—he fit in. We were scheduled to meet Russell Simmons at his Manhattan condo around the block from Def Jam. I always kept my gun on me, but I didn't want to disrespect Russell by bringing that type of energy into his home, so this kid Perry at Def Jam let me leave it in his office drawer until we were done.

Perry walked us to Russell's apartment on Broadway near NYU. Russell's assistant let us in. There was a big-ass Jacuzzi tub in the floor in the room next to the living room. The white carpet had just been shampooed and we had to take our shoes off and step on the soapy stinking carpet in wet socks. *Oh, so this is what it's like to have a million dollars and your own record label.* Nervous and excited, we waited around for fifteen minutes until the assistant said Russell wasn't going to be able to make it. He sent us back to the office to meet with Lyor Cohen instead.

Lyor listened to our best songs and told us that we cursed too much and our music was too violent. He said Def Jam couldn't do anything with us because we were too young to speak like that. They would get in trouble with the law for putting our album out.

What?! We couldn't believe it. We were pissed off but we weren't that mad because we knew we had some hot shit. If they didn't sign us it was their loss, not ours. Although a month later, they signed this group Onyx from Jamaica, Queens. These niggas were screaming, cussing, and waving TEC-9s in their videos, looking like black skinheads!

As we were leaving Def Jam, I went to get my gun from Perry's office. We walked in behind him and Perry passed it to Hav instead of me. I asked him for some De La Soul and Slick Rick posters I'd seen lying around, and he went to get them. Hav pointed the gun at me, playing around. "Don't play with me like that," I told him.

When our friend came back with the posters, Hav pointed the gun at him. "Nigga, give me them posters," Hav said, joking. The gun went off, hitting Perry in the stomach, his shirt catching fire where the bullet hit as he fell onto me. Hav dropped the gun and ran out of the building with Prince A.D. right behind him. *Yo, this nigga just shot this muthafucker!* I looked down at Perry as he tried to grab on to my shoulder. "Yo, get off me!" I yanked my arm away from him. *I'm going with my people.* I ran downstairs to catch up with Hav and A.D.

The most popular duo in rap, Run-D.M.C., was walking into the building as Hav, Prince A.D., and I came running out. My boys knocked them to the ground as they busted out of the front door and ran up Houston toward Broadway to the train station. I wasn't far behind.

"Stop those kids!" somebody screamed behind us. When I looked back, it was Ali Shaheed Muhammad, the DJ from A Tribe Called Quest. Hav stopped running and started screaming at me. "I didn't mean it, son! I didn't mean to shoot him! You gotta hide me, son, take me to Florida!" I saw some detectives riding past us in an unmarked car and told Hav to be quiet. The three D's got out of the car and came over to us.

"Is there a problem?" one officer asked. Hav started screaming again. "I didn't mean to shoot him, it was an accident!" The D pulled out cuffs and put them on Havoc. Ali Shaheed Muhammad caught up with us and told the cops what happened. I told them it was an accident, we thought it was a lighter, we found it outside, we didn't know it was a real gun. They took Hav to the bookings. Prince A.D. and I went home.

The next morning when Moms woke me up for school, she had the radio on Kiss FM as usual. While we were both getting dressed, they announced that some rappers got into an argument with Lyor Cohen at Def Jam over contracts and one of the rappers, Kejuan Muchita, shot an A&R because they didn't sign us. *What?!*

I explained the real story to my moms. "I have to go see the dude in the hospital to make sure he's okay and to make sure he knows how it went down," I said. I felt bad because we'd just met the kid through Q-Tip. Perry showed us love, helping us get inside Def Jam instead of having us stand outside like groupies, inviting us to industry parties. But my main focus was getting Perry to agree to tell the story to help Havoc get out of trouble. Moms said she'd come with me, so after school we went to see him. My mother felt more badly for him than I did.

Dude was messed up bad. The bullets were covered in green mold, causing an infection in his intestines. They had to take them out and let them heal outside his body so the infection wouldn't spread. They attached a shit bag to his body while his intestines healed.

"Listen, I'm here for a reason," I said, sitting beside the bed. "This is what you gotta say so Havoc doesn't have to go to jail. We found it outside the office, we thought it was a lighter, we didn't realize it was a gun. Say, *Yeah, that's true, I was there when they found it and they thought it was a lighter.*" Perry was our man so he knew it was just an accident. Hav beat the charges in court.

After that, Def Jam got security guards, big muscle-bound dudes at the front door. Wow, we were setting trends in the game already!

When my sixteenth birthday came around, my moms bought me *The Autobiography of Malcolm X* by Alex Haley, the same guy who wrote *Roots*. I'd never had the patience to read a five-hundred-page book before, but after the first fifty pages I realized that Malcolm X was a street dude before he became a great speaker and leader. Plus Malcolm X was once a part of the Nation of Islam and I wanted to learn more about the 120 Lessons of Islam. It took me two weeks to read, opened my eyes, and planted a seed in my brain. I still had a lot to learn, but I felt a change in my mentality coming, a drastic change.

Havoc and I started recording at this new spot, 5-10 Studio, on South Franklin in Hempstead. Paul, the guy who ran it, and his partner Kerwin, the in-house engineer, both made beats and had a similar style to Public Enemy's producer Hank Shocklee. Paul and Kerwin loved our style and wanted to produce a whole album for us, so we got to use the studio all the time. A lot of big names in rap music came from Long Island—Rakim, Biz Markie, EPMD, De La Soul, Public Enemy, Method Man, Busta Rhymes, and myself. I was proud to represent Hempstead, but I'm glad my moms got me out of there and moved to Queens because I was exposed to a different way of living. The first sixteen years of my life were incredible, but the next sixteen would be nothing short of history-book material.

October 10, 2008
Mid-State Correctional Facility
Marcy, New York
8:00 A.M.

The dorm I was in at Mid-State Correctional Facility held thirty inmates from all walks of life: ex-cops, judges, DAs, school superintendents, COs, a couple of Bloods, and a multimillionaire who ran Tyco and had an ownership stake in the Yankees and the YES (Yankees Entertainment Station) Network—a real motley crew, mostly white men in their late forties.

My homeboy Young, one of the few inmates I was close with, was twenty-two and serving five years for criminal enterprise. We'd laugh about how almost all the white inmates in our dorm had to take psychiatric medication because they couldn't deal with the reality of being in prison. They actually believed that they didn't belong there or should've received lighter sentences or gotten away with their crimes completely—that they were too good to be serving time because of their upbringing, academic background, or résumés. It was hilarious to sit back and analyze them. It made me appreciate being raised on both sides of the tracks. I know what it's like to live in the hood with poverty and in the suburbs with money, so I'm comfortable among savage street mentalities and highbrow squares.

I prefer a savage mind over a square one, because without money, expensive houses in safe neighborhoods, cars, and the other materialism that gives a false sense of security in their little fake-ass world, a square couldn't survive in the real world where poverty and savages are king. Just imagine for a moment, the apocalypse hits. Armageddon. Babylon (the corporate world) is falling. No electricity, bank accounts, gas stations, no calling 911, because there's no phone service. Who will survive longer, if at all? Mr. and Mrs. Square-Ass Lame with their master's degrees and Prada suits? Or Mr. and Mrs. Savage Mentality, who are used to having nothing and are close friends with all the neighborhood criminals?

I suggest you read the Book of Revelation if you're confused about the answer. Having a savage mentality doesn't necessarily make you an evil person. It just means you have a set of survival skills that can be used if needed. There are a lot of people who use it in a negative way. I used to be one of them, but while serving these three years in prison, I practiced keeping a very peaceful state of mind. For those of you who can relate, once you master that level of self-control, you'll notice your life start to drastically improve. It will help you avoid a world of unnecessary trouble. I wish I could've learned this on the streets at sixteen instead of in prison at thirty-three, but my life didn't play out that way.

In late January 1990, right after the new year rolled around, my mother woke me up to go to school at six forty A.M. I don't know what got into me that morning. "I'm not going to school anymore," I told Moms flat out.

She thought I was just talking in my sleep and tried to get me up again five minutes later. "I'm not going to school anymore," I told her again. "I'm going back to sleep."

"Okay," Moms said, and left for work. That was that.

I did eventually go to school again, but it wasn't to go inside. I'd park out front and kick it to the females at Art and Design, then do the same at the all-girls Catholic school down the street called Cathedral. The Cathedral girls walked past our school to get to the train station in their miniskirt uniforms. When I eventually succeeded at getting a Cathedral girl, it was like a dream come true. Her name was Jade, a real pretty seventeen-year-old dark-skinned dime with green chinky eyes from Harlem whose parents owned a brownstone by Convent Avenue. After a week, I had her cutting school to take rides in my Sterling, park, smoke weed, and get busy in the backseat. She was the first girl who would just pull her panties to the side so we could do it with her outfit on.

After three or four episodes with Jade, her phone number was changed. I never went back to Cathedral or Art and Design after that, not even to scoop girls. After Jade, I was on a mission. All I wanted was sex with the finest dimes.

CHAPTER 3

MOBB DEEP

Try to keep a positive mind
I walk a straight line, don't work
So niggas is forced to do dirt
And God made dirt
So this dirt won't hurt

"Shook Ones Pt. 1"

1991.
Havoc and I decided to change our name from Poetical Prophets to Mobb Deep. We needed something that described how we were living. When all the QB niggas got together to hang out, there would be thirty to forty of us, like a mob. The slang we used when we saw a whole bunch of guys together was, "Them niggas is deep." Both words together sounded

good. *Mobb Deep*. I decided to use two Bs because it just looked better with the extra *B*. It made it look even.

I was a high school dropout, full-time rapper stickup kid.

It wasn't long before Hav dropped out too. I was still doing my grand-larceny thing, sold my Sterling for three thousand dollars, and bought my second car, a used red Acura Legend, from the same car lot on Hillside Avenue. I paid nine thousand dollars—cash, of course—then took it to Earl Shieb on Peninsula Boulevard in Hempstead and got it painted money green. At Big Boy Toys on Queens Boulevard they put in white seats with money-green piping, a white dashboard, a Momo steering wheel, and money-green window tints. To top it off, I put hammers on it—rims.

I was sixteen with the illest car. I was on a rampage. My daily schedule was to buy a bunch of weed uptown, then drive around every borough bagging broads.

My man Dirty Harry, who lived around the corner in Hempstead, bought a BMW 5 Series—burgundy with gold trimming, five-star gold rims, and a burgundy ragtop. We used to stare at that car outside the used lot on Jamaica Avenue. "I'm buying that shit," Harry would say. And he damn sure did.

Carey was my closest friend from Hempstead. He lived on the corner of my block and we'd known each other since diapers. My father used to date his moms way back in the day, so Carey and I were like brothers. I stashed all my dirty money at his crib—thirty to forty thousand dollars. You know that's your homie, when you can trust him with that much dough.

Dirty Harry had a friend named Money No. Money No would thug him out for the new car Harry just bought—borrow and bring it back when he felt like it. Money No and I ended up getting real cool. Carey and Money No had some old beef with each other and would fistfight constantly, so I couldn't chill with both of them at the same time. Maybe it was because Money No's father also used to date Carey's moms.

But every Tuesday night we'd hang out at the Rink, a popular roller rink in Teaneck, New Jersey. Man, that was the spot!

We'd race the Beemer and Acura from Hempstead to Teaneck in fifteen minutes flat. Havoc, Prince A.D., Hav's brother T.J., and sometimes

Carey would ride in my Acura, and Money No had his crew in the BMW. Even if we didn't go inside the Rink, the parking lot across the street was a party in itself, packed with females and niggas and their prized possessions—their cars. Dudes walked around the lot selling drugs and temporary licenses for a hundred dollars. I bought like three.

Inside, the Rink was filled with females from all over the Tri-State. Everybody who was anybody was there every Tuesday. It was smaller and more exclusive than the popular Skate Key rink in the Bronx. You had to be in the know. I bumped into one of Hav's boys from QB, Yamit, a few times and we got real cool. He was a drug dealer and Golden Gloves boxer from Brownsville, Brooklyn, who'd moved to Queensbridge. Yamit was famous in the streets of New York, an official ghetto superstar. DJ Clark Kent would pass by us in the rink and the parking lot with our cars and jewelry and say, "You little niggas gonna blow up one day!" He didn't even know we were rappers, he just saw how expensive we looked.

Most of the sex I was having at sixteen came from hanging out at the roller rink and a small spot in Harlem called Ebony Lounge that had an older, well-dressed crowd with some good-looking females in minks and foxes. Derrick's homeboy from the Bronx, DJ Damage, played there. We were the youngest in the twenty-one-and-over spot with our fake IDs, big jewelry, and nice cars. The ladies were all over me, taking turns pinching my butt as I walked through the crowd. Harlem girls got a lot of style, and I wasn't shy about approaching an older woman. We always arrived dressed fresh—Pelle Pelle leather jackets in all sorts of colors and patterns, a different one every night.

The older dudes in the spots wanted to kill us, rob us, and both because we were taking their ladies. But we never had fear in our hearts; we would party anywhere. And we always had guns, so we didn't give a fuck.

I had guns galore. And I kept buying new ones, adding to my collection, different ones for different occasions. Little ones to sneak into parties and big ones in the engine of my Acura for crews that liked jumping people outside parties. We were very well protected from anything that might pop off.

•   •   •

At Ebony Lounge one night, this older female named Tonya, around twenty-six and wearing a gray mink coat, started buying me amaretto sours and other sweet drinks I'd never heard of. She was a nurse from the Bronx who worked at a hospital on the Grand Concourse by Fordham Road a few blocks from Derrick's crib. She was in love with me.

Some nigga Tonya used to mess with would come to the spot every week with his friends to stalk her. I was grinding up on Tonya while she was sucking on my ear in front of the dude to let him know what time it was. Later on, posted up on the wall next to the DJ table with Derrick and Money No, I saw the guy by the bar arguing with Tonya. Then he stormed out. "I think you should leave," Tonya came over to warn me. "He's talking about robbing ya'll when you go outside!" Ha! We laughed and kept partying.

When we walked out of the spot, the dude and six of his friends were standing on the corner watching Money No and me say peace to our people before getting in my car, parked across the street. I grabbed my gun from under the seat and stood outside my ride with it clearly in hand. The dudes whispered and walked away. Clowns, I thought. Dude's mad because a little nigga took his chick. Tuff shit.

Money No and I bounced to the Bronx to meet Tonya and her sister at her crib. Sitting on the couch in their living room, Money No and I were smirking at each other as Tonya served us drinks because the apartment was to' up from the flo' up. But those big asses Tonya and her sister had made us not care. Money No went into her sister's room and Tonya started giving me head right there on the couch. After thirty minutes, her sister called Tonya into the bedroom and Money No came into the living room, telling me that her sister and Tonya both had their period but still wanted to sex us. No thank you! I got caught my first time and it fucked me up for life. Never, ever again.

"P, look!" Money No said, pointing at the floor as we sat on the couch, gun in my pocket just in case. I didn't see anything. "You don't see all them roaches?!" I looked again. There were hundreds of them. As we were inspecting the roach population, a rat ran across the room. "Oh shit!" we both jumped on the couch screaming. We said our good-byes real quick.

Driving across the Triborough Bridge on the way back to Hempstead, a big roach crawled across the dashboard as if to say, "What's up, ya'll?" We pulled over at the first exit, took off our clothes, and shook them out in the street, jumping around like idiots. That was the first and last time I went to Tonya's crib.

We were having the time of our lives—superstars before we were superstars. Money No's and my most favorite thing to do was to drive to Philadelphia for the Greek Festival. There were a lot of little niggas our age with money in Philly, riding four-wheelers and dirt-bike motorcycles in the streets and through the park. Thousands of young people partying in the park, showing off cars, motorcycles, clothes, and females showing off their bodies . . . sweet.

In late autumn, Kid Capri threw a big party on Manhattan's Upper West Side. Derrick and his Bronx crew told me to meet them there, so I scooped Money No and headed to the city. I was wearing a brand-new black-and-olive-green butter-soft Pelle Pelle jacket with red trimming and a gold-barrel link with a Lazarus piece, looking real clean and ready to bag these older niggas' broads as always.

The block was packed when we pulled up. We parked around the corner and walked over to where Derrick and his crew were posted up across from the club entrance. Derrick told me they couldn't get in. We didn't care; it was like a party outside, with females roaming around who couldn't get in either.

One of Derrick's boys kicked it with me about this gun that I'd been trying to convince him to sell to me for five months. It was the illest gun I'd ever seen—still is, to this day—an all-plastic black TEC-22 with a forty-two-shot banana clip. He finally offered me some ridiculous price like eight hundred dollars. It wasn't that hot! I had a .22 revolver in my pocket so I wasn't pressed, though the gun looked sweeter than a muthafucker—like a toy.

On the walk back to the car after twenty minutes, Money No and I passed some guys lighting off firecrackers. *Is somebody shooting at us?* I pulled my gun out of my pocket discreetly. It was the night before Halloween, chilly. *Why are they still blastin' fireworks?* When I realized it was just firecrackers, I put my piece back quick as I pulled it out.

We stopped at the corner store for White Owl cigars and soda. As soon as I walked out of the store, I was surrounded by police squad cars pulling up from every angle. *"Freeze! Freeze!* Don't fucking move! Get on the ground!"* I complied with their demands. *Damn, I'm going to jail,* I thought.

It wasn't hard to find the gun, right in my jacket pocket. Before they threw the cuffs on, I gave the car keys to Money No. They put me in the squad car and took me downtown. It was my first time getting locked up. I flashed back to when I was eight in the backseat of the cop car holding my pops's cuffed hands. I dropped a few tears. I was only sixteen and didn't know what was going to happen. I thought I was going to prison for a long time.

At the station, they took my fingerprints, mug shots, and transported me to the Tombs. I spent the night in the Tombs in downtown Manhattan, a giant building with numerous courtrooms including the Supreme Court and, in the basement, hundreds of prisoners.

The Tombs stank, filled with bums and grimy New Yorkers, whoever they arrested off the street stuck in the holding cell together. It's every man for himself in there. I didn't have any problems. I knew how to carry myself. I didn't sleep, paid attention. The cops kicked and slammed on the door every couple hours as they moved people in and out.

Hours passed. The bullpen started to fill up and this white man began kicking on the steel door, yelling and screaming to be released. The kid I was smoking a cigarette with and I were laughing at that fool. The corrections officers came in and told him to wait like everyone else but he wouldn't shut up. "I've been in here for hours!" he shouted. "When do I see the judge?" The COs took him into another room and beat him up while we listened to him scream some more.

Moms and Uncle Lenny came to get me out the next morning. Since I was a youthful offender I got R.O.R., released on my own recognizance. My birthday was in two days. I was turning seventeen.

I ended up getting five years' probation and 150 hours of community service at St. Peter's Church in Midtown Manhattan, right around the block from Art and Design. My grandpops's old jazz buddy Reverend Gensel wrote letters on my behalf to hook that up. During my daily three hours at St. Peter's, he'd tell me stories about playing jazz with Grandpops. The church served free food for homeless people with AIDS so I helped set up the tables and chairs then put them all away.

My father left New York to hide out in California. He'd been on the run for like four years. After resolving his jewelry-store robbery case, he caught another case when the cops pulled him over on the highway and found a couple keys of cocaine and two Uzis in the trunk of his car, so he went on the run again. He made connections in Cali to change his identity, but he needed his moms's help. She couldn't send money or wire it through the bank because that would leave a paper trail, so Grandmoms caught a flight to Los Angeles and took me along for the ride. It was winter recess at school, so my moms let me go.

When we arrived in L.A., Michael Peters came to pick us up from the airport. Michael was a famous dance choreographer who my grandmother raised and taught to dance. He made a big name for himself by creating the dance moves for Michael Jackson's "Beat It" and "Thriller" videos. He was proud to show my grandmother how well he was doing and brought us to his mansion in the Hollywood Hills. They drank and talked about old times at the dance school while I walked around Michael's living room admiring the pictures on his walls of him smiling with celebrities.

We checked into a hotel room at Universal Studios. When I was a kid, my grandmother took me to the Universal Studios theme park right next to the hotel, where they showed us how they did the special effects in movies. Even though I was older now I still wanted to go, so Michael said he'd take me while we were in town. Michael was gay as hell but I grew up around a lot of gay dudes at my grandmother's school so it didn't bother me. Mike was cool. He was like family.

The next day, my grandmother and I met my pops at a grimy storefront on Malcolm X Boulevard in Compton to get the fraudulent identification. The fat dude behind the desk had a twelve-gauge shotgun leaning against the wall beside him. Pops and Grandmoms exchanged small talk with the dude for fifteen minutes like they had friends in common. Pops gave the guy a yellow envelope filled with twenty-five hundred dollars. After the fat fuck counted it, he gave my pops a bigger yellow envelope with his new paperwork. Pops opened and checked it all out—a birth certificate, Social Security card, driver's license, and utility bills, all with his new name, Carlos Johnston.

Back at the hotel, Pops told us he'd be living in San Jose. He'd met some broad out there and they were starting a new life together.

Pops and I went to see *Boyz 'N the Hood* that night near Marina del Rey. It was opening weekend and shootouts and stabbings were erupting at theaters across the country. The theater was packed. We jumped out of our seats when my song "Too Young" started playing during the backyard barbecue scene when Ice Cube came home from prison. He was proud that his son accomplished something like that. That was the last time I got to hang out with my pops.

Nine months later, the feds finally found him in San Jose. He had a good run, though—five years. He did two years in a federal prison in California, then they shipped him to a fed joint in Georgia for another few.

Back in New York, I hung out in QB every day with Hav's friends. Jamel and Jamal were twins—you could tell them apart because Jamel had two razor cuts on his cheeks, a long one on the right cheek and a short one on the left, from a brief Rikers Island bid. Someone came up behind him with two razors and cut him on both sides. We called Jamal Twin Gambino and Jamel the Scarface Twin.

Then there were Ron Gotti, Ty-Nitty, and Trip, who came to be known as Godfather; Karate Joe, who was a martial arts expert; Yamit, the Golden Gloves boxer; Free High, who smoked everybody's weed and never chipped in or bought his own; Capone, who had a reputation for supposedly shooting a cop and cutting people with razors; Draws, who we called Super Trooper because he survived numerous shootouts and had been shot multiple times; Rap and Spark, two older laid-back hustlers who didn't hang out with us much because they were wiser than us, though when they did come around, they'd advise us to stop all our young-minded shit and just get money; Prince God, who was always just coming home from jail; Opps aka Dead Arm 'cause he knocked dudes out with one hit; and Tejuan—they called him Noyd because he looked like the Domino's Pizza character the Noid. He was the only one in the crew with his own apartment, no parents. He was the same age as Hav and me but was on his own because his moms reportedly got locked up for cutting off her man's finger and left him with the crib. That was the hangout spot; we called it the Honeycomb Hideout.

Noyd had another nickname: the Natural Born Hustler. He had to pay the bills and support himself. He'd moved to QB five years prior from Red Hook projects in Brooklyn. He didn't speak to me much and wasn't friendly at first, but I was a new face so I didn't expect him to be. I'm that same way with people.

The Twins were also hard on me when I first came around. They told me if I wanted to be down with their crew, I had to battle every rapper in QB. So we got some E&J and weed and walked around the entire projects, and I had to battle whoever was outside who had a name. I was gettin' busy. The Twins would amp me up. "Yeah, this is my nigga P! Ya'll can't fuck with his verses!" Finally they told me I had to battle Nas.

It was around ten P.M. on a Friday night. We were all drinking outside in front of Havoc's building. "C'mon, let's go see if Nas is over there on the block," Twin Gambino said. Nas, Jungle, and Grand Wiz sat on the same bench on the Fortieth side of Vernon every night; that was their bench. Havoc's and Nas's blocks were on opposite ends of the projects. You had to cross a hill in order to get to the other side. You could go through the blocks, but most people crossed the hill. The two sides, the Fortieth and Forty-first sides, beefed with each other sometimes.

Nas and them were sitting on the bench as usual. "Yo, I got my man P right here, he wanna battle you," Gambino said. Nas was nonchalant like, *All right, corny little dude . . . who does this kid think he is coming around to battle me?* That's Nas—everybody knew how nice he was back then. I had a little liquor in me so I was feeling myself. It was time to battle Nas.

The Twins and I stood next to Nas and two of his boys on the bench. I was nervous as hell. I spit, Nas spit, then I spit some more. We lit a blunt and passed it around in between raps. When I heard Nas rhyme I thought, *Damn, I can't say no shit better than that! His was better than mine.* He told me my shit sounded cool and his boys said the same. I knew Nas had the better rap but the Twins were always encouraging me. "You the best P, you the best!" Nas was the best. Havoc was better than me, too.

We shook hands, and the Twins and I walked back over to Hav's block on the Forty-first side. "You're doing your thing, P, but there's one more person you gotta battle," they said. "If he says you good, then you good."

"Who is he?" I asked. "Where's he at?"

"You gotta wait, he's locked up right now. His name is Cormega. If you can hang with Mega, then you can hang with us."

Everybody in the hood said that Mega was a hundred times better than Nas, and Nas was fuckin' *good*. They had me scared to death to battle Mega. Mega was supposedly locked up for a crime he didn't even commit. Some white chick had been mugged and pointed Mega out while she was sitting in the back of a cop car and he was minding his business. He got five years for that bullshit.

I was seventeen years old in 1992, but in my heart and mind, I was more like twenty-five. I moved out of my moms's apartment and practically lived at Hav's moms's crib with him, his brother T.J., his sister Tameeka, his moms, and her boyfriend. Once I got a taste of the largest housing project in North America and became part of the action, it was addictive. Six blocks, ninety-six buildings. Every block had a crew. Hav's was the 12th Street crew from the Forty-first side of Twelfth Street. Mostly everybody sold crack and had money rolls in their pockets.

The excitement of QB hooked a lot of people with its new slang, unique style of dress, and cool characters. Queensbridge had its own way of doing things. We cuffed the bottom of our pants different, laced our shoes different—even tied them different, looping the laces through every other hole. People get sucked into that hood. They say New York is fast-paced—well, QB is triple that speed mentally. We had to think fast, react fast, and have animal instincts in order to survive in that hood.

Crackheads from different states and countries found their way to Queensbridge because in QB they sold big, loose rocks in their hands instead of a bunch of tiny pieces stuffed in a crack vial like other hoods. We called crack "he-mes," cigarettes "bogies," and St. Ides malt liquor "thainy." The word *thainy* came from our own cryptic speech code, something like pig Latin. This kid Bumpy started it and I dubbed it the Thun Language. For example, instead of calling each other son we said "thun," and "thorty" instead of shorty.

It got real intricate. Bumpy had a speech impediment that made him talk like that naturally, but we all turned it into our hood slang.

We even had slang terms for money—a one-hundred-dollar bill was called a "man," fifties were "half a man," twenties "dubs," tens "demons," and a five was a "fever." We called the police "jakes" from the eighties TV show *Jake and the Fatman,* and a phone was a "jack." Jewelry was "shine" or "special effects," oral sex was called a "head spin," and regular sex was a "back spin." We were doing and saying things nobody had seen or heard before.

One afternoon, Twin Gambino knocked on the door and told me Cormega was home and it was time for us to battle. I reluctantly got up and followed him outside to the card table where Mega was posted up on a set of crutches. I introduced myself, and he explained how he'd broken his leg in a motorcycle accident as soon as he got home. After the small talk, we started rappin'. Mega was definitely better than all of us. The way he put his rhymes together—his wordplay was extra unique. I was scared to rap after him, but I did. Mega said he liked my shit. I was in. I passed the test.

Twin Gambino told me that after I battled Nas, Nas told everybody that I sounded weak and corny and Havoc should go solo. I wasn't surprised. Even I thought I was wack compared to Nas, although Gambino never made me feel that way. He told me that in his opinion I could be better than him. "Man, fuck Nas!" Gambino said. "Don't listen to him, he's just jealous." To me, Nas was the best there was. I never had sour feelings toward Nas—I looked up to him. Gambino telling me that Nas said I was wack only fueled me.

I grew to love Havoc, his family, his friends, and Queensbridge so much that I wasn't going to let anything make them turn around and say, "P is wack, let's cut him off." From that day on, I went on a rap mission because I wanted to be accepted by my new friends. I didn't want Hav to go solo. It sparked a fire in me. I would like to thank Nas, the Twins, Havoc, and the entire 12th Street crew for bringing me into your world. I love ya'll.

CHAPTER 4

JUVENILE HELL

Buyin' new gear, nothin' but the best
Forget Levi's, strictly Polo and Guess
But how would I make the cash?
It gotta be easy and it gotta be fast

"Peer Pressure"

Hav and I did a few talent shows and went to a lot of industry parties in 1992, still trying to get signed after the Def Jam incident. Since we were so young and were the smallest dudes at the parties, music-industry people started to take notice. Matty C, a writer for *The Source* magazine's Unsigned Hype column, decided to feature us in the magazine. I bought like twenty copies when it hit stands. Slick Rick was on the cover. I was amazed—we were in a magazine!

Matty played our music for Bonz Malone, an A&R at 4th & Broadway Records. He wanted to sign us immediately and had a contract ready within a week with a twenty-thousand-dollar advance.

We had a falling-out with my moms just before we made the deal. We'd made it past the first few rounds of auditions at a New York State talent search and my mother had taken us to the main audition in the projects on the Lower East Side. When our song "Ahh Shit!" came on, the dude in charge was like, "Stop the tape, you can't curse!" We got into an argument, and they kicked us out of the show. "Fuck you, fuck this show!" we shouted. "You're gonna remember us!"

My mother didn't curse; she was a real positive person, into new age thinking. "You can't talk to people like that!" she said. "This is business!"

"Moms, Mobb Deep is the best that there is in rap music!" I said. "Guaranteed, we're better than anybody that's in that talent show."

"You can't go around thinking and talking like that," Moms said.

"Listen, if you don't think we're the best, you shouldn't be managing us," we told her. Moms was right. We shouldn't have cursed the dude out. But of course we're supposed to feel like we're the best.

Our new manager was this dude Dave, a well-dressed, soft-spoken guy from Queens with a good business mentality; Havoc found him somewhere. Moms was pissed. She spoke to her friend Brenda Dash, a real authentic psychic, about it. "Just leave them alone, they've gotta learn on their own," Brenda, who's Damon and Stacey Dash's aunt, told her. She eventually listened to Brenda and fell back.

Moms didn't think 4th & Broadway was a good deal, but we just wanted the dough and our videos on TV. Dave negotiated a good deal for us, in our opinion. We signed the deal.

Early the next morning, Havoc came knocking on my door, hyped up with the first half of our advance money. My moms had moved to Jersey City for a little while to get away from LeFrak after I was arrested for selling crack my freshman year. I wouldn't wake up until Hav eventually started banging. Still groggy, I opened the door and Hav stood there smiling with a mouthful of gold teeth, ten separate caps lining his top row, a brand-new Pelle Pelle leather jacket, and an envelope full of cash.

"What's this?" I asked.

"I picked up our advance today," he said. We split twelve thousand dollars—six thousand apiece. "C'mon, let's go shopping."

I learned how to make beats in my grandmother's basement with Grandpops's records. My grandfather left me his entire jazz collection from all his travels. Looking back at his life and the way he died, I realized that Grandpops did it real big. His friend Quincy Jones detailed a lot of their wild times on tour in his autobiography. Grandpops died while touring the world at age seventy-three. I used to think, *I wanna go out just like that*. But as I got older, I realized that I wanted to live much longer.

A handful of our songs were samples from his collection. We rushed, recording the whole album at 5–10 Studio, and didn't try hard to make hit records. I spent $2,200 on some studio gear and taught myself how to make beats.

Hav would come to my crib and watch me put ideas together in the basement. I taught him how to use the equipment. He picked it up fast. "Hold up, let me try something real quick," he'd say while I was working on a track, and then he'd hog it for hours. I swear it seemed like Hav was guided by spirits when he was on the sampler. He had this blank yet intense look in his eyes like he was possessed. I let him do his thing. It was really kind of amazing. After a while, I'd leave the basement while he was working on a track, smoke a blunt and drink a forty with my Long Island crew, come back with food and beer for Hav, and he'd be done. Then we'd work on the lyrics.

Havoc used to write some of my rhymes because my style and flow didn't match the unique style and flow he had coming from Queensbridge. He wrote my rhyme on "Peer Pressure" and a couple of other songs on that album, but after that I caught on just as fast as he caught on with the beats. I put my own twist on it, and when I wrote verses I always felt a higher power guiding me. It surprised me, what I wrote sometimes. Not the things I said, but the way I said it, like a force in my head was telling me, *No, nigga, say it this way!*

We made three beats on that album, but we'd just started learning how to make them, so that's exactly how the beats sounded—amateur. We shot two videos, one for a song called "Hit It from the Back" in Laurelton, Queens, and another for "Peer Pressure" in the Lower East Side of Manhattan.

Our album *Juvenile Hell* was released in 1993, a year after we recorded it, and was a flop. It sold a little over twenty thousand copies and the label dropped us quick fast. We learned a serious lesson: We had to take songwriting and producing seriously or we wouldn't get another chance. Our excuse was that we were only seventeen when we recorded the music, just kids, we were still learning. But there are no excuses in this business—you either do or you die!

While we were on our promo tour for the album, Nas dropped the *Illmatic* album; that really overshadowed our feeble attempt at rap music. *Illmatic* was and still is one of the best rap albums ever. Nas was an incredible songwriter, and the beats he chose were just as good. "Halftime," produced by Large Professor, was the best song out. During an in-store appearance in Washington, D.C., they were playing that song. *"When I attack there ain't an army that could strike back, so I react never calmly on a hype track . . . Whenever I freestyle I see trial niggas say I'm wow, I hate a rhyme biter's rhyme, stay tuned, Nas, soon the real rap comes at halftime. . . ."* It made us want to hurry home and start working on a new album.

Even though *Juvenile Hell* wasn't a big success, the U.S. promotional tour across California and the entire East Coast built us a cult following. While we were in Cali, it blew our minds to find fans who had cassettes of the entire fifty-song demo we recorded in Coney Island. For our demo to travel from New York across the map to Cali—before the Internet or mix tapes— meant that people were really feeling us! We did college and underground-radio interviews. In New York, Stretch Armstrong and Bobbito were among the first to show us love and play our music on Columbia University's radio station WKCR.

The Nas *Illmatic* craze helped boost our popularity because DJs and press people would always ask, "So you're from the same hood as Nas, huh?" The "Hit It from the Back" video was so erotic, filled with fat asses and explicit lyrics, that it started getting burn on the Playboy Channel: ". . . *cunt* little stunt with my butter dick shorty, you talk too much, so lay back and enjoy the blunt. . . ." So like I said, we made ourselves a little cult following.

One night around Halloween, we did a show at the Nottington House, a small spot right behind the Rib Shack restaurant on Linden Boulevard in Jamaica, Queens. While we were onstage performing "Hit It from the Back," a bunch of dudes in the crowd were giving us the cold stare. "We tired of all that Queensbridge shit!" they started yelling. "Fuck Queensbridge! Southside, nigga!"

Pandemonium broke out when we got offstage, people throwing bottles and chairs and running everywhere. Come to find out, it wasn't just Southside Jamaica niggas tired of all the Queensbridge hype. This kid named T who was onstage with us that night had beef with some dudes out there. Man, they were really trying to kill him! The brawl inside erupted into gunfire outside. Hundreds of shots were let off that night. The Camry we rode away in just so happened to be the car T rode in. We had to duck on the car floor because bullets were blasting through the windows. *This fool almost got us killed!*

When we got the news from our manager that the label dropped us after the album tanked, we were already working on new music so it fueled us. We fired our manager Dave and hired this girl Keisha, our man Lebraun from Art and Design's sister. Keisha had her own apartment in Harlem on 149th Street and St. Nicholas Avenue, almost directly across the street from the famous Branson "candy" store. Keisha invited Havoc and me to move in with her. We took her up on the offer. Havoc and I still used our little studio at my crib but spent most of our time at Keisha's.

The neighborhood had a ton of females. Keisha had this fine-ass cousin named Thalia who would come over to do Keisha's hair and nails. Thalia was bad as hell—light-skinned with chinky eyes, her hair in a wrap with colorful hairpins, slim body, nice curves in the right places. Thalia was at least six years older and had a man but I was a fly little nigga who was already taking other niggas' women. I was dead set on getting with her.

Keisha went out one night and left Hav and me with the apartment. After a few hours, Thalia and one of her girlfriends came over, a big Andre the Giant–looking creature with a slight Billy Dee mustache. Thalia sat at the dinette table with me and got right down to business. "I heard you wanted to see me," she said. I was shocked. She told me that she had a man, then grabbed her girlfriend and went into the bedroom to tell her something.

"Yo, she on you, kid," Hav said. "I bet you can hit that right now. If I were you, I'd take her into the bedroom when they come back out. Yo, what's up with her friend though? She's kinda wack, right?" I laughed in agreement as the girls came back.

Thalia and I went into the bedroom and started kissing, closed the door, and took off our clothes. She handed me a condom and started riding me. Her big brick cell phone rang. It was her man. She started arguing with him as I sucked her nipples and piped her at the same time. *She's actually talking to her man while having sex with me*, I thought. She hung up on him and we kept doing us. Thalia was a stone-cold freak.

A few minutes later, Thalia's phone rang again. Her man must've told her he was outside because she hopped off of me and looked out the window, saying, "Oh shit." Her man was standing in front of his Cherokee Jeep, a heavyset older dude with an Afro blowout. Thalia got some more young dick, then quickly got dressed as I kissed and sucked on her neck before she bounced.

From the window, I watched the girls hop into the Jeep with the dude and pull off. I asked Hav if he hit the big girl and he said, yeah, he took one for the team. That experience ruined my image of women. Females are grimy. But that shit made me like Thalia even more.

After like six months of living with Keisha, we'd overstayed our welcome and she stopped managing us. But our hoo-ra in Harlem was a good time, especially Thalia. Ha!

Havoc was tired of traveling to my crib in Long Island to record, so we agreed to move the equipment to his moms's crib in Queensbridge. Nineteen ninety-three in Queensbridge was a memorable year. Nas made everyone proud to be from QB. Not to mention the Juice Crew legacy, the generation of rappers that came before us in the early eighties when I was still in Reese Day Camp: M.C. Shan, Kool G Rap, Biz Markie, Tragedy, Craig G, Masta Ace, Big Daddy

Kane, Roxanne Shante, and superproducer Marley Marl, who lived in the building right next to Havoc.

One day, Havoc brought me to the hood photographer Dark Brother aka Riley's crib, a small QB apartment in the same building as the Twins and Noyd, right next to Hav's building. This dude had pictures of everything and anything that ever set foot inside of QB! It was like the Queensbridge Museum of History, with old pictures in frames of the Juice Crew members chillin' on the block like us before they were famous; old pictures of Havoc and Nas; a shot of Biz Markie, Big Daddy Kane, and Kool G Rap standing in the middle of one of the blocks. It blew my mind when I found out Marley Marl produced "My Melody" by Eric B. and Rakim. He produced the entire *Paid in Full* album. Wow, I was impressed. It gave me an understanding of how serious that hood was when it came to rap-music history.

We made a bunch of new songs that were on fire. We'd make the beats at Hav's moms's crib, then go to a new studio in downtown Brooklyn at Hoyt and Schermerhorn to record. One of Hav's older hustler homies from QB named Star paid for our sessions. Star was cool as hell—he was making so much dough that he didn't want anything in return. He just wanted to see us succeed.

From the studio, we'd rush back to the hood to let everybody on the block hear our new songs. That's how we tested all our music. If the hood loved it, then the world would love it, was our motto.

That spring we threw a big barbecue for Havoc's birthday on his block. One of his boys from 12th Street named Trev shared the same birth date, May 21, along with a soon-to-be rap star from Brooklyn, Biggie Smalls. It was the first time we threw our own party in QB, and we did it up with free food and alcohol for whoever came through.

We started shopping our new demo around. Uptown/MCA was one of the first labels we tried. We met with an A&R named Puffy. Derrick from school knew him from back in the day and set up the meeting. Puff loved our music. In Puff's office, he and Derrick were playing around and got into a wrestling match. Derrick scooped Puff up by his legs and slammed him on the desk hard, knocking stuff all over the place.

Bad Boy was just starting, and Puff didn't have any artists yet. He wanted Mobb Deep to be the first to come out on his new label. Puff had a little fame from working with Uptown/MCA artists Heavy D and Finesse & Synquis, a female rap duo known for their song "Soul Sisters" and for wearing green-and-yellow MCM suits. He introduced us to Andre Harrell, who was in charge of MCA's black music department. They wanted to sign us right then and there. We told them we'd think about it. Puff, who was a party promoter, invited us to a party he was throwing that night at a club called the Building on Twenty-fourth Street and Sixth Avenue in Manhattan.

Of course we agreed. We went back to the hood, gathered our boys, got some liquor and some mess tabs, and celebrated the offer and our new friendship with Puff.

At the club, the bouncer at the front door wouldn't let us in because we looked so young. We told him we were on the list and to go get Puff. Finally, Puff came and let us in.

Leaders of the New School were onstage performing when we walked in. The most hyper one in the group, Busta Rhymes, had a box of promotional cassettes he was tossing into the crowd. When he tossed the last cassette, he flung the box into the crowd and it hit me dead in my forehead. I was pissed, but more embarrassed than anything.

After the show, we went backstage and I stepped to Busta. "Yo, you hit me with that fucking box!" I barked at him. Busta's real tall, about six foot three, so he looked down at me and said, "My bad, shorty, it was a mistake."

I can't front, I was kinda starstruck, so I let it slide with a handshake. We proceeded to get drunk and high at the bar. Within the hour, a fight broke out between this crew the Young Guns from Mount Vernon and some other guys. Puff was visibly upset that they'd broken up his party, screaming and yelling from behind a few bodyguards who had guns out. We left and went home.

Around September 1993, we brought a copy of our demo to Matty C at *The Source*. He'd called a few days before and told us he'd gotten an A&R job at this new company, Loud Records, and that the president, Steve Rifkind, wanted to meet with us. Matty said he'd set up the meeting and give us a call.

That weekend, Hav wanted to chill at my grandmother's house in Long Island because he had a girl coming over and there wasn't room in his moms's crib to get busy with girls. "She has a friend for you, too," he said.

"Cool, you know I'm with that," I said. So we went to Long Island. It seems like yesterday.

It was a sunny Saturday afternoon. We had the crib all to ourselves because my grandmoms was at dance school. Hav's girl Shawna rang the bell. I was upstairs fixing up my room just in case I was gettin' some. Hav brought the girls to the basement and was playing records when I came down. "P, this is KiKi," Hav said, introducing me to Shawna's friend. "KiKi, that's P."

Shorty was real good-looking with chinky eyes and sexy lips. I kicked it with her in the basement, then invited her upstairs so we could be alone.

After talking in my room for a while, we ordered Chinese food. The girls wanted to go to the movies, but Hav and I had different plans. After we ate, it was right back to business. KiKi and I got busy in my room. KiKi was just my type of girl because she wasn't acting all prissy or scared. She's real pretty and didn't front with the punani. Who wants to be turned down when you're trying to get some?

I was feeling KiKi. We talked for a few hours after that. She told me how she's from Brooklyn but was living in Ridgewood, Queens. *I can see myself with KiKi,* I thought. *She's cute with the perfect body and a tough attitude . . . my dream girl.*

Back in Queensbridge, the new rapper Biggie Smalls started making a lot of noise with his song "Party and Bullshit": *"I was a terror since the public school era, bathroom passes, cuttin' classes, squeezin' asses, smokin' blunts was a daily routine. . . ."* The Scarface Twin constantly played it on his boom box out on the block. Puff signed Biggie soon after offering us that deal.

Queensbridge was tremendous. Everybody was a drug dealer—the Twins, Noyd, Trip, Ron Gotti, the whole hood. Niggas would be outside 24-7 selling crack like it was a candy store, making thousands a day. On Fridays, the top dealers would take everybody from the crew shopping.

There were almost twenty of us in the 12th Street crew. They accepted me into their crew like a brother even though I didn't sell drugs with them and wasn't from QB—treated me like I was one of them. They spent thousands on everybody—twenty pairs of Timberlands, twenty Champion hoodies, twenty army jackets, twenty pants, twenty everything. If one person got, we all had.

But later in life I realized they weren't doing it because they had good hearts. It was because they weren't properly paying their dealers, so they'd take them all shopping to keep them quiet, the same way a pimp does his hoes. "Keep 'em lookin' good, pretty and all that, but no dough!"

We went shopping on Steinway Street in Astoria and clubbing at night, mostly Puffy's parties at the Building and Red Zone because we could get in with no problem. We also hit the Muse, Home Base, 20 West, Club 2000, the Fever, and our favorite, the Palladium. A lot of fights, cutting faces open with razors, breaking champagne bottles over heads, gunshots, and drunken memories.

We were becoming immune to violence and danger. After Havoc's brother T.J. got heavy into the drug game, he started bustin' his gun a lot. We gave him the name Killer Black. He would shoot people in a heartbeat. We couldn't bring Killer to industry functions because he might murder somebody if they looked at us wrong. I started buying bigger guns and keeping 'em on me at all times.

Around three o'clock one afternoon during the school week, Dirty Harry from Hempstead, Killer, and I were walking from the Coliseum Mall on Jamaica Avenue to my car. A gang of forty high school kids came down the sidewalk looking to start trouble. Killer Black walked straight through the dudes, bumping hard into whoever was in his way. I knew Killer was going to do that before he even did it, so I rushed ahead to my Acura and popped the hood to get my Mac-11 out of the engine.

As I popped the hood, I looked to my left and saw the police posted up in a squad car on the corner. Turning back toward Killer, I saw the pack of dudes surrounding him, about to start swinging punches. I ran over, cocked a round inside the chamber of the Mac, and screamed, "What's up!" Everyone ran except for one kid, who dropped his backpack and stood frozen, scared to move. Killer laughed, picked up the kid's backpack, and threw it in his face. "Get the fuck outta here!" Killer yelled. The kid ran.

After that incident, Killer told the story to everybody in the hood, so I was looking good in the streets. At least niggas knew I was ready to bust my gun anywhere, even in front of the police.

Killer started selling drugs with this crew on Nas's side of the projects. The head guy over there was this dude Little Lord, a sixteen-year-old crack kingpin. Killer was also his gunman. Little Lord wanted to buy my Acura, so he took me to his grandmother's crib in Ravenswood—it's a crazy coincidence how all of our grandmothers lived in Ravenswood—and showed me his money stash. Little Lord had like two hundred thousand dollars stacked in shoeboxes in a closet. I was impressed. He offered me ten thousand dollars to buy my Acura, but I wasn't ready to sell it yet.

A few days later, my car was stolen down the block from my crib in Hempstead. Right away, you're probably thinking that Little Lord stole it, but he didn't even know where I lived or parked my car. I called the precinct and they found my car stripped down to the bone in Ozone Park, Queens. *I should have sold it to Little Lord for the 10K.* What made it even worse was that I had my Mac-11 in the engine and didn't know if the police found it or not. When I went to get the car, I took Killer and Little Lord with me. We were all nervous, wondering if they would arrest me for the gun. Nothing happened.

When I saw my car, I could have cried. They took my white seats with the green piping—$5,000—my rims—$1,500—my steering wheel—$1,000—my passenger-side air bag—$700. Dirty bastards even took my trunk lid—$1,200. $9,400 worth of shit! I popped the hood to see if my Mac was still there . . . *Yes!* At least they didn't get the burner.

Little Lord gave me two thousand dollars cash and towed the car to his crib. I was just happy to get my Mac back.

Soon after I sold the Acura skeleton to Little Lord, Havoc's little cousin from Crown Heights, Brooklyn, Ferg, moved to Queensbridge to live with us for a little while. Ferg was about fourteen or fifteen, a cool little muthafucker—crazy, but he was cool. He was laying low in QB because he'd been sticking up and shooting up too many people around his way.

While Hav was in the crib working on beats, Ferg and I chilled outside on the block. If I was broke and Gotti or Trip from the 12th Street crew were outside hustling, they'd give me five or ten bucks to get something to eat. I hit Gotti up a lot of times.

One of those hungry summer days, about a week after the infamous Colin Ferguson shooting spree on the Long Island Rail Road—the guy who shot all those white people dead—I took Ferg to my crib in Hempstead to get more bullets for my Mac from this dude named Blot who had everything. Blot came to my crib once trying to sell Killer and me grenades for forty dollars apiece.

We took the train all the way out to Hempstead, and Blot wasn't anywhere to be found. We chilled for a couple of hours, then got back on the LIRR to Jamaica. I boarded the train first and sat down. When I looked up, I didn't see Ferg. Two minutes later, he came walking on the train, his hand in his shirt with two fingers poking through like a gun. He told the passengers: "Shhhh! Nobody fucking move, this is a stickup! Put your wallets and purses on the ground now!"

I couldn't actually hear him from where I was sitting, but seeing him with his fingers pointed through his shirt while the passengers tossed their wallets and purses on the ground, I figured it out fast. This nigga walked over to where I was sitting. "Yo son," he said nonchalantly, laughing like it was a joke. "I told these muthafuckers it's a stickup and they believe me!" One of the passengers must have told the conductor, because suddenly the police rushed our train car with guns pointed at us. "*Freeze!* Don't fucking move!"

I couldn't believe what this little dude just did, not to mention that Colin Ferguson just killed all those people the week before. Ferg was charged as a minor and they hit me with twelve counts of attempted robbery. Man, this fool had us on the front-page news! Ferg went home immediately, but I was sitting in Nassau County jail for almost a week before I was bailed out. I beat all those charges. But that was the last time I took Ferg anywhere.

Before the LIRR incident, Ferg told me how he shot someone's arms off with a shotgun and other stuff that I won't repeat. Ferg was so young and spoke so freely, I didn't believe everything he said until he got locked up a year later for cutting up a fireman with a box cutter. Ferg was sentenced to nine years for the fireman and hit with more time for wildin' while inside. He should be home by the time this book drops if he'd calm his hot ass down.

•   •   •

When I lost my Acura that summer and found myself locked up again, I attempted to start making smarter decisions about my spending habits and how I was moving around. I bought a thousand-dollar hooptie, a 1984 Toyota Celica, light blue with white seats. Killer and I named it the Lil Nigga. The Twins almost died laughing when I told them my car's name. Havoc bought a burgundy 1990 Toyota Camry for four thousand dollars. Nas was riding around the hood in a gold 1995 Lexus GS and it wasn't even 1995 yet.

Nas's debut, *Illmatic*, had gone gold in October 1994, and he was having a party at the Melting Pot nightclub in Manhattan. The whole QB went. The party was poppin' for a few hours when some guy in a wheelchair started beefing with one of the QB homies. *How is somebody in a wheelchair still beefing?* I thought to myself. Everybody from the hood was upset because Nas's moms and baby moms Carmen were there and shouldn't be exposed to needless drama, so one of the QB dudes kicked the wheelchair gangsta in the chest, knocked him out the wheelchair, and started brawling with his crew. People got shot, stabbed, cut, and beat down. It seemed people didn't believe what we said in our songs or they didn't care and had a fetish for pain. It's mind-boggling. We went home and saw it on the news later.

We found out that the cops ran into the Melting Pot after the gunfire and saw T, the kid those guys were trying to kill at our Nottington House show in Jamaica, toss the gun. *Damn!* Meanwhile Little Lord, who bought my Acura, got locked up for carjacking somebody at gunpoint for their Maxima in Queensbridge while we were all at Nas's party. He was probably trying to get rims and an air bag for my stripped Acura. I heard he got five-to-ten years for that. At least he got to be in our "Peer Pressure" video before he got knocked.

After Nas's party, I started thinking about that girl KiKi who Hav hooked me up with. I kept thinking about her. I wanted to tell her how much I liked her and that we should be a serious couple. I asked Hav to get her number from his girl Shawna, and KiKi and I started being together every day. We just clicked, like we were made for each other. She'd come to QB, we'd go to the movies and dinner or to the park to talk, kiss, and stare at each other. You know, the young-love shit.

KiKi had just moved from Ridgewood to Corona, closer to QB. I knew Hav and I had some hit records on our hands and our whole life was about to change as soon as we dropped the album. I wanted to have KiKi with me before it all went down. KiKi was fucking with some other dudes on the side, but I was determined to change all that.

After about a month, KiKi started sneaking me into her crib late at night. She had a walk-in closet where I slept so her moms wouldn't catch me in the morning when she got up for work. It was better than sharing a bed with Havoc. Sometimes I slept at the Twins' crib, but they had two other brothers plus two sisters. I slept on the top bunk and there were mad roaches on the ceiling, so I had to wrap myself up in the sheets like a mummy. Fuck that, I'd rather sleep in the closet at KiKi's crib.

I would spend all day in Queensbridge, then get a small bottle of Hennessy and a blunt and take the 7 train from Queens Plaza to KiKi's crib in Corona. She lived directly across the street from the Hall of Science in Flushing Meadows Park. We snuggled up watching TV and getting nice off the Hennessy, then we'd get busy on the couch while her moms was sleeping. Sex with her was definitely the best I ever had. We fell in love quick but we were both still running around doing dumb shit.

Women advance faster than men, so I believe she was ready to be serious and I was fucking up. I really loved KiKi but I was still a young dumb-ass.

KiKi had a younger cousin Robby who came by the crib a lot to drink and smoke weed with us. He'd always sing along with James Brown's "The Big Payback" and had us cracking up.

KiKi had a three-year-old daughter from a past relationship named Keijzonna (pronounced *Key-Zonna*). A lot of people would run away from a female with a kid, but I was willing to accept her with her child because I was feeling her a lot. Shawna and Havoc warned me to be careful with KiKi because she used to mess with this dude from Brooklyn who still came around to see her sometimes, but I didn't care about no nigga. If it was going to be a problem, then I was equipped to handle it.

When I asked her about it, KiKi claimed that she didn't mess with the kid anymore but I didn't know what was true or false because we were still learning about each other. I was more than willing to find out, though.

KiKi's favorite music was Jodeci, an R&B group Puffy had just signed to Uptown/MCA. She also loved Teddy Riley's group Guy. But her all-time favorite was Prince. I mean this girl was in love with Prince and *Purple Rain*.

One thing I learned about KiKi right away was that she had a passion for music and poetry. She told me she dreamed of being a singer or song-writer someday, so she understood my passion for rap. The number-one thing I loved about her, besides her inner and outer beauty, was how she never ha-rassed or interrogated me when I spent long hours in the studio. I would see other dudes' girlfriends paging and calling them nonstop while we were trying to work. But KiKi encouraged me to work harder and gave me my space. She got major points for that.

CHAPTER 5

THE INFAMOUS

Life is a gamble we scramble for money
I might crack a smile but ain't a damn thing funny
I'm caught up in the dirt where your hands get muddy
Plus the outcome turns out to be lovely

"Eye for an Eye (Your Beef Is Mines)"

Matty C called to set up a meeting with Loud Records. The Twins, Killer, Havoc, and I went to Times Square to meet with Matty C, Scott Free, who was another A&R, and Steve Rifkind, the founder and chairman of the label. Loud Records was just four cubicles in the RCA building representing the Alkaholiks, PMD, and a new group from Staten Island called Wu-Tang Clan, none of whom had any hit records. Wu-Tang's single "Protect Ya Neck" had just started playing on the radio. Steve had long hair like a surfer and didn't look like he knew what he was doing. He did, though.

Sitting around a table, they listened to our songs in a big conference room with a good sound system. Their favorite was "The Patty Shop," about a weed spot uptown, plus a song called "Shook Ones Pt. 1." These were the same songs we played for Puff and Andre Harrell and, just like them, Steve offered us a deal right then and there.

After the meeting, sitting in the hallway with Scott Free and Killer, Scott asked us about QB and the lifestyle out there. I just so happened to have a TEC-9 in my pants, so I pulled it out. "This is how life is," I said. Scott's face looked shocked that I could have such a big gun on me without him knowing it, like, *This little kid's got a big-ass gun in a corporate office.* I wasn't showing off—he asked, and that's how we were living.

A week later we signed to Loud and started working on our second album. They gave us a sixty-thousand-dollar budget, twenty thousand for our pockets. We decided to call the album *The Infamous.* Yamit from Hav's block gave us the name; he had THE MOST INFAMOUS tattooed on his biceps in black ink. We were already Mobb Deep, but he dubbed us the Infamous Mobb Deep. This was our second chance to show the world that Mobb Deep was something special, so we focused on our lyrics and production skills, bringing Q-Tip in to help us master our sound. We finished the whole album in four months.

I started sniffing and smoking coke in 1995 during the making of *The Infamous.* A lot of niggas in the hood were selling and doing it, so it was easy to get. It was just a phase.

Wu-Tang Clan had just gone gold and they were pulling in a lot of money for the record company. Scott Free, who's from Staten Island, brought Wu to Loud. His dream was to have Raekwon and Ghostface collaborate with Mobb Deep, so he took us on the ferry to Staten Island. We walked from Scott's house to the Harbor projects and chilled in Wu's hood, smoking angel-dust blunts with Rae and Ghost and two white kids in a silver Benz. Rae and Ghost drove us back to QB and dropped us off on Tenth Street in Rae's navy-blue Acura Legend. Raekwon was working on *Only Built 4 Cuban Linx* and said he wanted to work with Nas, so we hooked it up when we saw Nas the next day.

A few days later at Platinum Island Studio in downtown Manhattan, we made "Eye for an Eye (Your Beef Is Mines)" featuring Nas and Raekwon and "Right Back at You" featuring Rae, Ghost, and Noyd. There was an ill energy in the air, like, *Damn, everybody in this room is hot right now!*

The Infamous took off like a rocket before it was even released. The "Shook Ones" remix, "Shook Ones Pt. 2," was the biggest song on the album, and then came "Survival of the Fittest." While we were shooting the video for "Survival of the Fittest," even though we'd signed with Steve Rifkind instead of him, Puffy pulled up on the hill in Queensbridge in a white stretch limo and made a cameo appearance out of nowhere, unannounced. Even Nas made a cameo in that video. That was how we convinced Noyd to start rapping; he saw that we were really going somewhere. Noyd used to kick great verses on the block and in the Honeycomb but he wasn't into rap, he just wanted to sell drugs. Noyd ended up kicking some of the most memorable verses on that album—on "Right Back at You" with Rae and Ghost, people still say that Noyd killed it the most.

Our singles and videos started getting major burn on radio and TV. We were on fire and the album wasn't done yet. While we were wrapping up the last few songs in Hempstead, some strange white dude with long hair and a beard came walking through Queensbridge with a Bible in his hand. He walked up to random people asking, "Do you know Prodigy? I have to speak to him." People looked at this fool like he was a basket case. The white dude walked around the projects for hours asking how he could find me. Finally, he walked up to my man Opps, who told him to go to Havoc's apartment, 3A. The dude knocked on Hav's door; Killer, Havoc's uncle La, and Twin Gambino opened it.

"Is Prodigy here?" the dude asked.

"Who the fuck is you?" Killer said. "What you want with P?"

"I've got a message for him," the white dude said. "Please get him, it's important."

"What message? Who are you?" Killer asked.

"The message is only for Prodigy, I've been sent to give it to him my-self. It's very important," the white dude said. "Please go get him."

Killer thought the kid was a lunatic, so he pulled a gun on him and pushed him down the staircase. Gambino had to stop Killer from hurting him. Then Gambino asked the dude, "What's the message? I'm gonna tell Prodigy for you. He's not here right now."

"I've been sent to tell Prodigy who he is and his purpose on this planet." The white dude started telling Twin bugged-out stuff. "Prodigy is an angel and people have written about him in the Book of Revelation. He's pow-erful and people want to kill him."

"Who sent you?" Gambino asked him. "And who wants to kill P?"

"God sent me," the white dude replied. I won't reveal who he said wanted to kill me, but it sounded very crazy.

Gambino and Killer kicked him out of the building, and he continued to walk around the projects in search of me. When I came back to the hood the next day, I saw Opps outside and he told me about the dude. I didn't believe Opps, but Twin and Killer confirmed it was true. Twin explained every-thing he was saying, and it was the weirdest shit I ever heard in my life of liv-ing. Our music was affecting people in all kinds of ways. People went nuts for "Shook Ones" and "Survival of the Fittest." So I just figured the white dude was a Looney Tune and an early Mobb Deep fanatic.

We were making groundbreaking hit records for the hood and quickly becom-ing the most elite rappers in the world, responsible for helping create one of the best eras in rap-music history, the nineties—Nas, Mobb Deep, Wu-Tang Clan, Biggie, and Jay-Z—a changing of the guard.

The West Coast had been dominating rap right before we all came out. Death Row was the biggest thing in rap. But when '95 hit, that changed. Shit, we were all influenced by one another, in one way or another. The West Coast inspired us to do better, and I'm sure we inspired them. So it was all good.

Everything was going perfect.

Just as we were completing *The Infamous* . . . gunshots. I was taking a catnap late at night at Hav's crib when shots rang out through Hav's open bedroom window. Fifteen minutes later, Killer rushed upstairs drunk with a set of Walkman speakers in one hand and my .22 revolver in the other. "Hide the gun," he said coolly, handing it to me.

"What happened?" I asked.

"I think I just murked somebody for his Walkman speakers," Killer said.

Wow, he just killed a dude over nothing, I thought. *Walkman speakers?* I tucked the gun away under a mess of balled-up clothes in Hav's dresser for the time being and tried to figure out exactly what had happened. From Hav's window, I could see the crime scene, police lights, yellow tape. Cops were everywhere, but they had no clue as to what happened either. All they had was a body.

Killer was trying to calm down and figure out his next move. He definitely had to leave the hood. Hav walked into the crib within an hour and Killer explained what happened. We stayed up all night talking about what he should do, where to hide, how to flee the projects without the cops spotting him. I took Killer to lay low at my crib in Long Island until he could get down South to his people in North Carolina.

The next day, Hav's moms found the gun in the dresser and gave it to the pastor at her church. She didn't know what had happened. She found a gun in her house and the first thing that came to her mind was to give it to the church.

Killer hid out in a hood in Hempstead called Terrace by the bus terminal, then skipped town. After we found out the cops were officially looking for Killer, we made the song "Temperature's Rising" about that situation. *"What up Black? Hold your head wherever you at, on the float from the cops with wings on your back. . . ."*

The Infamous went gold in thirty days and we were off on another promo tour, this time across the entire East Coast, Midwest, West Coast, and Europe. We brought the whole crew with us. We were getting a lot of love on the East, but out West in California and the U.K. they were die-hard Mobb Deep fans—you could tell by the intense looks on their faces as their heads bobbed.

On the East side, our friend Puff Daddy was turning his new company Bad Boy into a powerhouse. Biggie Smalls dropped his hit debut *Ready to Die*. The Scarface Twin loved Biggie. "I told you!" He was hyped. "I told you this nigga's hot!"

We were cool with Puff. Even though he was mad at us for not signing with Bad Boy, he put us on the Big Mack tour with Biggie and another new rapper named Craig Mack, performing at big venues across the East Coast, getting paid.

The wildest night on that tour was at a club in Cleveland, Ohio, with a real rowdy crowd. Our crew was always prepared for drama. Before the show that night, we had a big steak dinner and stole three steak knives. We would make weapons out of anything. We'd order room service and I'd take the fork and bend down the two prongs at each end, squeezing together the two prongs in the middle to make an ice pick. At the venues, I might have to poke somebody in the eye or neck. Fuck that, we were performing in hoods all over America. Better safe than sorry.

At showtime, Craig Mack opened up, then Mobb, then Biggie. But when Craig Mack took the stage to perform, somebody from the crowd jumped up and snatched the microphone from his hand before spraying mace in his face. Mack ran backstage, warning everybody: "Don't go out there, them niggas is crazy!"

Backstage, I overheard Biggie tell his manager to let him go next instead of Mobb Deep so he could get the money and get out of there. Our crew just laughed and sat back to watch. Biggie and Lil' Cease went onstage and sure enough, five seconds later they came tripping down the stairs, running out of the club. Mace flooded the air—it was hard to breathe. People were running all over the place and fighting with the police: pandemonium. Them Ohio niggas were not playing; I guess they wanted to show us Ohio was gangster too.

My man Ron Doo—a hustler from Queensbridge—and I pulled our knives out and made our way to the exit. We couldn't find our car or driver in the side alley, so we hopped into the van with Biggie and Cease. That was the first time on tour that we really kicked it with each other. I had a copy of *The Infamous* in my pocket and gave it to them; we played it on the way to the hotel while passing blunts, then got some groupies back at the hotel. For the remaining month of the tour, we'd get drunk and high together before and after all the shows.

Next it was off to tour on our own in California. We had three days off so I chilled at home with KiKi. When it was time for me to bounce, she wanted me to leave my hooptie, the Lil Nigga, with her.

I thought about it for almost ten minutes. All I could think about was her driving to see some other nigga in my car. *Hell no!* I told her no and she was mad at me.

The night before leaving town, I went to Long Island to smoke angel dust and drink with my niggas. The next morning, I got up early and was weaving in and out of lanes on the Long Island Expressway blasting Raekwon's "Glaciers of Ice." Flying through traffic, I tapped the back of another car and Lil Nigga did a 360 spin in the middle of the highway. Buses and sixteen-wheeler trucks were coming at me full speed but the higher powers were on my side. My car spun around and landed safely on the shoulder of the road and smacked into a concrete wall. My Lil Nigga was destroyed.

Whoa! My hands were shaking. *That was a close call.* I didn't have a license or anything. I grabbed my bag and boom box (my car radio didn't work because it was a hooptie), snatched the plates and stickers off the car as fast as I could, and walked quickly to the next highway exit to catch a cab to the airport. It was definitely the dust. And Raekwon's *Purple Tape* had me wanting to drive extra fast.

In the cab, all I could think about was KiKi asking to borrow the car while I was gone. *I should have left it with her! Fuck it. Lil Nigga only cost me a thousand dollars. I'll buy a new one when I get back from Cali.*

In California, Loud had a West Coast office. A rep called Bigga-B showed us all over Cali. I'd been visiting Cali since I was a little kid with my grandmother, but this time I got to see the real deal on the West side, from L.A. to the Bay, Sacramento, and San Jose. Bigga-B was the man out there. He made sure the entire state was hip to Mobb Deep by the time we were done with the tour.

After the West Coast promo tour, it felt good to be back home and finally have everybody recognizing us in the street, asking for autographs and telling us they loved our music. But disappointment hit when we found out the D's caught Killer down South. They had his pager tapped. The D's had shown up at Carey's crib in Long Island, where Killer had used the phone a few times. They traced the calls and came asking Carey and his mother about his whereabouts but they didn't say a word.

Killer did about a year in Rikers Island when Havoc started getting word from the lawyer he hired for his brother's case that somebody from QB was snitching. He didn't have a name yet, though.

That summer, Raekwon dropped his solo album *Only Built 4 Cuban Linx*, and to promote both Rae and Mobb Deep, Steve Rifkind invited thirty of the top DJs from all over the country to Long Island to play paintball with us—rappers versus the record label and DJs. A video station called the Jukebox Network came to film. I didn't last more than thirty minutes before I got shot up and killed off the team. Yo, paintballs hurt!

Later that night, Steve surprised us by throwing a small private after-party at the Marriott in Long Island where the DJs were staying. We were chilling on the couches talking with Rae, Ghost, and other Wu-Tang members when Steve walked in and surprised us, presenting us with our gold plaque for *The Infamous* album. *Wow, a gold plaque!* I really didn't give a fuck. I wanted money, not plaques, but it was definitely a great achievement. I was still staying at my grandmother's house sometimes, so I just propped it on the floor against the wall.

Method Man from Wu-Tang was also gearing up to drop his solo album that summer. A couple of weeks after the paintball game, Meth performed at the Jones Beach Greek Fest. Yo, that nigga ripped it! I was with Illa Ghee, his boy Ant, Carey from my block in Hempstead, and his boy Ali. We were super high and drunk, walked around for a few hours, and kicked it with some broads. Thousands of girls, yo. It started pouring rain, so we took it back to my crib for more blunts and liquor. I did a few lines of coke on the low in the bathroom. Nobody knew I was sniffing coke. I used to see my pops do it when I was younger and I always wanted to try it. I got addicted right away. It's a real nasty habit.

If you watch the "Shook Ones" video, I was real coked up—you can see it in my eyes. I was sniffing about five to six grams a day, rolled with my weed and in my cigarettes. The more I used, the more I needed to get high. Coke makes you hyper with quick blasts of energy. At parties in Queensbridge, some of the older gangsters would be in the bathroom doing lines. They'd pass it right over like, "Here you go, shorty. Take it easy now."

None of Havoc's boys were into coke. If they'd found out, they probably would have punched me in my chest, told me, "You're playing yourself," and tried to take it from me. The only thing they were into was getting high off weed, getting drunk, getting pussy, and selling crack.

Puffy signed a female R&B artist to Uptown/MCA, Mary J. Blige, who had a few hits out—"Real Love," "What's the 411," and "You Remind Me"—and was celebrating her album-release party at the Supper Club near Times Square. We shot our video for "Give Up the Goods" in that club; it's a nice-looking place. Mary J. wanted Mobb Deep to perform.

Havoc, Gotti, Trip, Ty, the Twins, and I all wore black Infamous T-shirts. As soon as we walked into the Supper Club, all eyes were on us because most everyone was dressed upscale. Mary J. stepped right to us, thanked us for coming to perform, introduced us to her little brother, and asked if we wanted anything to drink. We told her Hennessy, so she got us a bottle and we chilled in VIP.

Mary J. introduced us to the stage and we killed "Shook Ones," "Survival of the Fittest," and "Give Up the Goods" while Mary J. and her girlfriends were wildin' out in the front row. We kept the show short and got back to the party, which was packed with so many females we didn't know where to start.

Some girls with different-colored minks followed us to the projects in a white Benz. We took them to the Honeycomb and niggas ran the train on two of them. I took one of them to Pebble Beach and got some head. We called all project roofs Pebble Beach because they're lined with pebbles and it sounded better than "Let's have sex on the roof." She didn't let me hit it. She said she wanted to be with me and didn't want me to think she was a ho. I wasn't interested in being serious with anybody but KiKi anyway.

Shorties used to be open to go to Queensbridge. They'd be mesmerized by the hood, asking where Nas was at.

The next night we had a show at the Velvet Room on Twenty-third Street by the West Side Highway. KiKi came; this was her first time coming to one of our shows. A limo picked twenty of us up from Queensbridge and we all wore Carhart suits: black, brown, gray, navy blue, and forest green. I had a pint of E&J in my pocket to drink with KiKi after the show. I told her to hold it for me until we were done onstage. When we finished performing, I asked her for the bottle of E&J and she laughed, passing me an empty bottle. *This girl drank the whole bottle dolo!* I couldn't believe it. *E&J is strong! Oh well.*

The crew got back in the limo and rode back to the hood. After everybody got out, I told the limo driver to drop KiKi and me off in Corona at her crib, but Havoc wanted to take the limo to his girl's crib in Astoria. We started arguing. "Fuck it," I said. KiKi and I got out and walked to Queens Plaza to catch the train in a damn blizzard. As the limo pulled away, I picked up a bottle off the street and threw it, trying to break the back window, but I missed. I was pissed off that Havoc couldn't just drop us off.

On the train, KiKi had her face inside her bubble goose collar. It was cold but her face had been in there a little too long, so I asked if she was okay. Then I saw her shoulders jumping like she was throwing up. *This girl threw up in her coat because she was too embarrassed to throw up in front of me!* I told her she was crazy but it was okay.

Stumbling drunk, I held her up on the walk home from the train station. Luckily, her moms wasn't home. I helped her get undressed, put her in the shower, and then we fell out until late the next afternoon. I woke up and bounced back to Queensbridge because we had another show in the city that night.

Onyx was shooting a video at Irving Plaza by Union Square in Manhattan, and they wanted Mobb Deep to do a cameo. Chillin' outside with the Twins and a few of our boys between scenes—Irving Plaza was right across the street from my old summer school, Washington Irving—this rapper Keith Murray walked up and asked if I was talking about him on the intermission skit on *The Infamous* when I vented all my frustration from our first album flopping.

Slick with my mouth, I said: "Nigga, if the shoe fits." This bitch-ass nigga just walked away and never said anything else. Can you believe that? If you listen to the skit, I didn't say any names or direct it at anyone in particular: *"And oh yeah, to all them rap-ass niggas with your half-ass rhymes talking about how much you get high, how much weed you smoke, and that crazy space shit that don't even make no sense, don't ever speak to me when you see me. Word. . . ."* So if someone thinks that skit is toward him, he must have some insecurity and feel that way about himself. Fuckin' punks.

There was a club on the West Side of Manhattan called the Tunnel, and oh my God, Jesus Christ, we would be there every Sunday like church. Funkmaster Flex DJed along with his fill-in, Big Kap. This was the mecca of all clubs, the best club that ever opened in America, capacity four thousand with coed bathrooms. It was our generation's Studio 54. We ran through the Tunnel like we owned it.

This dude Chris Lighty, a well-known manager and party promoter, ran the door. If you weren't cool with him, you waited outside for hours and paid top dollar to get in. Chris managed the Jungle Brothers, Q-Tip, and LL Cool J. He let all forty of us in without paying. We got so comfortable with him that one night I pulled him to the side and gave him a gun to sneak in. He did it.

One gun became two, two became three, and the next thing you knew, I was handing him book bags full of knives, shanks, screwdrivers, guns, plus other sharp and blunt objects. Chris handed the bags off to me in the bathroom, and I passed the tools out to the boys. Try to understand, number one, we're famous, and number two, every hood in the Tri-State area was in that club and it was dangerous. We never started trouble, but just imagine how we could have finished it.

Chris was a corporate dude who dressed in hoodies, jeans, and Timberlands and came up working with Def Jam, practically raised in the industry by Russell Simmons. One cold night, on our way inside the Tunnel, Havoc and I pulled Chris to the side and asked him to manage us since he had so much experience in the business. A smile spread across his face. "Hell yeah," he said. "I'll do that."

We walked into the jam-packed Tunnel one night with a crew of fifty. Heading toward our favorite spot, the side of the bar opposite the exit, Yamit led the pack, pushing people out of our way. "Oh shit, that's Mobb Deep!" We saw like fifty other niggas walking toward us, pushing people out of the way too. It was Wu-Tang Clan, with a sweaty, shirtless Ol' Dirty Bastard leading the pack. "Prodigy?" Ol' Dirty said, looking at me. "Oh shit, come here, man!" He grabbed and hugged me mad tight, getting his sweat all over me. *Nasty.* "I love you, P!" ODB said, kissed me on my cheek, then walked away with his crew.

Every time Funkmaster Flex played Nas or Mobb Deep, we lost control slam-dancing, tossing girls in the air, spilling our drinks on ourselves. Chris Lighty pulled me to the side one night, knowing he just gave us a small armory of weapons. "Please don't kill anybody in here," he said. "They have cameras all over the place now."

"Don't worry, if we do something we gonna do it right," I assured him.

KiKi always wanted to come out with me, but the Tunnel was just too wild. We went for sex and war and to promote Mobb Deep. The coed bathroom on the second floor had about ten stalls, and it was easy to have sex inside them. I think Money No was the only one of us who did that.

Nasheem, one of Puffy's Hitmen producers from Cambria Heights, Queens, and his boys had this big idea of renting a yacht and sailing around Manhattan to celebrate Mobb Deep going gold. It sounded real high-class, so we agreed. They'd make all the money from the ticket sales and we'd enjoy a yacht party with free drinks. They promoted it at beauty shops all over Queens and Manhattan, and a lot of ladies were talking about it in the streets.

My lady KiKi had gotten close with my boy Stobo's girlfriend Fawn. They found out about the yacht party and wanted to come, but we weren't planning on bringing them. We wanted to stunt like single men for the night— it was my time to shine, and I didn't want my girl around.

The day of the party, I chilled with KiKi all afternoon. My plan was to bounce on her around party time. I felt bad because she was picking out her outfit all excited. "I'm coming with you to that party!" she said. Around six P.M., she was in the bathroom taking a shower when I snuck out. I picked my cousin up from Flushing and we headed to the boat dock. Yes! We both ditched our girls and were ready to have the night of our lives.

When we pulled up to the dock, I couldn't believe it: KiKi and Fawn were already there waiting. They'd taken a cab and somehow made it before us. Fuck! I was mad as hell. How did they know where to go? It felt like I was going to a party with my moms.

There were so many chicks on that yacht. You always see the best ones when you're with your girl. Havoc and my QB niggas were making fun of me because they were free to do what they wanted, while Stobo and I were the only two dickheads with our girls. I could have flipped on KiKi, started an argument before we got on the boat so she would go home, I thought. Fuck it.

The yacht took off around seven P.M. DJ Clue was spinning, and even though my girl was there, I had crazy fun drinking overproof rum, open bar all night. As the yacht circled Manhattan, Hav and I snuck off to the bathroom to do some lines and get coked up.

Toward the end of the night, Cormega wanted to get a rap session going, so we told Clue to play instrumentals. We ripped it—Cormega, Havoc, Trip, Noyd, Capone, Tragedy, and some niggas from Jamaica who were down with the dudes who threw the party for us. There was already animosity between Southside Jamaica and QB from back in the day. Mega and I grabbed the mic first, the dudes from Jamaica spit their rhymes, and the battle began.

Tension filled the air as the session became a battle between Jamaica and QB. Everybody was drunk from the free liquor, arguing over who got next on the mic as the yacht pulled into the dock. "Back up!" three security guards ordered as everyone moved toward the exit. "Let the boat fully dock! It has to be tied to the pier before you can get off safely." But instead of waiting for it to dock, a few QB niggas tried to hop off early. My man Ice went first. A security guard started spraying mace in my man's face. Ice knocked him down. It was on after that—an all-out brawl. Through all the commotion, KiKi and I lost each other, so I hopped off right behind Ice, Money No, Ty-Nitty, Scarface Twin, and Capone to wait for her on the pier.

A guy was standing at the top of the steps that we were running up to try to make it to the parking lot. Capone walked straight up to the dude and cut him across his left cheek for no reason with a little Gemstar box-cutter razor. Nitty and Money No dropped a giant flowerpot on his head and kicked him into the Hudson River. That kid's boys came running off the boat straight up to Pone and jumped him. Twin Gambino started letting off shots and everyone on the pier was ducking, running, and hiding, people getting tossed into the water. I pulled my orange box cutter out of my pocket and started searching for KiKi.

I didn't see KiKi anywhere. *Maybe she stayed on the boat until things calmed down,* I hoped. I watched person after person until everyone was off the boat. When I turned around, Twin was swinging a long metal pole, cracking people in the head. They were dropping. I walked to the parking lot to see if KiKi was already at the car. Sure enough, she was sitting on the trunk of Lil Nigga Part 2, waiting and watching. She had a look on her face like she'd been there for hours. "I don't know how you got past me," I said.

Capone came walking over to my car all bloody. Somebody must have hit him with a bottle. Police were pulling up, so he took his bloodstained shirt off, wiping the blood off his face with it and tossing it to me before the cops saw him. I threw it into the bushes and gave him a T-shirt from the car while more gunshots were fired from the pier. My cousin Stobo and his girl ran over and we jumped into my car and pulled off.

On the way back to drop Capone in the projects, we drove past this kid Mone from QB pedaling fast down the side of the Grand Central Parkway on an NYPD mountain bike. In the "Shook Ones" video, Mone was riding in the passenger seat while I'm driving a Saab across the 59th Street Bridge. He must have grabbed the bike while the cops were cuffing everybody and made a smooth getaway amid all the excitement. *This nigga's on the Grand Central Parkway riding a NYPD mountain bike! Wow.*

Later that night we crashed in Hempstead. Money No, Stobo, and I were sitting around my kitchen table talking and watching the news when the clips of the "Survival of the Fittest" video flashed on the TV screen, then footage of all the bullet holes in cars at the pier parking lot and the shell casings on the ground. The news reporter called it "An Infamous boat ride." We were open. Our yacht party actually made the news!

A couple of the dudes who got their heads cracked open with that pole tried to sue us for hospital bills and pain and suffering a few months later. Niggas kill me—they act thug, and then when they get whupped out, they try to sue you. That shit is pathetic.

A month after that yacht party, we did a show at some small club on West Twentieth Street in Manhattan called 20 West. Another new group, the Lost Boyz from Jamaica, Queens, was also on the bill to perform. They were supposedly some gang who started rapping and had a semihit record called "Lifestyles of the Rich and Shameless." Of course the whole 12th Street crew came with us. Even if we didn't invite them, the whole hood would show up and get mad if everybody couldn't get in. I never understood that. If nobody invited you, how can you be mad that you can't get in?

I was extra drunk. Some girl climbed onstage and was dancing in front of me while I was performing. *Who the fuck is this jumping onstage acting like a fool?* I felt that she was disrespecting our show, so I kicked her in her back and she went flying into the crowd. I kicked the shit outta her! I was bugged out back then.

A big muscle-bound bouncer was standing in front of the stage ice-grilling me. He must've been upset 'cause I kicked that girl. After the last song, I jumped offstage and punched him in his mouth. He started pounding on me. I was so drunk I didn't even feel his punches. My man Bumpy from QB helped me fight him, and then more bouncers surrounded us. Next thing I knew, all the bouncers were jumping us. Knocked to the floor, I looked up and they were carrying Bumpy up in the air while dragging me outside by my shirt. They dropped Bumpy on his head and pushed me to the curb.

After that we tore that club up, all thirty of us. We broke the windows and all the mirrors behind the bar. As we were walking back to the train station to go home, we saw like forty dudes walking toward us from the Twenty-third Street train station two blocks away loudly chanting, "Lost Boyz! Lost Boyz!" So we started chanting, "Mobb Deep! Queensbridge!" It was inevitably about to be a royal rumble.

Already hyper from the club, we walked straight up to them. Capone set it off, pulling out a razor and cutting the closest nigga across the face. Niggas were getting stabbed, hit with metal garbage cans. No gunfire, though.

A police riot squad pulled up. Suddenly we all stopped fighting each other and started fighting the cops so we wouldn't get arrested. Garbage cans were flying, some of the Lost Boyz got stabbed, everybody fighting everybody, someone started swinging a long blue wooden police barricade. Hav and a bunch of us ran to the train, but a lot of niggas got locked up that night.

On the train ride home, two white boys were standing on the platform with bloody faces. They said that a bunch of black dudes had just jumped them and cut their faces up. Wow, everybody was wildin' that night! Now that I think about it, it might've been the Lost Boyz.

To this day, my people from Jamaica tell me they heard about that fight. Some say they saw the Lost Boyz come home all bloody that night. It sounds like a scene from a movie, but it was real.

Steve Rifkind informed us that we were banned from performing in Manhattan for two years after that 20 West show. We were getting into too many fights and destroying clubs, so somebody with power banned us. We never found out who it was, but that bullshit ban didn't stop us—we were still doing shows worldwide. Our music was on fire all over the map.

We didn't know our music would affect people's lives the way it did. It made us work hard to keep that feeling going. We saw people dressing like us, talking like us, and even drinking like us. They tried to make beats and rap like us. A lot of people started using "Infamous" and attaching it to their name. I wasn't feeling that. Get your own shit. Get off my pole. Even Biggie started calling himself the Notorious after that. *Hmmm* . . . I wonder where he got that idea from.

CHAPTER 6

HELL ON EARTH

Your store-bought rap ain't shit my category
Is that of an insane man who strikes back
I draw first blood it's over with and that's that

"G.O.D. Pt. 3"

Life was hectic when we were young. The night after the 20 West brawl, the whole 12th Street crew was on the block drinking, smoking, joking, and playing dice. A chick from the hood came walking by with a dude who wasn't from QB. She was a slut who everybody ran through so the crew started calling her over, she came, and my man Karate Joe met her halfway. The dude she was with didn't look too happy about this and kept his distance. Joe spoke to shorty for a while and the kid got frustrated and told the girl to hurry up.

"Mind your business," Joe looked over and told him. The kid said something slick back to Joe and about five of my boys responded by walking toward him. The kid acted like he had heart, walked over to us, and exchanged more words. Then the kid reached in his pants and pulled out a gun but was so nervous that he dropped it on the ground in between him and Joe.

Everyone paused. Joe looked down like he wanted to reach for the gun, but it was closer to the kid. The kid reached down quick, picked it up, and everyone hauled ass. Havoc ran top speed into a pole and busted his forehead open. I wanted to run from the bench where I was sitting next to the kid but I couldn't because I was too close. *He'll definitely shoot me if he sees me get up.* So I just sat there. He squeezed the trigger at my boys but the gun was jammed from being dropped. He scrambled to fix it, looked over at me, and pointed the gun at my face. My adrenaline was going crazy. I wanted to run or duck, but something told me to just be still.

The kid started squeezing the trigger toward my face but the gun still didn't work, so he ran out the projects. Everybody came back to the benches. "Why didn't you run?" my boys asked.

"He was too close. If I ran, I would've been the last one," I said. "I would've been the one shot in the back."

After we laughed it off, I went upstairs to lie down because my sickle-cell was acting up. I thought I was about to get shot in my face, shit, I thought I was about to die. I took about six Advil and went to sleep in Hav's room. A few hours later, loud shouts from outside woke me up. When I looked out the window, the 12th Street niggas were beefing with niggas from another block. Some tall dude kicked Noyd in the chest and knocked him down. Karate Joe walked over and everyone backed up. Nobody wanted to fight Joe: He was a boxer and knew karate. He and Yamit were our secret weapons.

The argument spilled onto Tenth Street, and from the window, I had the best seat in the house. Trip, aka Godfather, chased some guy around a car twenty times with a knife. Noyd cut someone across the face with a razor.

The next afternoon, the nigga who Noyd cut shot Noyd three times on Twelfth Street right next to the hill: bullets in his leg, arm, and middle finger.

Noyd wanted us to put out his solo album, but we didn't have our own label or the money to sign and promote him properly. We told him to have patience and it would happen soon, but he didn't listen. He got Karate Joe to manage him and they started shopping for a deal without telling us. We were upset, but Noyd explained that he had bills to pay and couldn't wait around for us to get a label deal. We understood and let him go.

After Noyd got shot up, fans, radio stations, and magazines were all talking about it, amazed that we were living the life we were rapping about. Feeling all that fake love from people boosted Noyd's ego and made him want to be a star on his own. You know how that story goes. Like when 50 Cent first came out and nobody gave a shit until he got shot and almost died. *Fake love.*

A few months later, Noyd landed a deal at Tommy Boy Records. We helped him with the production. He dropped *Episodes of a Hustla* and sold a disappointing thirty thousand copies, but the streets loved Noyd. It could have been way bigger than it was. The original plan was for Havoc and me to convince Steve Rifkind to give us our own label, Infamous Records, and sign Noyd and the whole crew—the Twins, Ty-Nitty, Godfather, and Gotti, plus Chinky, a female R&B singer who was Harlem hustler Alpo's niece.

No one had patience and we all needed money, so we split up with separate plans. Havoc and I were mad at Noyd, though: Mobb Deep was responsible for making him a star, so he should have stuck it out with us.

Right after Noyd's album was released, he got locked up for shooting this kid three times in the stomach for messing with his baby moms. It happened right in front of his building in Queensbridge and the police were looking for him. I told him to dye his hair blond and wear a fake nose ring for disguise. We all laughed at that one, but it wasn't funny when Noyd got caught and sentenced to a one-to-three-year bid.

Tommy Boy dropped Noyd. We kept his name alive by performing his verse from "Give Up the Goods" at all of our shows: *"Yo, it's the*

R-A-double-P-E-R N-O-Y-D, niggas can't fuck with me!" The crowd chanted his verse along with us word for word.

In August 1995, *The Source* magazine hosted the second annual Source Awards at Madison Square Garden. We were cool with the owners of the magazine, so we got a bunch of tickets and the whole crew went. I even brought KiKi. I'd always tell her that it was too dangerous to come out with me, but I wanted to bring her along and make her feel good. We all got drunk and high, then went inside and took our seats.

Havoc and I were presenting an award with Wu-Tang Clan, so we kicked it backstage with them in the dressing room. Hav was so bent that he fell asleep on the floor. KiKi and I walked back to our seats to watch the show. In the middle of Biggie's performance, Havoc came out into the crowd screaming, *"Somebody took my fuckin' chain! Somebody fuckin' robbed me, son!"* We jumped up to help find his chain. Come to find out, Raekwon saw Havoc drunk on the dressing-room floor and took his chain off his neck so nobody else would snatch it. Rae pulled it out of his pocket, gave it back to Hav, and we all calmed down.

Death Row hit the stage and did one of the illest shows ever. Their stage setup had jail cells that opened one by one as they performed "Stranded on Death Row." After the song, Snoop Dogg started screaming on the mic, "New York ain't got love for Death Row?" I sat there wondering, *What the fuck is he talking about?* He was really feeling himself because of all the money and power they were displaying onstage. But he took it too far. All the whoopin' and hollerin' made Snoop look stupid and left a sour taste with everybody from New York.

After Death Row was done, Mobb and Wu-Tang hit the stage to present an award. When we went back to our seats, Suge Knight, the cofounder and CEO of Death Row Records, came out in a tight red shirt and tight-ass pants with his ass crack hanging out the back. He started dissing Puffy, talking about how he danced in all his artists' videos and how niggas should come to Death Row. "To all you artists out there who don't wanna be on a record label where the executive producer's . . . all up in the videos, all on the records, dancin'," Suge shouted, "then come to Death Row!" After Suge's little hatred speech, Biggie took the stage to perform and won the award for Best New Artist.

•   •   •

The New Year passed. During the summer of 1996, sitting in my grand-mother's house, I drew an idea for a pendant to go with my chains and brought it over to my man Manny in Midtown Manhattan's Diamond District. He did custom work for rappers way before Jacob, David, and all those other guys. Manny loved my drawing—a miniature MAC-10, about six inches long and one and a half inches thick, all solid gold.

"Make it so I can take the clip in and out," I requested. He charged me $5,000 and it was the illest piece ever made in the history of rapper jewelry.

The only pendants that could compete with mine before or after were Run-D.M.C.'s miniature gold Adidas sneaker—the first sneaker pendant; Ghost-face's giant gold Versace head—the biggest pendant ever made; Big Pun's giant gold tombstone—the heaviest chain and pendant ever made; my platinum and marquise diamond Infamous Records piece—the first pendant made with marquise diamonds and the first forty-inch-long chain; Nas's giant platinum QB piece; 50 Cent's spinning platinum G-Unit—the first pendant that could spin.

Jewelry was a bad habit and a competition as far as I was con-cerned. If you couldn't compete then put your chain in your shirt when you're around me because I'd make your little bullshit look stupid. Some people hooked up their car. Some people were heavy into designer clothing. My thing was my sixteen bars and my jewelry.

Toward the tail end of the summer, we chilled in Queensbridge, tak-ing a break from touring and recording. Havoc and his crew loved basketball, NBA and college; they were real serious about it. Everyday, they'd play for money on the court in front of Hav's building. They all played on school teams when they were younger. Ty-Nitty and Twin Gambino were the best.

In the Honeycomb Hideout, I'd sit on the couch while they were all excited and I didn't even know what the hell they were screaming for. They'd try explaining the game, but I just wasn't into it. When they played on Hav's block, I'd sit on the bench and try to learn the rules. I never got into any sports because when I overworked my body it triggered my sickle-cell pain.

One of Havoc's close friends from Queensbridge, Ron Artest, played for the St. John's University team. Anytime his games were on TV, we made an event out of it and hit the Honeycomb with a bunch of weed, liquor, and beer. Ron was real good and everyone was hyped that he was gonna be in the NBA soon.

In autumn 1996, almost half the 12th Street crew went to North Carolina to get out of New York for a few months. Most niggas went down South to hustle, but Havoc, Twin, Gotti, Godfather, Nitty, and I were there for a vacation and to get driver's licenses for the first time. We couldn't get them in New York because of our driving records. The DMV computers weren't connected back then, so my New York record didn't show up in North Carolina. And the test was easier down there—we got them in one day!

Down South, they got something you won't find in New York—Southern hospitality. Girls moved us into their homes, cooked for us, let us drive their cars, and a whole lot more. Mobb Deep was real popular in the South, so we had it extra easy. We loved the dirty South.

Havoc's homie Star from Queensbridge, the one who paid for the studio time for our demo, had moved down to North Carolina and was doing well for himself. He had the streets on smash and opened up a few strip clubs and nightclubs in Fayetteville and Greensboro. Havoc, Ron Doo, the Twins, Godfather, Nitty, Gotti, and I were all living in a small two-story shack on Juniper Street by Duke University in Durham. Star paid us to perform at one of his spots in Fayetteville. It was packed. After the show, we were so drunk that Twin Gambino and I fell asleep in the spot.

When I woke up in the morning, Twin Gambino and I were lying on the carpet in Star's office in the club. *Where is everybody?* I was disoriented. *Why am I on the floor?* We were locked in the club with no way out. "Yo, Twin, wake up!" I said. "Where's everybody at?" He didn't know either. Neither of us had a cell phone, so we just had to wait. Luckily, the club was huge and had pool tables, video games, and a kitchen with a freezer full of french fries and chicken, so we fried up some food.

After our meal, we turned on the DJ equipment, went behind the bar, and mixed Seagram's gin and orange juice, our favorite drink at the time, and played a few games of pool. Five to six hours later, Star, Havoc, and the rest of them came back for us. They said they tried to wake us up the night before but we were both out cold. Twin and I reminisced about that night for years.

Around that time, this new truck came out called the Tahoe. There was a Chevrolet dealership by the house in Durham and I finally had my license. *It's time to buy my first brand-new car.*

Gotti and I went to the dealership and right away we saw a black Tahoe with gray leather seats that we liked. This badass saleswoman worked there—brown skin, real pretty, with the big dirty South fatty. You know we went straight to her. She took us for a test drive and after two minutes it was sold. Impressed that some black kids from New York bought a truck that fast, she gave us her phone number and told us to come chill with her later. We did.

My man Doo was making scrambled eggs for breakfast the next morning when Snoop and Tha Dogg Pound's "New York, New York" video came on TV. These niggas were in the video stomping all through the New York landscape and kicking over our buildings! Ron Doo, Gotti, and I immediately looked at each other and said, "These niggas is trying to play us!" First Snoop was flippin' at the Source Awards, and now this! It was time to get back home.

Right before Christmas we made the ten-hour drive back to New York. Havoc bought a green Chevy Blazer from the same spot I bought my new Tahoe; we drove back to back. We had been in North Carolina for three months, the longest Havoc and I had spent away from the recording studio. We immediately got started on our next album.

The first song we made, "L.A., L.A.," featured Capone-N-Noreaga and was aimed at Snoop and Tha Dogg Pound. Marley Marl made the beat and we shot the video a week after we recorded it.

We blocked out a few months at Axis recording studio in Manhattan next to the famed nightclub Studio 54 and stayed there 24-7 making the new album. After *The Infamous* had so much success, Havoc always let me choose the names for our albums. "I leave that up to you, P," he said when I asked for his input. "You good at the album-title shit." I came up with a good, strong name: *Hell on Earth.*

While we were recording at Axis, DJ Premier and Lil' Dap and the Nutcracker from Group Home started hanging out at the studio a lot, smoking blunts with us while we worked on our music. Lil' Dap was laid-back and Nutcracker was literally a nut. Our engineer Mario didn't like us smoking cigarettes in the control room. He'd get pissed off and scream, "Would you guys please take the smoke outside?" Mario was a good engineer, so there'd be like ten of us smoking Newports on the balcony.

A big pair of binoculars on the balcony brought us directly into the high-rise apartment windows all around. We saw naked women, couples fighting, people having threesomes, all kinds of stuff. The studio management complained to Mario and Steve Rifkind at Loud because we left cigarette butts and Philly blunt guts all over the floors and spilled beer and liquor everywhere. We tried to clean up our act so we could complete our album.

After pulling a late session one night, Havoc, the Twins, Lil' Dap, Nutcracker, Ty-Nitty, Gotti, and I left the studio around three A.M. Havoc and I were the last two to come down to the lobby, and when we got off the elevator, we saw Nutcracker sitting Indian-style on the lobby floor clutching the studio bathroom air-freshener can in his hands. We looked at him like, *Okaaay . . .* and left the building.

The next day on our way to the studio we got a call saying that somebody in our session the night before took a shit on the carpet. We started cracking up, but the studio wanted to ban us from coming back. The only person who seemed capable of taking a shit on the carpet was Nutcracker, but we never found out for sure. Lil' Dap and Nutcracker were our homeboys, though, we got love for them whether Nutcracker did or didn't leave a pile of shit on the studio carpet.

One of Premier's friends told me that one day Premier let Nutcracker use his car and he brought it back crashed up pretty bad. Nutcracker didn't mean to crash it, so when he had to face Primo and show him the crashed car, it hurt him so much that he pulled out a nine-millimeter and shot himself in the foot to show Premier how sorry he was. That incident happened in the hometown of Group Home and DJ Premier, Brooklyn, just in case you were wondering. Yeah, Nutcracker was bugged-out.

"L.A., L.A." quickly started getting airplay across the country. The press turned a rap battle between Tha Dogg Pound and Mobb Deep into an all-out coastal war between the East and West.

Tupac had just signed with Death Row. When he heard "L.A., L.A.," he decided it was time to prove his loyalty to his new camp. Pac put out a song called "Hit 'Em Up," going at Mobb Deep, Biggie, Nas, and Jay-Z. Somebody in QB played it for us on a little boom box outside. "Yo! Pac's dissing ya'll!" It was cool, but he couldn't fuck with us. *Why the fuck is Pac coming at us . . . ?* It took me a minute to figure out why he was dissing us. Then it came to me that he had just signed to Death Row and Snoop was his labelmate, so Pac decided to take it upon himself to jump into the drama.

That night, we went straight to the studio and recorded "Drop a Gem on 'Em," going right back at Tupac: *"My rebellion, retaliate, I'll have the whole New York State aimin' at your face. . . . I got a hundred strong-arm niggas ready to rock ya shit, clocks tick, your days are numbered in low digits, you look suspicious, suspect niggas is bitches, get chopped up, Grade A meat, somethin' delicious. . . ."* We were the only ones to make a comeback song. Biggie made his little jokes about his wife Faith Evans having two Pacs, but that wasn't a war song. And Nas and Jay-Z? Well, I guess they just decided to fall back. Jay-Z wasn't even that popular yet—he had only one single out with Foxy Brown called "Ain't No Nigga." It was weird that Pac targeted him too.

There was tremendous tension in the air. All of Queensbridge was ready to ride with us and I'm sure Pac had plenty of soldiers ready to kill for him. We talked about it on the benches on the block every day. It would have been a mess if we ever crossed paths. Pac bumping into Nas at the MTV Awards was nothing compared to running into us. Nas was like the older wise man. Mobb Deep were the little wild niggas you couldn't control. There wouldn't have been any talking.

Tupac started doing interviews displaying his hatred toward us. In one of the interviews, Pac spoke about a time he and his crew bumped into Mobb Deep in Atlanta and how they had us scared. When I heard that interview I didn't know what Pac was talking about. We never crossed paths with him or his crew. After a while, I remembered some dudes screaming "Thug life!" as we left a *Juvenile Hell* in-store appearance. That must've been what Pac was talking about, some meaningless bullshit. Tupac was just furious that we were going at him and Snoop without a care. Mobb Deep held it down for New York when nobody else would because they were scared of them Death Row boys.

Less than a month later, in September 1996, Tupac was murdered in Las Vegas after a Mike Tyson fight. He and Suge Knight got into an altercation and jumped a member of the Crip gang inside the MGM Casino. Didn't these fools know that casinos have cameras covering every angle of the joint? Right after they jumped the guy, Pac was shot four times while leaving in Suge's BMW. He died six days later.

When we found out what happened to Tupac, we immediately pulled our single "Drop a Gem on 'Em" off the radio out of respect for his family. To tell you the truth, we felt sad that he was killed, but relieved at the same time. It would have seriously been a problem if we ever clashed with homie. We were glad it never got to that point.

Years later, I found out that my peoples E-Money Bags, Majesty, and Stretch were real tight with Tupac. One of the members of Tupac's group the Outlawz, Young Noble, is Majesty's blood cousin, so, though we didn't know it back then, we were all on the same team anyway.

Back in Queensbridge, Tragedy's man Noreaga aka N.O.R.E. started hanging out on Twelfth Street. He told me he was from LeFrak, but I didn't ever see him when I was living out there. N.O.R.E. had just came home from jail, where he'd met Capone after Capone had gotten locked up for supposedly shooting a cop in the neck right in front of Havoc's building. He only did a few years for that case and somehow came home early.

One night that winter, Hav and I were on the block with Karate Joe, Gotti, Nitty, Trip, this kid we called Bill Cosby, and this other kid Johnny. Havoc started flipping out, saying he heard Tragedy was fucking with his lady Shawna on the low and he wanted to step to Tragedy about it. We all walked over to Capone's building next door where Tragedy, Capone, and N.O.R.E. hung out. Hav knocked on Capone's door and asked him to tell Tragedy to come outside. Tragedy came out with N.O.R.E. and Capone.

"What's up, man, you fucking with Shawna?" Hav asked. Tragedy said it wasn't true but Hav wasn't trying to hear it. "I know you fucking with Shawna, stop lying!"

Hav punched Tragedy in the face and knocked him down. While he was getting back up, Karate Joe warned Tragedy, "You better not hit him

ALBERT "PRODIGY" JOHNSON

104

back!" Hav punched Tragedy and knocked him down again while we surrounded them, watching. N.O.R.E. was getting nervous seeing the nigga who he thought had strength in QB getting his ass beat—he was worried he was gonna be next. So he reached for his gun, pulled it out, and shot one bullet at the ground in between all of us.

The bullet bounced off the cement and hit my man Johnny in the shinbone. N.O.R.E. ran for his life out of the projects. Tragedy and Capone ran into the building and someone drove Johnny to the hospital right away. The next day, Johnny came through the block on crutches with a cast on his leg. N.O.R.E. could never show his face in Queensbridge again.

About a month passed and some unknowing fool set up a show for Mobb Deep and Capone-N-Noreaga at a little club called Krystals on Merrick Boulevard in Jamaica, Queens, across the street from the bus terminal and up the block from my grandmother's dance school. The only reason we went was so we could catch N.O.R.E. and torture him for what he did to Johnny.

The whole crew pulled up and parked our trucks in the bus terminal facing the club to get a good look at everybody out front. Tragedy and Capone were standing at the front door facing us. Nitty spotted N.O.R.E. walking over to them. "Anyone got a razor?" Nitty asked Twin and me, but we didn't. Nitty, Twin, and Money No approached N.O.R.E.

"Come over here so we can talk," Nitty told him, putting his arm around N.O.R.E.'s neck and walking him into the street. After a few steps, Nitty started punching N.O.R.E. in the face while he had him in a headlock. N.O.R.E. dropped to the ground and the crew jumped him. Gotti, Havoc, and I stood by the trucks and watched them beat the clothes off that boy. *Man, I never saw somebody get jumped so bad!*

They were like dogs fighting over a piece of meat. Karate Joe grabbed N.O.R.E. by what was left of his shirt and dragged him to the corner so he could have him all to himself. He focused strictly on his rib cage, destroying N.O.R.E.'s ribs with punch after punch. Nitty snatched N.O.R.E.'s Jesus piece from the ground and we hopped back in our trucks.

While N.O.R.E. was getting jumped, his boys Tragedy and Capone didn't move. They just stood in front of the club watching the whole thing.

Some of N.O.R.E.'s people carried him to a parking lot around the corner. I already knew what was going to happen next. "You know they're about to come back from the parking lot with guns," I told Twin Gambino. We sat and waited.

I popped the hood and told Twin Gambino to get my gun out. I'd just bought an automatic .22 with a twelve-shot clip, but like an asshole I'd never tested it out. After a few minutes, just as I predicted, a few of N.O.R.E.'s people came dragging him from the parking lot with a TEC-9. I was sitting in the driver's seat; Gambino was outside, standing at my door. We had the drop on them, meaning we could move on them before they saw it coming. "Start shooting," I told Twin calmly, but the gun didn't fire. The piece of shit was broken! N.O.R.E.'s people started unloading their gun on us. As their bullets started to explode, Gambino got frustrated with my broken gun and threw it at them. Ha!

"Shoot him!" N.O.R.E. pointed at Nitty, who was in between my truck and Havoc's truck. "Right there!" Whoever had the gun shot Nitty in his back as he was trying to jump into my backseat. Plus the shooter dumped the entire forty-two-shot clip at us and not one of the shots hit our two trucks. I was shocked. The only target they hit was the person they were after.

Luckily, Mary Immaculate Hospital was right around the block from Krystals. Nitty was screaming and bleeding like a pig in my backseat as I sped to the hospital in less than five minutes. When we got to the emergency entrance, Money No, Twin, Karate Joe, and I dragged Nitty inside. The D's showed up within a few minutes to question everybody. Two detectives came over and questioned me while I was smoking a cigarette outside the emergency room door. I told them we were about to do a show and somebody started shooting at us for no reason. "We don't know who it was," I said. They asked me over and over to see if I was lying, but I kept saying the same thing. Eventually they got tired and left.

Havoc thought he found out who was snitching on his brother Killer. At the trial at Queens Criminal Court, the whole crew sat in the middle of the courtroom waiting to see who the DA's star witness was going to be. We couldn't believe it when he came walking up to the stand. It was Capone! Was Capone the fucking snitch?

Capone got up there and said he saw Killer pull the trigger and shoot the man in the back of the head. He pointed at Killer. "I saw him do it," he said. "He shot the man." He was on the stand snitching like it was cool! Later I heard he was trying to lower a sentence for a case he'd caught for a direct sale to an undercover. *Wow.*

The false testimony Capone gave wound up backfiring. The autopsy report said that the man was shot in the front of the head, not the back. Killer beat the case. After that, Capone tried telling people that he did that on purpose to help Killer beat the case. *What!?!?* I don't know for sure— Maybe he did know what he was doing, maybe his testimony did help. But from then on, instead of Capone and Noreaga, the whole hood called them Canary and Nore Faker.

While Killer was locked up, he became a full-fledged Muslim. When he came home, it took awhile to get used to. *This wild-ass nigga is a peace-loving Muslim now?* I liked the new Killer, though; we'd have deep conversations about life. I started reading books by Dr. York, a spiritual leader from Bushwick, Brooklyn, who taught about the origin of all races and religions. If you listen to the *Hell on Earth* album, you can hear how my rhymes started changing at that time. I started rapping about the Illuminati, secret societies, and the corrupt government and becoming more conscious of my surroundings, going through a mental and spiritual change just like Killer. That seed that my moms planted in my head with Malcolm X's autobio was starting to grow.

My lady KiKi and I had to move because she wasn't getting along with her moms. After a while, her moms busted me sleeping in her closet, so I stayed over a lot now that her moms knew. My cousin Stobo and his baby's mother had just gotten a two-bedroom apartment underneath the train tracks in East New York, Brooklyn, and offered us an extra room.

KiKi was four months pregnant and we found out we were having a boy! I was happy. *Yeah, I'm ready to have a son!* I didn't even know what being ready to have a kid meant, I was just ready. We were really in love. I had been all over the world and realized that KiKi wasn't one of those money-hungry hoes. She was a special girl.

KiKi was eight and a half months pregnant when my man from Art and Design, Illa Ghee, came back to New York from Virginia. Remember that kid with the Scorpio ring who was scheming on me in the school bathroom?

He ended up being one of my closest homeboys, the rapper Illa Ghee from Sumner projects in Brooklyn. Ghee had taken over his cousin's dope neighborhood down South in Richmond, Virginia, while his cousin was serving seven years. His cousin called Ghee like, "Yo, take over my neighborhood for me." Ghee approached me and I'd given him some start-up money before he went back. "P, put a little bit of money up and I can get you a whole lot," he promised, and he'd been down there getting mad money. He was shining with a huge Mary Mother of God piece hanging from a big gold link similar to the one I bought for Havoc back in the day, but without the ruby in the middle.

Ghee told me he had the hookup with some guns in Virginia for dirt cheap. I was in need of new toys so I decided to drive down on a Friday, get the hardware, and head back to New York by no later than Monday. Ghee and I slept at two girls' crib on a block full of dope addicts called Church Hill, the same place Ghee had been staying while he was out there getting money.

Saturday morning, Ghee got in contact with the connect and told him what we wanted—two nine-millimeter Rugers—and that same afternoon the connect came back with the hammers and we gave him the bread. Things were going even faster than planned. I should've left as soon as I got what I came for, but instead I stayed to hang out at some club that night. Stupid move.

On the way back from the club to the girls' house, we ran into a roadblock. Ghee was driving my black Tahoe, he didn't have a license, and the two girls were in the backseat. There were at least seven cars ahead of us before it was our turn to show paperwork, so Ghee and I climbed over each other to switch seats. The hammers were in the engine but I kept the clips in the car because the temperature was so hot—I didn't want the bullets to explode in the engine. When we got to the roadblock, the cop asked for my paperwork. "I saw you guys switch seats," he said. "Step out of the truck."

The officer searched the truck, found the clips, and asked where the guns were. "There aren't any guns," I told him. While he was searching my truck he saw the bloodstains on the floor and seat belts in the back right-side passenger door from when Nitty had gotten shot. "What's this?" he asked. "Blood?"

I told him the truth: "Yeah, my friend got shot, I had to take him to the hospital."

ALBERT "PRODIGY" JOHNSON

108

"Oh yeah, when did this happen?" He was acting like we had just committed a murder and he was going to get promoted to captain for busting us. He read me my rights, impounded my truck, and sent me to the Richmond City jail for the clips. They didn't have anything on Ghee and the girls because I took the blame for the clips, so they caught a cab home.

When I was finally allowed to use the phone a couple hours later, I called home and told KiKi to call my uncle Lenny so he could contact his sister Connie in Richmond to get me a lawyer. "I told you not to go down there, I told you so!" she said. "Now I'm gonna have the baby while you're in jail. I told you so!" After two days on the Richmond County tier, Illa Ghee and the two girls came to visit. We laughed about what had happened and laughed some more. Ghee is a funny nigga; he always cracked me up. I was locked up for two weeks before I saw the judge.

Aunt Connie had a government job and had me transferred to the county medical ward so they wouldn't send me to the penitentiary while I was waiting to see the judge. After two more days, they moved me to the medical ward and gave me shots of Demerol every five hours for sickle-cell pain that I wasn't even having. Shit, I'd rather be chained to a hospital bed getting high on Demerol around the clock than sitting in a jailhouse with a bunch of dirty South criminals talking about, "Yo Mobb Deep, I can rap too! I know ya cousins out here, just ask them!"

Three days later I went to court. Aunt Connie had gotten me one of the best lawyers in the state of Virginia. I got out that same day on one thousand dollars bail. Aunt Connie was waiting for me outside. Aunt Connie's a tough lady, smoked a lot of cigarettes and drank a lot of Jack Daniel's. "C'mon, I'm taking you to see your cousins," she said. "You know you owe me big-time now." She took me back to her crib to visit my cousins Monu and Dialo. I hadn't seen them since I got my first tattoo. As a kid I was scared of them because they used to always fight and fuck each other up—I figured if they did that to each other, then they might do the same to me.

My cousins were way more calm and cool now. Monu, the older, bigger brother, had been shot in the face a few times with an Uzi submachine gun a year before. He was heavy into the streets in Richmond. I heard about the shooting from Uncle Lenny, but Monu's face didn't look as bad as I had imagined. He had two bullet-hole scars next to his right eye that looked like little bubbles. I figured an Uzi would Swiss-cheese his whole face.

Monu and Dialo were happy to see me because now they had a famous rapper in the family. It was a big thing for them. They showed me off to their friends and took me around the neighborhood. It was filled with heroin addicts. Young kids out there thought it was cool to smoke weed and sniff heroin—they called it diesel. I wanted to check out the mall across from their house, but my cousins were banned for starting too many fights. I was just as happy to hang with them.

It was a coincidence that my cousins' friends were hustling with my man Illa Ghee from New York. They told me that he was doing his thing in the streets. Richmond was a small community and anybody who's somebody knew each other. I had to stay until the court case was over. The lawyer promised he would make it as quick as possible. They also kept my truck impounded until the case ended.

I called home every day because KiKi was about to give birth, plus she was planning a baby shower in Brooklyn and wanted me to get DJ Clue to do the music. She was mad at me because I got locked up and couldn't be there with her. A whole bunch of I-told-you-so's. I felt bad, but she was going to be all right; I had to make sure my freedom was going to be all right. I contacted Clue and he said he would do it.

DJ Clue made a big name for himself by using a lot of Mobb Deep songs on his mix tapes before the songs were even supposed to be out. We found out later that he was getting them from an engineer we used to work with named Duro. Little did we know, Duro was Clue's partner while he was our studio engineer; Clue owed us a lot of favors.

After a couple of weeks hanging out at local clubs and in the Richmond hoods with my cousins and Illa Ghee, I finally got my case thrown out. At my last court date my lawyer was like, "Look, you don't have a gun so you don't have a case." To top it off, my lawyer was so good that he made the DA give me back my clips right there in the courtroom, fully loaded with black talons. *Holy shit! I never saw or heard of nothing like that in my life!*

Illa got me a ride to the pound to pick up my truck. *Man, this is feeling like déjà vu.* I thought that as soon as I told them my name and that I was there to pick up my black Tahoe, they were going to lock me up again for the guns in the engine.

Two guys behind a desk were giving me dirty looks and told me that I had to wait while they processed my information. Twenty minutes later, a black detective car pulled up and two D's walked inside the pound lot and started searching my Tahoe all over again, taking their time. *For sure, they're gonna pop the hood and find them . . .* but they didn't. They gave me my ride back and I was out.

Back at my cousins' crib, Illa, Monu, and Dialo helped me wash the remaining blood out of the carpet before I drove back to New York. When Nitty got shot, I'd washed the blood off the seats and door but never got around to the carpet. It still wasn't all the way out, but it was the best we could do. I thanked my cousins and Aunt Connie and got the fuck out of Dodge.

Even though I had a minor setback and paid an extra twenty-five hundred dollars for the lawyer's fees, it was a mission accomplished. I had two new guns with full clips, all together inside the engine this time, and I was on my way home. When I got back I wanted to kiss the dirty New York streets, I was so happy. I went straight to KiKi's crib and we packed our stuff and moved in with Stobo and his baby moms in East New York. It was a small railroad apartment, but we had our own space and we weren't going back and forth between KiKi's moms's or my grandmoms's anymore.

Nineteen ninety-six was a year of tremendous joy and pain.

A few weeks later, Illa Ghee's brother Tim called and told me Ghee got locked up in Virginia. "He was in somebody's crib when it got raided by the task force," he said. "They found weapons, drugs, boxes of money, bullet-proof vests, and charged Ghee with kingpin charges!" They sentenced Illa to five years in the Virginia penitentiary. *Crazy, I was just with this nigga.*

Killer Black started bussin' his gun again. He had a smart mouth and got into an argument on the hill in Queensbridge with this drug dealer named Dope who was clashing with Little Lord. Dope pulled out a .22 revolver. Killer tried to grab the gun, but Dope squeezed the trigger. A bullet went through Killer's hand. He let go and started running. Another bullet hit his arm, then another the back of his head. Killer dropped to the ground. When he realized he wasn't dead, he got up and kept running home.

Later that night, Killer called and I went to his crib to see him. He was wrapped in bandages and you could actually see the bullet sticking halfway out the back of his head. One of his boys found pain medicine from some girl, but he needed me to take him to a hospital in Long Island to treat his wounds. He couldn't go to a hospital in Queens or the D's might come for questioning and lock him up for parole violation. So I took Killer to Mercy Hospital around the block from my crib in Hempstead.

The bullet in Killer's hand had gone in and out; the other bullet broke his arm. He didn't even tell them about the head shot—the bullet was just stuck in his skull. After they put a cast on his arm, he lay low at my grand-mother's crib for a week before going back to QB. All that Muslim stuff was out the window and Killer went right back to business.

That bullet to the head had him acting strange. He wasn't the quiet, no-nonsense Killer Black we all knew. Late one night, I pulled up on the hill at two A.M. and like twenty dudes were up there hustling, drinking, and doing the regular. A bunch of them called me over asking me to take Killer home because they couldn't control him. "You need to take care of your homie, he's bugging," they said, scared he might do something to one of them. Killer leaned against a wall with a look in his eyes like he was about to snap at any minute. I put him in the car, drove to his block, and walked him up to the crib. On the way, he was slurring his words and I realized that he was just drunk and needed sleep.

The next morning he called early asking to borrow money, so I left my bed in Brooklyn and went to Hav's crib to give Killer some dough. Since coming back from North Carolina, Havoc had moved out of his moms's crib and was living in the Best Western City View hotel in Long Island City, Queens, bringing girls by and living the life.

When I got to his crib in Queensbridge, Killer showed me how he had been picking at the bullet in his head, which finally came out after a few weeks. "I've been seeing things in my room at night," he said. "I've been having conversations with the Egyptian King Tut! I know it sounds crazy, but I'm really seeing and talking to King Tut!" I listened real close because even though he did some wild shit, Killer wasn't crazy at all; he was very intelligent. The only time he ever shot somebody for no reason was when he killed that guy for the Walkman speakers, and he was extra drunk that night. Any other time he fired his gun it was because somebody was messing with him or us. We spoke for a few hours. I gave him the money and left.

Killer walked me down to the door and we had a few last words. While we were talking in front of the building, this little dude named Worm rode past us on a pedal bike and shouted out, "Oh shit! Yo, Prodigy! What up, kid!" Killer and I were ending a deep conversation, so I didn't pay the kid much mind. "What up," I said. He stopped his bike but I just figured he was mumbling, excited to see me. Killer and I gave each other a pound when the little dude rode off shouting, "Oh word? It's like that? All right!"

What was that about? I wondered, brushing it off. Twin Gambino and Money No were waiting for me in the Tahoe. We drove to the corner store to buy a White Owl blunt. Money No hopped out to get it, and while he was in the store, I saw my man Bumpy riding a pedal bike across the street on Fortieth Avenue with the little dude Worm on the back, standing on the pegs.

"Yo, that little dude over there got a gun out," Money No said when he got in the truck. I turned and saw Worm swinging a chrome .45-caliber in his hand, shouting something. "So what," I said, grabbing the White Owl from Money No, opening it to roll up the weed. Gambino was staring at Worm.

"Pull off, P. This nigga's buggin'," he said.

"I'm not pulling off 'cause he's got a gun," I said. "Fuck he gonna do, shoot us?"

"Yo P, pull off," Gambino said again.

"Son, I'm not pulling off for this little clown. What, I'm supposed to be scared 'cause he's got a gun?" If we pulled off he might think we were scared of him. If somebody's waving a shiny chrome gun around, then that person's obviously trying to scare somebody. If he was going to use the gun, why would he wave it around for five minutes first? Gambino demanded that I pull off, and as soon as I bent the corner onto Twenty-first Street this little chump shot the gun in the air just like I thought. *I'll deal with him when I'm back on this side.* I dropped Money No and Twin off and bounced to see my baby KiKi.

That night I took KiKi out to eat at a diner on Jackson Boulevard down the block from Queensbridge. She ordered her favorite dish, shrimp scampi, and I ordered my usual, the broiled fillet of sole. Ten minutes into our meal, KiKi's water broke. She'd been having some contractions all day, and we later found out that seafood induces labor. We rushed to St. John's Hospital on Queens Boulevard and they pushed her in a wheelchair straight to the delivery room. "The baby's coming," the doctor said. "It might take some time."

Man, I was happy, nervous, anxious, shook, and a whole bunch of emotions all at the same time. I held KiKi's hand; she was crushing mine while she breathed and pushed in and out, in and out. After an hour, I started seeing my son's head, his shoulders, and then finally, with her last push and crushing hand squeeze, our bloody little boy was born into the world. It was truly the most amazing and nastiest thing I ever saw.

The worst part about watching my child's birth was seeing them pull out the placenta after they cut the umbilical cord and seeing my woman shake uncontrollably because her body temperature dropped extremely low after the baby came out. The nurses wrapped like seven blankets around her. I was definitely scared for her as I held her hand.

The Dr. York books I was reading spoke about how hospitals inject babies, especially black babies, with microchips and diseases at birth when they vaccinate them. I followed the two female nurses when they took my son to another room for the shots. I was going to refuse the shots, but I let them do their job and kept a close eye on every move they made. I figured if they wanted to do something they could just do it late at night when I was gone, while KiKi was sleeping. *Fuck it.* They let me stay with KiKi for thirty minutes before kicking me out.

The first thing I did was call my pops from the pay phone in front of the hospital. He'd just gotten out of jail and was living in Atlanta with his new wife. "I just had a baby! I'm a father!" It was like I hit the lottery. "You're a grandfather!" Then I called my moms and everybody else I knew. My first baby boy! T'Shaka Keion-Maliq Johnson, and I was there when he was born.

I spent all kinds of money on baby Polo, Nautica, Hilfiger, all the fly gear for Shaka. I bought clothes he couldn't fit into until he was three years old and kept it all in a stash. Then I realized I was wasting my money because my little man was growing so fast.

My pops came to New York a month later to see his grandson. He was cheesing like a muthafucker when he saw Shaka. I hadn't seen Pops in five years. He looked old and had lost a lot of weight. He stayed with my grandmother in Long Island for two weeks. I didn't get to see much of him, but we hung out two or three times.

One winter day while we were at Axis studio, the worst thing that could ever happen happened. Havoc, the Twins, Godfather, Gotti, Money No, and I had all stayed at my crib in Hempstead the night before, planning how we could become a stronger team. I suggested that we take it easy on the drugs and alcohol. "It's slowing down our progress," I said as we sat in the basement smoking and drinking. "We should do whatever work we need to do first, then get high when the work's finished. That way we're more focused on getting and staying rich." Everyone agreed, but they weren't really ready for a new way of thinking and living.

My leadership qualities began to manifest. I started becoming the more enlightened one of the crew because I was the only one reading about the past, present, and future of the world—current events, politics, proper nutrition, spiritual health, and the origin of all things. Dr. York's books are truly one of a kind. Nobody alive on this planet has the comprehensive understanding that Dr. York has on such a vast array of topics. That man's books boosted my intelligence level beyond this physical dimension and gave me the information I needed to step out of the sleep spell that almost all of us are in. I was wide fuckin' awake and was able to see if another person's eyes were wide shut or wide open.

I started looking at the world differently, seeing things nobody else could or wanted to see. Passing by a billboard advertisement on the street or watching a movie, I saw hidden messages and symbolism while almost everyone else just saw the outer layer of information. The things I was learning about the origins of symbols, secret societies, and civilizations gave me the ability to see the spell we're living in and those responsible for casting it. It's all around us. It's rather spooky.

The 1988 movie *They Live* by John Carpenter starring Rowdy Roddy Piper explained exactly what I'm talking about, using sunglasses as a metaphor for learning information. When Roddy Piper put the special sunglasses on, he saw all the evil in the world. When the glasses were off, everything looked normal. He tried to tell his friends to put the glasses on so they could see what he saw, but his friends were so comfortable with their lives that they didn't want to try. He had to force them to put the glasses on, and they finally saw the spell that these aliens had the entire world under.

I wish learning this information was as easy as putting on some glasses and suddenly waking up to the real world, but it's not. It takes time, dedication, patience, and a hunger for knowledge to grasp it all. That's why many try but only a few succeed.

I was no longer understanding the world; I was now overstanding it. Among the first major things I overstood were the popular sayings "ignorance is bliss" and "misery loves company." We were all living in a state of blissful, ignorant misery. People would rather have a good time than deal with the dark realities of the world because that's easy and learning is hard. Learning is a never-ending process. Hence the term "knowledge is infinite."

The crew noticed that I was changing and gave me two nicknames: the God and Science. Trip came up with the names the same night I came up with the chorus for the song "G.O.D. Pt. 3" on Hell on Earth. We were drinking lime Bacardi on Hav's block and I started chanting, "G.O.D. Father Part Three Q.B.C. sip lime Bacardi, heavy on the wrist cube link and ice ring, drama we bring, yeah, that's a small thing. . . ." That's also when we started calling Trip "Godfather."

We stayed up most of that night talking about how slavery began, how religion was created to control people, and how the U.S. government was really a puppet for the British royal family. Mostly I spoke to them about not getting high or drunk until our daily business was handled. "In order for us to have continued success in this business we have to start adapting to the corporate world," I urged. The Twins, Gotti, and I spoke the most because they were the only ones who showed interest. Everyone else listened for a little while and got frustrated because they didn't want to overstand, so they conveniently removed themselves from the conversation. Hey, for some people change takes longer than for others. I knew I had to be 100 percent clean and sober soon. Mentally, I just wasn't ready for that yet. But I was off to one helluva start.

The next day we woke up around noon and Hav had already left for the studio in Manhattan. Havoc always got up early in the morning to start working on songs. He had this saying: "The first to wake and last to sleep."

The Twins, Godfather, Money No, and I were in my truck a few hours behind him. When we got to the studio, Havoc had this ill beat and I immediately started writing my verse for "Nighttime Vultures" from *Hell on Earth:* "*Flashbacks of gunshots shot past my head, I can recall an eight-man brawl, three men fall, bullets flew I had to drag my man behind a wall, left a wet trail, delivered these slugs like air mail.* . . ." While I was writing my verse, I kept dozing off from staying up all night. "*An eye for an eye you know my science of life, Is you men or mice, thugs or the cowardly type.* . . ." I balled up my leather jacket as a pillow and took a power nap on the studio carpet.

Three hours later, I woke up and noticed several missed calls from a strange number. I called the number back and it was a detective! He told me that my Tahoe had been in an accident on the West Side Highway and I needed to come to the precinct on 125th Street in Harlem. That woke me up quick fast. Somebody must have taken my keys from my pocket while I was asleep.

Gotti and I took a cab uptown. Inside the precinct, the detective sat me down and explained the accident. "Your truck flipped over more than ten times while getting off the 125th Street exit," he said. "Get up and put your hands behind your back." The muthafucker started reading me my rights! He said I had warrants in Long Island for traffic violations. "By the way," he said after he cuffed me, "your friends are dead."

I heard detectives screaming at Godfather in a nearby room. They put me in a holding cell and brought Godfather to the cell soon after. "We took your truck uptown to get some trees," Godfather explained in the cell. "I lost control when I switched from the fast lane to the exit." He was damn near having a nervous breakdown. As mad as I was, I felt bad for him. He had just killed his lifelong friend Jamel the Scarface Twin. Scarface flew out of the window and his neck got cut from ear to ear. His other friend Ghostface from QB was decapitated; he'd just started hanging out with us. They found his head and sneakers on one side of the highway and his body on the other. Jamal, Twin Gambino, stayed strapped in the passenger seat with a broken collarbone. Money No was in the backseat, his spine almost crushed. Another one of our homeboys, La-Skally, was found up in a tree with his head split open. He was lucky to survive. Godfather was driving and unscathed, not even a scratch. Nassau County Police came to take me to the county jail and the NYPD took Godfather to Rikers.

It was Friday night. I didn't get bailed out until Monday. That was the foulest feeling ever, sitting in my cell in complete shock. I couldn't imagine what Jamal was going through, losing his twin brother. *I wonder how Jamal's gonna take this.* Everybody loved the Twins. They were outgoing and always ready to party. They showed me more love than Havoc and anybody in QB. Hav's more of a recluse; the Twins introduced me to everyone, took me everywhere.

Uncle Lenny came to pick me up from jail. When I got in the car, he told me that my father had just died of AIDS from sharing needles with other dope addicts. *What the fuck else can happen?* I knew Pops didn't look healthy when I last saw him, he'd gotten so skinny, but I thought it was old age. *Damn, AIDS?*

KiKi was waiting at my grandmother's crib. I lay on my bed and cried about everything.

Gilmore's Funeral Home on Linden Boulevard in Jamaica, Queens, was packed for Scarface Twin's wake later that week. Man, people loved the Twins. A bunch of girls who the Scarface Twin had relationships with were there. He was in the casket in his favorite outfit, a denim suit; his face looked real swollen.

Afterward, some of Twin's friends from 40 Projects in South Jamaica threw a block party. The Lost Boyz' DJ, Grand Master Vick, DJed, and we were all doing our best to keep Twin Gambino in good spirits. I let him hold my big Figaro link with the Mac-10 pendant and we drank, got high, and got on the mic for a rap session, trying to have as much fun as we could. Southside Jamaica and QB partying together in 40 Projects without drama—a monumental moment.

The following night, Twin was mourning his brother's death on Twelfth Street with a broken collarbone and a bunch of friends from QB, drinking, smoking, reminiscing on old times, and lighting candles. The block started clearing after a few hours but Twin stayed on the benches drinking. This little nigga Worm came through the block and saw Twin wearing my big chain. Worm walked over to Twin and pulled a TEC-9 on him. "Take the chain off!" I don't know why he wanted to mess with Twin just days after his brother died. Twin looked at Worm and told him: "Pull the trigger!" Worm got scared and ran away.

The next day, Twin gave me my chain back and told me what happened. We wanted to kill the kid. He was a problem that needed to be dealt with.

Then, as if we weren't going through enough emotional pain, we found out that Yamit had gone upstate to take over the crack game in some town by the Catskills. "Yamit had the town scared of him," Yamit's brother Buddha told us. "One of the local drug dealers ran up behind Yamit with a bat and cracked his head open!" Yamit was in a coma on life support because he was brain-dead. *Damn!* Yamit was one of the strongest niggas I knew: He gave us the name Infamous. A Golden Gloves champion who could kill you with his hands and would kill you with a gun. He loved us, he loved Mobb Deep, and was always very protective of us. *Fuck! Not Yamit too.*

A few days after Worm's disrespectful, botched robbery attempt, I went to Atlanta with my moms and Uncle Lenny to identify my father's body before they cremated him. KiKi and our son Shaka joined me. When we got to the crematory, I saw my older sister Kim, my father's daughter from another relationship. We never saw much of each other growing up; she's about the same age as my brother Greg, twelve years older than me. My father was in a black plastic bag on top of a gurney. They zipped open the bag and there he was, laid out stiff. I looked at him real close and saw a drop of blood trickling from his nose.

My mother shed some tears but I was tired of crying. I looked at him for a while and left. It took about thirty minutes to cremate him. They handed me his ashes in a plastic bag inside a small cardboard box. My father's girlfriend gave me a leather briefcase with his watch, pictures, and notebooks filled with computer-tech writing. He was working for IBM at the time of his death, setting up computer systems for colleges.

I missed my pops. There were a lot of questions about life that I never got to ask him. The deepest question I ever asked my father was the night that we saw *Boyz 'N the Hood* while he was on the run in California.

"Is there a God?" I asked as we walked from the movie theater to his apartment.

"Yes," he answered.

"How do you know that God is real?"

"I've seen God before," he said.

"If you've seen God, then what did God look like?"

"God looks like water."

"Water?"

"Yeah," Pops said. "God looks like water."

We finally finished *Hell on Earth* and did the album photo shoot. I came up with the idea for all of us to sit at a roundtable and leave the chair next to Twin empty so we could insert a ghostly image of his brother Scarface. We let Money No from Hempstead sit at the table with us since he was part of the crew now. It wasn't a small thing for us to add a new face to our family. It was big for him to be in that picture. Noyd came home from jail just in time to get in the picture too. We missed having him around. In that roundtable picture you see Gotti, Nitty, Twin Gambino, Noyd, Money No, Godfather, Havoc, myself, and the ghost of Scarface Twin—it was the best crew picture we ever took.

At a show in Boston the night after the photo shoot, the Lost Boyz finished performing as we arrived and the promoter wanted us to start right away because the crowd was getting rowdy. As "Shook Ones" came on, a dude with dreads in the front row started slamming into people and the whole front row beat him up. The venue owner turned on the house lights and the DJ stopped the music, but it only got worse. Chairs were flying. "Put the fuckin' music back on!" I screamed, but the promoter wanted to stop the show. Mr. Cheeks from the Lost Boyz approached me and said, "I know we had beef in the past, but we gotta stick together tonight." I laughed and agreed.

Gunshots started poppin' as people stampeded toward the exit doors. We slipped out and got in our cars, talking to females as they left the spot. The dreaded dude walked up to our car, chest naked with his pants ripped, blood all over his body and splattering from his mouth. "Mobb Deep! What!" he screamed. "I'm still standing, they can't stop me!" We've been cool with the Lost Boyz ever since that night.

· · ·

Then more bad news.

I got a 911 page on my beeper while driving and pulled over to use the pay phone to call back Hav's boy Bolo. "Killer Black is dead," Bolo said.

"Don't play with me, man, don't joke like that," I said. "It's not funny."

"I'm serious, he committed suicide."

I didn't believe it so I went to QB to find out what happened. Havoc told me it was true. Killer shot himself in the head with a nine-millimeter in the bathroom.

People were saying Killer was with Tragedy at a club that night and Killer might have smoked some weed with dust in it. I knew Killer. He might have been crazy with the guns when it was time, but he wasn't mentally crazy or suicidal. This was totally out of character. Hav's mom said Killer closed the bathroom door, turned on the sink, and she heard a *pop!* She didn't realize it was a gunshot. She heard water running. She went into the bathroom but it wasn't water, it was her son's blood, his head slumped in the sink.

It felt like a black cloud hovered over us all the time. There was so much death around us during that short period, it felt like we were cursed for all the wrong we'd done.

We shot a video for our title track, "Hell on Earth," just before Killer shot himself, and Killer Black made his final cameo in that video. Killer was in our first video, "Peer Pressure," and in the verse that Havoc wrote for me I rap about a kid named Kenny who started drinking, smoking weed, and messing up in school. At the end of the verse, Kenny committed suicide. It's spooky that Killer Black played Kenny in that video.

Upset about his brother Killer's death, Havoc started drinking heavily. I became addicted to the prescription pain pills like Percocet that hospitals sent me home with for my sickle-cell. The high made me forget about the stress and death, at least momentarily.

We took a two-year break from doing shows, radio, and interviews. We still made music in the studio and did a lot of features and movie sound tracks within those two years: Nas's "Live Nigga Rap," Das EFX's "Microphone

Masters," Mariah Carey's "The Roof," LL Cool J's "I Shot Ya" and "Queens Is," RSO's "The War Is On," Shaquille O'Neal's "Legal Money," Xzibit's "Eyes May Shine," Big Pun's "Tres Leches," Blondie's "No Exit," KRS-One's "5 Boroughs," PMD's "It's the P '97," A+'s "Gusto," "Crash the Boards" from the *Hoodlum* sound track, "Rare Species" from the *Soul in the Hole* sound track, and *America Is Dying Slowly*'s "Street Life."

I also appeared on a bunch of songs with drug dealers who paid cash to have a song with Prodigy from Mobb Deep. A twenty-thousand-dollar check here, ten thousand dollars in cash there: It was good money. Hav did production for Biggie, Foxy Brown, Nas, and a bunch of drug dealers who paid cash for a Havoc beat.

Havoc was doing beats for LL Cool J at the Hit Factory in Manhattan one night, and LL asked me to rhyme on one of the songs. When I arrived, Hav was passed out drunk on the couch. LL's A&R Benny was with him plus a camera crew. LL told the cameras to film us as we listened to my verse, stopping the music midway to talk shit to the camera. "Yo Hav! What're you doing?" Benny suddenly yelled out. Havoc was standing up, taking a piss on the gear rack—about thirty thousand dollars' worth of equipment and mad electrical wires—still half asleep. Then Hav lay back down on the couch and kept sleeping. He didn't even realize what he'd done.

"Your man is out of control," LL said. I told the camera crew that they had to erase that part off the tape, and LL agreed.

That was far from Hav's first drunken blunder. A year before, Hav invited me to the studio where he was producing a song for Biggie Smalls called "Last Day," featuring the Lox. "Big wants you to come by the studio," Hav said. "He wants you to get on the song."

"I don't wanna do a song with Biggie, he's corny," I said. I wasn't a fan of Biggie's music at that time. "Go ahead without me." After a long studio session, Hav was so drunk that he left his beat disc in the machine—leaving behind all six songs he crafted that day instead of one. Somebody ended up using one of the beats for Black Rob's "I Love You Baby," on the Puff Daddy and the Family album. I could tell as soon as I heard it because it had Hav's signature drums, bass line, and all. "Hav, that's your beat!" I said when we heard the track. "That muthafucker stole your beat!"

After Biggie's *Life After Death* album came out with that track "Last Day" that Hav produced, I became a huge Biggie fan and regretted not doing the song. I was a hardheaded young fool back then.

In March 1997, we got more bad news. Biggie Smalls had been shot and killed in Los Angeles after a party. There was a lot of tension between New York and California, but the media was turning the Mobb Deep and Biggie vs. Death Row feud into a coastal war, making it seem worse than it was.

Now that Big and Pac had been murdered, it felt like we were next on the hit list. The feeling of death lurking around the corner enhanced our already existing "I don't give a fuck" mentality. Of course, we didn't want to die but with all that was going on in our lives, we became extremely fearless and ready to defend Mobb Deep at any cost.

My five-year probation for the gun charge I caught at sixteen was coming to an end and I transferred my probation from Manhattan to Hempstead, Long Island, because it seemed easier out there. Wrong move. I was always ripping and running and missed a few phone calls to my probation officer, so that little meat-face PO violated me. When my lawyer, Irv Cohen, and I took it to trial, I must've had the most racist judge in Nassau County. The Archie Bunker–looking bastard sentenced me to a one-to-three-year bid to be served immediately. They threw me in cuffs and took me to Nassau County jail.

After three long weeks in the county jail, I beat the case with my appeal. I was finally free. One to three years? Fuck that. I'm gone. Archie Bunker, kiss my ass.

The whole gang still went to the Tunnel every Sunday like church. One Sunday, a few weeks before New Year's 1998, we saw Keith Murray by the bathroom on the second floor. We'd just arrived and met Chris in the bathroom to get our bag of weapons. I finished passing out the weapons and we walked out and this punk-ass nigga was standing there, looking scared to death when he saw us because he was by himself and had probably heard all the stories of us beating people raggedy. Noyd and Twin were fienin' to get him. "What's up?" they were in my ear asking. "We got the drop on him!"

"Yeah, we got the drop on him, but for what?" I said. Even though he asked if I was talking about him on the skit, he never said or did anything offensive to me, so I told them to fall back. "Leave him alone," I kept telling them. "Leave the boy alone." We had so many weapons we would've killed the boy, and it wasn't my style anymore to take advantage of a weak, defenseless person.

At that point, I realized that it was wrong to abuse the destructive power that we had. *You only hurt people when it's necessary*, I told myself. My boys were upset with me for not giving them the green light, but I knew it was the right choice.

After a few hours of partying, Money No, Godfather, and I left early with some girls. It was close to Christmas 1997 and snow and ice lined the ground outside. Money No and I walked to the parking lot to get my car while Godfather walked with the girls. Money No and I were waiting for the light to change to cross the street when we saw Keith Murray with four of his boys standing ten feet to our right. "What's up now?" one of his boys said to him. "Let's see what's up now!"

"Pass me your gun," Money No said. I had a big nine-millimeter on my hip all night.

"Nah, chill," I said. I wanted to fire the shots.

"What's up with all that shit you was talkin' on your album?" Keith Murray walked up and asked after his boy pumped him up with gas.

"Are you serious?" I looked at him and asked. *How am I gonna shoot this dude and get away with it?* I was thinking. *All right, I'm gonna take him down to the dark shadows toward Tenth Avenue.*

One of Keith Murray's boys and Money No started beefing about who could fight better. I suggested that we take it across the street, out of sight so the cops couldn't break us up. They reluctantly agreed. As we crossed the street, Money No kept asking for the gun but I refused. I couldn't wait to get in the shadows of the next block and see the look on their faces when I started squeezing bullets at them. *Should I shoot to kill, shoot to wound, or shoot to scare them?* I decided to just shoot Keith Murray and wound him.

A police squad car came up on my left when we got to the double yellow lines in the middle of Eleventh Avenue. Keith Murray jumped in front of me like he'd changed his mind about stepping into the shadows across the street. I could see him ready to swing. "The cops are right there," I warned him. "Chill until they pass." But he decided to punch me in the mouth in front of the cops. How corny is that?

My first thought was, *This nigga punches like a girl.* My second was, *Get distance between you and these cops immediately before backup arrives and we all get frisked.*

The police put on the siren and lights. I ran to get rid of the gun behind a van, tossing it in the snow, covering it with more snow. When I looked up, Money No knocked out Keith Murray's man. He hit the ground and slid on some ice underneath the cop car. As I was walking back toward them, Keith Murray was talking to the cops, pointing at us, saying that we started it. The police were cool and simply said: "You guys go that way, and you guys walk the other way."

Them niggas don't even understand how lucky they are! God was truly on their side. I guess God was on my side, too, because I might have gotten locked up. Keith Murray must have felt death down that dark street. When he saw that squad car coming, it must have been like Jesus Christ coming to save him.

New Year's Eve 1998 fell on a Sunday and the Tunnel was on fire as usual. Godfather and I stole two hoes from their pimp—Diamond and Strawberry, Puerto Rican dimes from Albany. They told us homie was lame, pimping them in the club every Sunday, and they wanted to work Queensbridge. We headed out of the club with them. I realized that I left my car keys with Gotti, gave my gun to Godfather, and told him I'd be right back.

Inside the Tunnel, I walked all over trying to find Gotti. I noticed dudes wearing Deaf Squid hats, Keith Murray's crew. I saw two hats, four, then more. Minutes later, with the dudes following, I bumped into Karate Joe, Bill Cosby, Nitty, Twin, Gotti, and a bunch of the 12th Street crew. I told Gotti to give me my keys.

"These dudes are following me," I told Karate Joe. He didn't even wait for me to tell him who: Karate Joe punched the face off the poor dude behind me, who wasn't even down with the Deaf Squid. The 12th Street crew started fighting everybody behind me. Twin grabbed me out of the way, holding me behind him, slicing and dicing faces with a razor. I asked him to give me one. Twin just kept cutting, not hearing me. We chased the Deaf Squid pussies through the club. I ran outside and told Godfather to give me my gun, thinking that whatever was left of the Deaf Squid would come running, but nobody came.

Ten minutes later, the crew strolled out laughing. "Where's the Deaf Squidron?" I asked.

"Them niggas in there bleeding," he said. "They probably need an ambulance."

Godfather, the girls, and I walked to the parking lot to my new black Lexus GS300, which I'd bought with some of my feature money. We drove the hoes to a cheap motel next to the Holland Tunnel where their pimp kept them to get their clothes from their room. They ran out of the hotel with two stuffed garbage bags. We took them to QB and started pimpin' them the next morning.

Diamond and Strawberry were good-looking Puerto Rican broads with fat asses and nice bodies. We took them to Chang's Chinese food spot on Fortieth Avenue. Mr. Chang and his employees were our first customers, in a car behind the restaurant. Then we walked around the hood with them and made a few thousand dollars. It gave me a new respect for pimps. *Pimpin' ain't easy, it's a full-time job and I ain't got time for it.*

My run as a pimp was over within a week. Godfather kept Diamond and Strawberry for another month and got tired of it too, so he left them somewhere in the city. I told KiKi what we were doing but she probably didn't even believe me.

A spiritual war was going on within me. All the things I was learning about life and health had me wanting to stop doing drugs and living the grimy way I was living, but at the same time all the stress and pain, drama and criminals around me made me not care about being peaceful and cleaning up my act. My coke habit and drinking were affecting my sickle-cell. All the partying was finally starting to catch up.

Not long after my little pimping episode, an OG in Queensbridge went to cop a bag of coke for me in the projects late one night—this was our regular routine—because I didn't want people to see it was Prodigy buying from them. Never send a broke cokehead to buy coke. The OG came back and gave me a bag of something that wasn't coke or coke mixed with something that smelled and tasted like plastic. I don't know if the dealer gave him a bad bag or if he dipped in my bag and replaced what he took with some bullshit. Later that night, my head hurt and my sinuses swelled up above my eyes.

My sickle-cell started acting up and I had to go to the hospital. They told me I might have spinal meningitis and stuck a needle in my spine to remove some fluid. I didn't have meningitis; I knew damn well it was from the coke. My head looked like E.T.'s and I felt ugly and embarrassed when KiKi came to see.

The doctors asked KiKi and Uncle Lenny to leave the room for a moment. They told me that they found cocaine, PCP, and marijuana in my blood. When KiKi and Lenny came back, I admitted that I was using cocaine and angel dust. KiKi was mad as hell, and when I explained how long I'd been using, she couldn't believe it.

After I healed, KiKi told me when she saw my face and head swollen like that and found out about my drug habit she wanted to leave me. That scared me into wanting to change my life. Sickle-cell pain had brought me close to death many times, but the thought of losing KiKi was worse. It was time to put all the righteous information I was learning about into serious practice. It took a few more bangs on my hard head for me to finally get my shit together. But from that night on, I never used cocaine again.

Twin and I waited for an hour in the freezing cold to get inside the Tunnel one night about a week after my hospital stay. Chris Lighty wasn't at the door and the bouncers were hating on us, making us wait outside forever. The cold triggered my sickle-cell. By the time I got inside, I was in superpain. With no medicine, I thought of my own remedy. I drank Hennessy until I was numb.

The next day I went to the hospital and had to stay for a week. My man Shameek from LeFrak came to visit and brought fish, biscuits, and shrimp from the Red Lobster next to LeFrak City. He made surprise visits with Red Lobster a lot when I was in the hospital. We talked about the latest jewelry, fashion, and rap drama. Shameek was a cool dude. He'd come up since the nickel-and-dime days, become real big-time in the drug game.

A few days after I came home from the hospital, Shameek invited me to Gordon's strip club on Hillside Avenue in Jamaica, Queens. He was meeting his homeboy E-Money Bags and Nas, so I went. Shameek was selling drugs for E-Money Bags and they were talking in code language about their dealings while Nas and I spoke about the Nation of Islam's 120 Lessons and the rap game. We drank for a few hours, then we left. My niggas and I were never into giving our money to strippers or getting lap dances. I always looked at dudes who did that like they were herbs, suckers, or cornballs. "Tricks" is the pimp terminology for those types.

While I was driving Shameek back to LeFrak, I asked him to give me the 120 Lessons. Sha was what we called God Body from the Five Percent Nation now known as the Nation of Gods and Earths. Males are called God Body and women are Earth. They believe that the black man is God and that we shouldn't be praying or waiting for Jesus to save us. We should be creating our own destiny, and if we want life to be better then we must make it that way by doing positive things. They have some very interesting concepts. I didn't want to join them, just acquire their knowledge.

Sha had been given his God Body name, Shameek Allah, when we were little kids in Lakeview. Growing up, there were a lot of Gods in Hempstead and Lakeview, Long Island, and ever since I started reading Dr. York's books, I wanted to study the 120 Lessons and learn knowledge of self. Dr. York teaches that we should know the origin of all things and I wanted to learn their origin.

Sha ran up to his apartment and came back with an unbound booklet of the Lessons. People Xeroxed loose copies and passed them around; some people even hand-wrote the Lessons with a pen and pad. I went home and didn't stop reading until I was finished.

Like I said, I wasn't planning on becoming a follower anyway—I'm just an addict for information, especially the facts. I started realizing that all religions were created to control the masses on this planet. They control the people through the fear of God and the devil, heaven and hell, my dick and my nuts. I'm not into race-hating and I don't rely on religion for my spiritual health.

I've got my own relationship with the Creator. The only thing I believe in are the facts, and the fact is that when we were in Africa living in peace with the universe, we didn't have bibles or corrupt corporations. We were spiritual people with our own way of life.

We didn't need for anything because it was all there for us naturally in infinite abundance. Africa is the cradle of all humanity and civilization. We were advanced in technology, agriculture, architecture, medical procedures, math, science, astronomy, astrology, and health practices, long before the Greeks and Romans. Don't believe the lie when they say Caucasians came to Africa and found black people living in destitution as unruly cannibalistic bush babies and they had to save us from our evil savage ways, clean us up, civilize and transform us into wholesome, upstanding Christians. This is all propaganda created by the Caucasian pirates to conceal their true agenda of the largest land, natural resources, knowledge, and population heist in history, not to mention the largest mass genocide. We thrived independently for millions of years before they invaded our lives with their wickedness and lifestyle of the beast.

When we were enslaved and shipped to America, the Europeans forced us to follow fairy-tale religions so that they could control our minds. They forced their banking system on us to control our lives with money. If we don't agree with their system and refuse to believe in their religions, then we get killed, sent to jail, or locked in a mental institution.

I could write an entire book on that subject alone, and I will.

MURDA MUZIK

Envision a canvas, I'll paint a picture
similar to Ernie Barnes nigga
But mines is more ghetto more guns
more drugs mostly thugs all of my thuns
they baby moms daughters and sons

"Streets Raised Me"

In early 1998, Havoc and I decided to open up a new album budget with Loud Records so we could get a new check. Loud agreed that it was time for it, so they gave us six figures and we started working on our fourth album. I came up with the title *Murda Muzik* because the songs we'd been making sounded so sinister—like murder music. I told Havoc that we should buy a house with a studio and live together as a team—Godfather, Twin, Gotti, Nitty, Havoc, and myself—so we could constantly bang out songs. We found the perfect brand-new five-bedroom minimansion in Freeport, Long Island, built a studio in the basement, and we all moved in—KiKi and Shaka too.

That tan house with forest-green shutters, a front porch, and small backyard was the first piece of property that Havoc and I ever owned. I put the entire house together by myself—the gray carpet, wooden blinds, furniture, TVs for every room. Hav let a couple extras move in: Poppa Mobb, aka M.C.-T, from Queensbridge—he was pushing fifty-something—and Ty-Nitty's cousin Bolo. I knew it was a bad idea but Havoc wanted them in, so I agreed. I even let Hav take the biggest room in the house so he could feel good about being home.

Determined to live a peaceful, positive life and make smart business decisions, I tried my best to get all my boys to do the same, but we were a bunch of savages and I was the only one ready for a change. I posted house rules on the refrigerator and gave everybody a job to do. From the beginning, I could tell that Bolo was lazy. He didn't rap or produce and was just a dead-beat.

Once a week I called house meetings in the living room. "Get a hotel room if you're with a girl 'cause I don't want nobody to know where we live," I told them. "Or blindfold your girls before you get off the highway exit so the broads won't know where they're going." I had KiKi and Shaka with me and had to make sure my family was safe.

Within six months, the guys were breaking every rule. Havoc was the main one breaking them, and the others followed him. It felt like they were talking behind my back: "P's crazy with all these house rules! We're partying in this bitch when he's not looking!" And they were.

KiKi was disgusted with the way my friends were living, the number of girls she saw coming and going. She found a list of the symptoms of HIV/AIDS and taped it to the refrigerator next to my house rules. The next day the paper was gone. I guess it made somebody feel insecure about their health.

Godfather, his boy Ty-Max, and I were heading home from Soundtrack Studios at three o'clock one morning. Just as LeFrak City was coming up to our left on the Long Island Expressway, a giant bright-green fireball about the size of a falling planet shot down from the sky. I almost crashed the car. "Oh shit!" I yelled. "Did you see that?"

"See what?" Godfather asked from the passenger seat.

"Son, you didn't see that big green fire just now?"

"No, I just closed my eyes to go to sleep," he said.

"Ty-Max, you ain't see that?" I asked.

"Nah, I just closed my eyes too."

I couldn't believe it. We were all wide awake and having a conversation just seconds before. The clock on the dashboard read 3:33 A.M. I had been studying books on numerology and to see something that extraordinary at that exact time was obviously a sign and a sign meant for only me. In Dr. York's books, he said that God's angels, the Elohim, used green fire, and evil forces used amber or red fire. My pops and I used to watch shooting stars and comets at certain times of the year, but there was no comparison to what I had just seen. Pops and Grandmoms told me that when Pops was young, they saw a multicolored UFO in Virginia hovering above a store for several minutes and then take off with light speed.

At the crib in Freeport, nobody believed what I had seen except Godfather, Twin, and Gotti. I had been praying and asking the Creator to show me a sign or some type of proof that all the things I was learning about the origin of life on earth were in fact true. I was grateful to receive a sign but furious with the Most High for not giving me a witness. *Maybe I'm buggin'*, I thought. They had me doubting my own eyes.

The brand-new minimansion in Freeport was slowly but surely becoming disgusting. Carpet stains, sticky shit on the hardwood floor, garbage overflowed, and dishes piled up in the kitchen. KiKi was seven months pregnant and fed up.

Bolo was lying on my eight-thousand-dollar gray suede couch with his stinking feet up when I came home one afternoon. *Yo, this nigga Bolo is a bummy, dirty-ass muthafucker.* I told Bolo to clean up or get out, calling him Benson and Mr. Belvedere so he'd get mad and want to fight. He laughed it off and started cleaning.

Havoc and Noyd were at the Platinum Island Studio in Manhattan working on *Murda Muzik*. I arrived a few hours into the session and Hav had this ill beat playing while Noyd was writing a verse. I rolled a blunt, kicking rhymes in my head. *I put my lifetime in between the paper's lines I'm the Quiet Storm nigga who fights rhyme. . . .* Hav left with Noyd to meet some girls. *What?* I couldn't believe they'd rather meet girls than make a new song to that incredible beat. It was one of the best beats I'd ever heard.

I smoked my blunt and started writing one of my best rhymes ever: *"Are you the same too? Goin' through the emotions of gun holdin' long shotguns down my pants leg limpin' Killa B you still livin' even my pops too he taught me how to shoot when I was seven yo I used to bust shots crazy I couldn't even look because the loud sound used to scare me POW! I love my pops for that I love my niggady Black I'll take the life of anybody tryin' to change what's left . . . I spent too many nights sniffin' coke gettin' right wastin' my life now I'm tryin' to make things right . . . nigga please, don't make me have to risk my freedom we worked our whole life for this. . . ."*

I finished the song in three hours and named it "White Lines" for the time being because the sample was from the old Melle Mel song of the same name. When I played it the next day, everyone liked it but they didn't understand the power that song had. I immediately gave it to DJ Clue, who started playing it a lot.

Meanwhile, I got a new budget for my solo album *H.N.I.C.* and rumors flew that Mobb Deep was breaking up because Prodigy was going solo. "You guys are breaking up?" radio interviewers and random fans on the street would ask. "You're going solo?" It wasn't true. I had a hustler's mentality, and doing a solo album only meant more money in my bank. I wrote so many songs, I couldn't let them all pile up and collect dust. Plus the fans always said I was the best rapper in Mobb Deep.

I never felt that I was better. Havoc used to write *my* rhymes and he spit some of the best verses I ever heard. But that's what everybody told me, even Havoc, so it was inevitable. "See, I told you that you was better than Nas!" Twin said. "Do you think you're better than Nas now?" he'd always ask.

"No." But when I was sitting writing verses in my head I was thinking, *Shit . . . I'm the best rapper that ever lived.*

• • •

Stobo, Twin Gambino, and I linked with rapper Big Pun at his crib in the Bronx one night to head to a club called Carbon on Fifty-sixth Street and Eleventh Avenue in Manhattan, the same spot where the Scarface Twin once carved QB in a kid's face with a razor. Pun, or Big Punisher, as some called him, was our new labelmate at Loud Records. We got real cool after collaborating on the song "Tres Leches." In the kitchen at Pun's house, Pun was sitting in front of the refrigerator with the fridge and freezer doors open and a table fan inside blowing the cold air on him—true ghetto air-conditioning. "Please, Pun, you gotta stop doing all this gangsta shit," Fat Joe was begging and pleading with Pun. "You're a celebrity now. You can't keep beating and trying to kill people. You gotta chill with all that."

"Listen, I'm not trying to hear nothing you're saying right now," Pun said. "First off, I wasn't trying to kill him, and second, P is here so shut the fuck up. Yo P, what's up man?"

"Pun, I saw you with the knife in your hand about to stab the guy," Joe said. A big knife with spiked brass knuckles attached to it was lying on the couch in the living room.

Pun walked into the living room where Twin Gambino and I were checking out his knife. "That ain't shit," Pun said, turning to one of about fifteen friends hanging out at his house. "Show P your gun." The kid reached down to his ankle and pulled out a federal-issued mini .45-caliber—all black, plastic, and about three inches long. Then Pun looked at another one of his friends. "Show P your gun." One by one, all the dudes said, "Look at this one," "Look at my gun," "Check this one out," until thirteen guns were out. Pun looked at me and said, "Show us your gun, P."

"My gun is in the car," I said, feeling dumb.

"Don't ever do that again," Pun said, disappointed. "If we were foul we could have the drop on you right now."

Pun's debut album *Capital Punishment* went platinum that year and, sadly, while he was recording his follow up, *Yeeeah Baby*, he died from a heart attack and complications from being overweight. I really miss that dude. R.I.P., big homie.

Ray Benzino from the rap group RSO and co-owner of *The Source* magazine had a production company called Hangman 3 that made good beats. He invited me to his mansion in Boston where he had a studio so we could work on music for my solo album. My fake cousin Stobo came with me. We met Benzino and his *Source* partner Dave Mays at JFK airport and caught a quick flight to Boston.

Toward the end of the flight the captain made an announcement. "This is your captain speaking. We seem to be having a problem with the landing gear. We're going to circle around for a while and see if we can get it working so we can land. I'm sorry for the inconvenience." Ten minutes later, the captain got back on the loudspeaker. "Ladies and gentlemen, I'm sorry to announce that we're going to have to make an emergency landing without the landing gear. We have fire trucks and ambulances waiting on the ground for us. Try not to panic."

An East Indian guy sitting in front of Stobo and me pulled out his credit card and used the airplane phone on the headrest to call his wife. "Baby, my plane is about to crash. I love you," he said. "I probably won't ever see you again!" It was Stobo's first time on a plane. He closed his eyes. We were both scared to death. Just as the plane was nearing the runway, the wheels dropped down and we landed safely.

The driveway outside Benzino's mansion was lined with Ferraris, Bentleys, and Lamborghinis. Stobo and I stayed for two days and I found two beats. One I never used and the other became "What U Rep" featuring N.O.R.E.

N.O.R.E. had just dropped his self-titled solo album and a new rapper from Harlem, Cam'ron, was starting to make some noise with another Harlem rapper, Mase, who was already on fire and signed to Puffy. Dave and Benzino put together a *Source* magazine tour with N.O.R.E. and Cam'ron as headliners. I hadn't spoken to N.O.R.E. since he shot Johnny in the leg by mistake and our crew jumped him in front of club Krystals in Jamaica, Queens, and he got my man Ty-Nitty shot in his back, so it was weird to reach out and put him on my album. But he was hot at that time and it was a good business move. He came and did the song with no problem and we deaded the tension.

The *Source* tour started soon after N.O.R.E. and I recorded the track. Money No, my cousin JM, Stobo, and I drove to the Philly Greek Festival and ran into Dave Mays, Benzino, N.O.R.E., Cam'ron, and Big Daddy Kane at the park where they were performing. Dave, Benzino, and N.O.R.E. suggested that we follow them for the rest of the tour and hop onstage to do a song or two. So we followed them from Philadelphia to Washington, D.C., Delaware, Maryland, and Asbury Park, New Jersey, where DMX made a surprise appearance onstage with a bunch of pit bulls, performing "Get at Me Dog."

While I was working on *H.N.I.C.*, I started eating healthy food, putting myself on a strict diet and lifestyle. I cut out red meat, pork, fried foods, white bread (it's bleached white), white rice (it's bleached white), mono- and diglycerides (animal fat), artificial coloring, juice, animal milk (for baby animals, not humans), alcohol, soda (only ginger ale occasionally), canned foods (aluminum causes Alzheimer's disease), artificial sweeteners, candy, fluoride (fluoride is poison), weed, and cigarettes.

My new diet consisted of fish, chicken, turkey (broiled, baked, or grilled), brown rice, yams, potatoes, green vegetables, bottled water (all night and day), margarine (instead of butter), soy milk (instead of animal milk), wheat bread (without mono- and diglycerides), pure cane brown sugar, vegetarian chili (the frozen kind), original oatmeal, Honey Nut Shredded Wheat, Post Raisin Bran, turkey sausage, fruit (fruit contains acid that kills germs, so you're only supposed to eat it when you have a cold; if you eat it every day, the acid will no longer have the same effect), nuts (for protein), protein shakes, multivitamins, and minerals.

That's my word to everything I love: After a year of following that plan, I stopped getting sickle-cell attacks and felt the best I'd ever felt in my life. When you clean out your body and mind, that's when you start receiving your blessings from the universe. I was now 100 percent clean and sober.

After the *Source* tour, I bumped into Shameek's boy E-Money Bags at a barbecue in Queensbridge. He gave me a videotape of some guy in a church speaking about spirituality and health. He broke it down like this: There is a positive energy all around that we can't see, here to help guide us through life. But when we have bad food, alcohol, drugs, smoke, and negative thoughts in us, it's like a thick cloud of black smoke inside and around our body blocking us from receiving or giving that positive energy at its maximum potential. That energy is alive and real even though we can't see it.

Doctors and teachers won't tell you this because this world is set up to keep us down. It's against the law for a medical doctor to prescribe natural or holistic remedies for diseases. If caught, they may lose their license or spend time in prison. Some doctors don't believe in an alternative way of thinking and living, others aren't in tune with it, others blatantly keep the information secret because medicine is big business and if everyone were healthy then hospitals, pharmaceutical companies, and mainstream doctors would go out of business.

I felt like a machine. My brain was moving a million miles per hour. I pitched Steve Rifkind the idea for my *Murda Muzik* movie. Master P's movie *Bout It, Bout It* pushed me to write my own script, and Steve encouraged us to do our own thing. I convinced him to give me a budget for the sound track. I got $650,000 for it—yes, 650K!—plus $450,000 for my solo album *H.N.I.C.* and $200,000 for my cut for Mobb Deep's *Murda Muzik*. I never had so much money in my life!

That summer I bought a black buggy-eye Benz with charcoal seats and a stash box for my guns along with a burgundy J30 Infinity with white seats for KiKi. She was real happy when she saw that car—she finally had her own shit.

Raekwon had his birthday party at some bar on Staten Island and Mobb Deep went to celebrate with him and all of Wu-Tang. It was a cool get-together and we left fairly early. Havoc, Noyd, and everybody got home twenty minutes before me. They were in the kitchen laughing and talking, still drunk from the party, when I got to the house. Tired, I went upstairs and got in bed with KiKi and Shaka.

As I was dozing off, Noyd and Bolo started screaming and I heard them mention my name. "Call P downstairs and let him know you don't like it when he calls you Benson!" Noyd told Bolo. *What?* I put my clothes back on and went downstairs.

"Bolo says he's not feeling all that Benson and Mr. Belvedere shit," Noyd said.

"I told you if you don't clean up every day you're gonna have to get out," I told Bolo.

"If Havoc don't tell me to do it then I don't have to do it," dirty-ass

Bolo said. "I'm not here with you, I'm here with Havoc. If Hav says I can stay then I can stay." I punched him in his mouth. Gotti grabbed Bolo, holding him from fighting back. I was screaming at Bolo, calling him pussy, Benson, Mr. Belvedere, asshole, taunting him to break free from Gotti. I even tried to get Gotti mad at me so he would let go.

"Don't let little-ass Gotti hold you!" I yelled. Bolo's a big dude. "Look how little he is!" Gotti finally let Bolo go, but he acted like he didn't want to fight because I was smaller than him. So I punched him in his mouth again. "Get outta my house!"

"No, I'm here with Havoc," Bolo said, his face dripping blood. "I'm here with Hav."

Why am I fighting and screaming? I thought to myself. *I should just go upstairs, get my gun, and shoot him in the leg.* Upstairs, KiKi stopped me from getting the gun and calmed me down. I banged on Havoc's door and told Hav what happened. He told me to give Bolo another chance! *Hav's got these slouch fools destroying our house and he just lets it go down. Man, fuck another chance!*

"If you don't kick Bolo out then I'm gonna leave," I said.

"I'm not kicking him out," Hav said. "You're overreacting."

"I'm dead serious—if you don't kick Bolo out, I'm gonna leave and not come back."

Havoc decided to let Bolo stay, so I left the next morning. I couldn't let it get to the point where Havoc and I were beefing, because then both of our monies would stop flowing. Bolo was lucky I didn't shoot him in his leg.

KiKi, Shaka, and I moved temporarily into a duplex apartment in Bushwick, Brooklyn, in a brand-new building on Linden Street and Knicker-bocker. The rent was only five hundred dollars a month. The only downside was that we were back in the hood. But as long as I was far, far away from the idiots we'd been living with, that's all I cared about. I went to the Long Island house to visit and record, but that was it.

Early one morning at the Freeport house, a guy named Larry knocked on the door and Gotti answered. Larry was an independent film director and producer looking for Mobb Deep to make a cameo in his first flick, *Statistic*, with

Redman, the Lost Boyz, and old-school rapper Dana Dane. I had just completed my first script for *Murda Muzik* the movie and was looking for somebody with the equipment and knowledge to shoot it. I told Larry that if he'd help shoot my movie, I would make a cameo in his. "No problem," he said.

A month later, we put a budget together for *Murda Muzik*. My intentions were to spend no more than sixty thousand dollars. But I wanted real gunfire, mansions, helicopters, police cars, a jail, and more, so the initial budget ended up being $120,000. Larry and I made a verbal agreement that he would get 5 percent of the profit and a codirector's credit.

We started filming immediately and finished half of the movie in a few months. I wrote the script so that Noyd, Godfather, Prince God, Twin, Hav's uncle Lamiek, and an OG from Queensbridge named Tim Lord who's Nas's right-hand man were the stars, while Havoc, Nas, and I had small roles. Noyd, Godfather, Twin, Hav, and I sat up all night rehearsing lines at the crib in Freeport.

The Housing Authority wouldn't allow us to shoot guns in Queensbridge, so the gun-shooting scenes had to be filmed in Red Hook projects in Brooklyn. Noyd's whole family is from Red Hook, so some of them were in the movie as well.

My number-one mistake was that I should have had Larry ink the deal first. Larry seemed cool and down-to-earth, so I didn't rush the contract. That was the last time I made that mistake.

Havoc and I got a call that month from Charlene Thomas, who worked in the product-management department at Loud Records. Mary J. Blige had contacted Charlene requesting that Mobb Deep be featured on one of her new songs, "Deep Inside."

At the recording session in Manhattan, Mary was sitting in a lounge chair with her legs hanging over the armrest, lighting a slender cigar, wearing big sunglasses. She looked good, like a female pimp. She hopped out of the chair and greeted us with hugs and kisses. The beat sounded hot, so I grabbed a seat, a pen and pad, and Mary told the engineer to play the song so we could hear her lyrics. I finished my verse in about twenty minutes. Havoc laid his next and we were done real fast.

A month or two later, Charlene from Loud called again. "What's up, today is Mary J.'s birthday and she wants to take you guys out to dinner with her," Charlene said. "Just you and Havoc. She's sending a car to pick you up around six P.M., okay?" Hell yeah it was okay! I got fresh, met up with Hav, and we hopped in the S500 Benz that she sent. We stopped to buy Mary birthday flowers before the car dropped us off in front of an exclusive Chinese restaurant in Midtown Manhattan. We figured it would be a dinner party with a bunch of her friends and family, but when we walked inside the spot, we saw Mary and one of her girlfriends seated at a table for four.

We gave Mary her flowers, said happy birthday, and sat down. "Where's everybody at?" I asked.

"It's just us," Mary said. "I wanted to take ya'll out to eat and thank you guys for working with me. You know Mobb Deep is my favorite rap group." Havoc sat next to Mary's friend, a good-looking light-skinned female, and I sat next to Mary. Mary asked me what kind of drinks I liked. I told her I was drinking whatever she was drinking. "You ever had a cosmo?" she asked.

"A what?"

"A cosmo," she repeated. "It's more of a ladies' drink, but it's good. Try one with me."

"A'ight, cool," I said. Mary ordered a round of cosmos, pink and chilled in large martini glasses. Mary ordered another round. The first one gave me a crazy buzz because I hadn't been drinking, but how could I refuse drinks with Mary J. Blige on her birthday? *I ain't drinking no more after tonight,* I promised myself. *This is a special occasion.*

The next round of cosmos came out with our main course. Mary was feeling the drinks and started getting comfortable, asking me questions. "How old are you, P?"

"Twenty-four."

"What's your sign?"

"Scorpio. November second."

"You got a lady?" she asked. "You married?" Mary was flirting and giving me all kinds of signs, but I didn't realize it until I looked in her eyes and saw she was dead serious. I got real shy and nervous, stuck like a deer in headlights. Man, this was Mary J. Blige! My mouth wanted to say no, but my brain forced my mouth to give an honest answer.

"Yeah," I said.

"How long have you been together?" she asked.

"For about five years now."

"That's good, that's what I'm looking for in my life," Mary said. "I need somebody to be serious with." Mary was cool as hell, beautiful, and very down-to-earth. I felt like a fool for not pursuing her but I was really in love with my woman. Havoc hooked up with Mary's girlfriend that night and I went home to KiKi.

Our manager Chris Lighty became more popular than ever with his companies Violator Management and Violator Records. When other rappers found out that Chris was our manager, they wanted Chris to manage them too. His roster was growing and in order to handle that, he was going to need some help.

Chris's brothers were also in the music industry. His older brother Dave Lighty worked at Jive Records, his younger brother Mike Lighty had a booking agency, and his youngest brother Jonathan started helping us book studio sessions and contacting outside producers and guest features for *Murda Muzik*.

One night Jonathan, Havoc, Gotti, Noyd, and I were in the studio tossing around ideas about who should be featured on the album. Jonathan came up with the idea of getting somebody from the South so that we could bridge the gap, and Havoc suggested we get 8ball from the Memphis rap group 8ball and MJG. Chris hooked it up and we flew to Houston, Texas, to Swisha House Studios. 8ball was standing at a table cutting up weed with a pair of scissors next to Bun B from UGK. "Man, ya'll niggas don't even know, me and my niggas love Mobb Deep!" Bun B said. "Ya'll got them burnt biscuits, nigga! That's that ice-pick shit."

8ball rolled up some of his weed in a Swisher Sweet. As thick clouds of strong smoke filled the studio, we listened to some Swisha House beats and found one that we all liked and knocked out the song "Where You From" featuring 8ball in about two hours. Afterward, we went to the hotel to get some rest for the morning flight back to New York.

Back home, I started coming up with more and more ideas for my solo career. Since Havoc and I weren't seeing eye to eye with something as serious as our house, I had to plan for my and my kid's future. I'm always Mobb Deep to the death, but I decided to invest all my time and energy into my solo album, shoot my movie, and start a clothing company because the future was looking unpredictable. I needed to have my own career going in case things didn't work out between us.

Before Sean John, Rocawear, and all the other rapper-branded clothing existed, my inspiration came from Wu-Tang's Wu Wear and Russell Simmons's Phat Farm. Watching how RZA and his crew raped the corporate world, I admired Wu-Tang's business savvy. They made over eleven million dollars from Wu Wear within a couple years, so I quickly came up with a concept for a brand called Infamous.

I had Infamous T-shirts printed and wore them in photo shoots so Loud's art department would add the photos inside *Murda Muzik* to start promoting the brand. One of the art dudes at Loud had friends in the fashion industry who put together a four-season look book—like a demo for the clothing line to present to possible buyers and backers—and had a few samples made. I met with several investors and backers but none of them saw my vision. *Fuck it! If you want something done right . . .* you know the rest.

My man DJ Hot Day from Queensbridge had a record store on 147th Street and St. Nicholas Avenue right near where Havoc and I used to live. I had connections in that hood, so instead of waiting for some investor to pick my brand up, I opened my own store in Harlem—Infamous on 132nd Street and Eighth Avenue. I wanted to open up in Queens but it was ten thousand dollars a month for a small spot on Jamaica Avenue, while a way bigger spot in Harlem was two thousand. I was moving too fast, but you have to move on ideas fast, so I got my first storefront.

Dave Mays and Benzino ran ads in *The Source* to promote the clothing brand and store. After my first Infamous ads, all of a sudden Rocawear, Sean John, OutKast clothing, Fat Joe's FJ560, and others began to emerge. I was pissed because in the business it's all about who does it big first or at least second. If you do it third or fourth, then it's called dick riding and biting. But after 1999, all the rules of the game went out the window and everybody was copying off of everybody. It wasn't about who did it first anymore, it was about who did it best.

I put twenty thousand dollars into building the store, which was a gutted-out, empty storefront when I moved in. The Tats Cru painted a mural of all five New York City boroughs on the ceiling: Everything was on fire and it looked like the apocalypse. I had a hookup at Home Depot and put in stone floors and gates with barbed wire so it looked like a prison in there. On the store awning, our dragon logo lit up at night.

My man Keith owned the women's clothing boutique next door to my spot. A week before our huge grand-opening block party that he helped me put together at the park up the street, some people tried robbing Keith's store while he was opening up. Keith popped one of them and killed the other. I was glad he did that because it let other would-be robbers know not to fuck around on our block. He wasn't charged because he had a legal firearm to protect his business.

Busta Rhymes came to the block party. My brother Greg came from New Jersey to help run the opening and brought his daughter Kenisha and son Kenny. No more than ten minutes after my brother, niece, and nephew arrived, a kid passing by on a pedal dirt bike shot a man right in front of us. After shooting the victim, he got off the bike, picked up the gun shell, hopped back on the bike, and rode off slowly like nothing happened. The day wasn't off to a good start.

Queensbridge came deep and the whole hood bought at least one Infamous shirt. We walked to the park and chilled for about an hour. Sadat X from Brand Nubian was there and everybody was having a good time until some Harlem dudes started beefing with my Queensbridge niggas and QB shut the park down. Those Harlem boys got their asses whupped in their own part of town. We walked back to the store to let things cool off. I locked up and told my brother and KiKi it was best if they left. I didn't want them around if somebody tried to shoot at us. Before they left, KiKi and I snapped a picture in front of the park. She's holding our son Shaka, leaning up against the car I bought her. We hung out at the park all night just to prove a point: We're not scared!

On grand-opening day I started thinking about putting my money elsewhere. I was already overspending to run that business and I needed all the money I had to shoot my movie, so I made a quick decision and chose the film over the store.

I shut the store down a month after the block party and some dude bought it and turned it into a weed spot. They kept the dragon up over the door.

My crib in Brooklyn started getting hot right before we released *Murda Muzik*. "White Lines" was playing in clubs and on the airwaves more than any of our past songs and the whole neighborhood knew that Prodigy from Mobb Deep lived there.

One summer night, a bunch of kids and teenagers rang my bell, screaming up at my window for me to come outside and battle them. It was time to move. I was the only one on that block with a buggy-eye Benz, Lexus GS300, and Infinity J30, so I had a spotlight on me. Coming home from the studio at four A.M., I'd walk up to my apartment with my gun in my hand inside my pocket and my finger on the trigger. That part of Bushwick wasn't particularly active with gun violence, but I was always ready. When KiKi and I took our son to the movies, the park, a restaurant, or shopping, I always had my nine-millimeter Ruger in the baby bag under the stroller or on my hip. Instead of waiting for trouble to happen, KiKi and I started looking for a new crib.

Meanwhile, at the minimansion in Long Island, Poppa Mobb was hungry one afternoon, scrounged two dollars in dimes and nickels lying around the house, and walked six blocks to the Chinese spot. He got back to the crib and had eaten two of his three chicken wings when Bolo rang on the doorbell. Poppa Mobb let him in, then ran upstairs to use the bathroom. Bolo ate Poppa Mobb's last chicken wing.

"I was hungry, man!" Bolo said defensively when Poppa Mobb flipped out. Poppa was just as tired of Bolo as I was. He got his gun, went into the living room, and shot Bolo in the leg, just like I'd wanted to do! Bleeding like a pig, Bolo called the police and told on Poppa, but Poppa got off in the end. I wanted to hug and kiss Poppa Mobb, I was so glad he shot that bitch-ass nigga.

During radio interviews, they'd bring up that situation. "So, I hear people were getting shot at your house over a piece of chicken. . . . Mobb Deep's hungry, huh?"

At around ten P.M. on March 18, 1999, KiKi, Shaka, and I were in our Brooklyn apartment watching TV. KiKi went to the bathroom and came out all frantic, telling me her water broke while she was on the toilet. In the delivery room at St. John's Hospital, the doctor said that she wasn't ready to give birth yet but the baby could come at any time. I stayed with her for a couple of hours, then walked to White Castle to get fish sandwiches, onion rings, and apple pies. I loved White Castle apple pies and ate like four back to back. KiKi kept asking for some onion rings; the doctor said she couldn't eat anything, but she demanded that I give her some.

At 3:03 A.M. on March 19, 1999, my daughter Fahtasia was born. Watching my second child's birth was just as amazing as the first. I followed the doctors again, paranoid about them injecting my baby girl with those suspicious vaccines. Tasia looked like a little old Jewish lady when she was born, all wrinkled up and tiny, but I was excited to have a daughter.

Around that time, Twin kept bugging me about this rap duo from Queensbridge called Bars'N'Hooks. "You need to sign these kids to a deal, they've got talent," Twin said. I finally got tired of him harassing me so we found them and they started rapping for me outside on the block in QB. I couldn't front; they were hot.

The front man of the duo, Mike Delorean, aka Hooks, was from Hav's block and was famous in the hood because his parents were both heavy into the drug game and had close ties to the Queens gang the Supreme Team. Delorean always had the best new clothes, mopeds, and motorcycles. Delorean was also famous in the hood for this verse he spit on a Cormega song dissing Nas. Nas started a group called the Firm with Foxy Brown, Cormega, Nature, and Nas. When it came time to promote the group, Nas didn't tell Mega about important photo shoots, including magazine covers. Mega was furious after that. Then Nas kicked Mega out of the group. Mega was on a Fuck Nas mission ever since.

Mega and Mike Delorean killed Nas on a popular mixtape freestyle, so I knew Delorean was nice with rap. Mr. Bars, Delorean's rap partner, had some slick punch lines too. They reminded me of a younger version of Mobb Deep. I signed them to Infamous Records right away.

Bars'N'Hooks said they were getting threats from guys at Lynchman Entertainment, a record company they had signed a deal with before signing with me. Delorean explained to me that when Lynchman found out that Bars'N'Hooks signed with me, they tried to intimidate him and Bars by claiming that they were responsible for getting Tupac shot at Quad Studios, and if Bars'N'Hooks didn't want that to happen to them then they had to pay back whatever money Lynchman had spent on them or dead the Infamous deal. (They later denied any involvement in Tupac's shooting.) To resolve the situation, I set up a meeting with Lynchman for Friday of that week.

Havoc and I recorded the entire *Murda Muzik* album in Soundtrack Studios on Twenty-first Street and Broadway. The sessions started at noon and usually ended around five A.M. Along with *Murda Muzik*, I was grindin' on *H.N.I.C.*, my movie sound track, and revisions of my movie script.

Early one afternoon Mike Delorean came by the studio with his uncle Green Eyes, who'd just come home from doing fifteen years for a robbery he claimed he didn't even do. Green Eyes was a member of the Supreme Team, and when a few of them got pinched for bank robbery, the police arrested Green Eyes and he took the weight for whoever was involved. When he first introduced himself, I wasn't feeling him at all. He was real cocky, like, "What up, my name is Green Eyes, you've probably heard of me in the streets," bragging how he was locked up with this one and that one. . . . My only focus was music, so I really didn't give a fuck about all the shit he was talking.

Green Eyes was living with Delorean at his moms's crib in QB and started coming to the studio with him every day. He wasn't really Delorean's uncle—I think he used to sex Delorean's moms and they used "uncle" so the little nigga wouldn't feel bad. After a few days, I realized Green Eyes was cool. He was just an OG suspended in time, 1984 to be exact. He told me how the gang leader, Supreme McGriff, didn't take care of him while he was locked up and never sent his family money. *Damn, and this nigga did fifteen years for them!*

Friday came and I told Green Eyes I was meeting with Lynchman about the story I'd heard from Bars'N'Hooks. Delorean hadn't told him about it. He asked if he could come and said that he'd just sit there and not say anything. "Lynchman will think twice about all the thug shit they're popping when they see me 'cause they know me from the streets," Green Eyes said.

At the Lynchman offices, Delorean, Green Eyes, and I listened to Lynchman's appeal. They said that Bars'N'Hooks couldn't sign with Infamous Records, and they wanted to be paid back for the studio time, electric bill, and the phone calls made on the group's behalf. Lynchman had a compilation album coming out, so I told them Bars'N'Hooks and I would do a song for it free of charge if they would squash everything. They agreed.

I decided to introduce Bars'N'Hooks to the world through two free-styles, one over Melle Mel's "The Message" and another over Frankie Beverly's "Outstanding." I pressed up five thousand records with Bars'N'Hooks stickers and the Infamous Records logo, got the national DJ mailing list, and contacted thousands of DJs about my plans for my new label and group, then shipped records to all of them. I'd seen how the Loud radio staff did it, so I just did it myself. My brain was working like a robot and my energy was through the roof.

Late one night at Soundtrack Studios, Twin called saying that he was bringing by this kid who had some hot beats and was down with DJ Muggs from Cypress Hill. Twin showed up a couple of hours later with a white kid dressed in khakis and an Adidas jacket like he was straight outta Compton. He introduced himself as Alchemist and put a DAT tape in the player. The first few beats were cool, but one made me go crazy. As soon as I heard it, I claimed it for the Mobb Deep album.

We put Kool G Rap on the song and called it "The Realest." I wrote a real crazy verse: "*Never prejudge it be the humble that'll squeeze slugs, it be the nigga standing still that'll peel guns, spill blood for my niggas thugging for me, man you don't wanna get involved fuckin' with P. I spent more nights illin', less nights chillin', the more shots it hold the better they feel it, what be the dealings. . . . *" Alchemist had many more where that beat came from and has been a part of the team ever since.

I'm very leery and suspicious of new faces and initially thought Alchemist was a fed or some type of undercover agent trying to dig up some dirt on me and my boys. My initial thoughts were, *The police think they're slick. They've got agents who know how to make beats now.* But when Alchemist came around with those dope beats and I saw how serious he was about his career, I embraced him like a brother. He was like a gift from the heavens. That white boy's got a lot of soul. We made up nicknames for him like White Chocolate, the White Vulture, and the Rare White Bird.

Just as we were ready to hand in the album, Loud Records switched distributors from RCA to Sony/Columbia and our album was pushed back three months until the deal was finalized. We were pissed. Loud had a whole new staff after the deal was done, and while they were going through those changes our album got bootlegged. *Murda Muzik* was one of the most bootlegged albums of all time. We had to record four new songs before we put it out so the fans would still want to buy it.

My song "White Lines" was getting hot and it was time to give it a real name, so I called it "Quiet Storm." Havoc and Chris Lighty wanted "Quiet Storm" for *Murda Muzik* instead of *H.N.I.C.* because Mobb Deep needed a big single, but I refused to give it up at first. After a week of Havoc and Chris's convincing, though, I gave in and gave my solo song to Mobb Deep. Lil' Kim and Havoc were on the remix and we shot videos for both my version and the remix. Rumors had been going around that Kim didn't write any of her music, so I was impressed when I saw how Kim killed her verse and wrote it herself.

The four new songs we made for our album were "Spread Love Not War," "Adrenaline," "Where Ya Heart At," and the "Quiet Storm" remix featuring Lil' Kim.

The Sunday before *Murda Muzik* dropped, one of Havoc's homies from Queensbridge, Fakey, came home from doing nine years for shooting at some cops. I went to Freeport to visit Hav, and Fakey was sitting in the kitchen looking happy to be home, being real cool and humble. I didn't know Fakey very well, he was Havoc's boy. I met him once or twice when I first came to Queensbridge but he got locked up right after that. I told Fakey we were having an album-release party at the Tunnel the following Sunday and that I'd give him twelve VIP passes.

Sunday rolled around and I called Fakey to meet in the early evening on Twenty-first Street in Queensbridge so I could give him the passes. Fakey pulled up in a white limousine with a gang of people—Cormega, Ice, Spank, Nut, and a bunch of others. I gave him twelve passes and told him to arrive early because the passes were only good until eleven P.M. He agreed, then I jetted to Alchemist's crib to meet Havoc and the crew.

Club security tried to rush us into the Tunnel after midnight because the cops were shutting the doors down. "You've got a bunch of people at the side door trying to get in—they say they're with you," one of the security guards told me.

"How many people?" I asked.

"Twelve."

It was Fakey and his crew. I told the security that they had VIP passes. Two cops walked up. "We're closing the club doors for good—you people are either going in or out! Make up your mind!"

I tried my best to talk to the cops and let them know this was our party, but they started getting pushy. "Either go in or you're staying out!"

"Fuck them niggas, P, we gotta do this show," Havoc yelled, heading through the door. "Let's go!"

I told Havoc to wait a minute. I didn't want to leave Fakey and his boys outside without trying to help them get in. "Can I leave one of my boys here with you to point them out so they can get in?" I asked club security. "Please, man, they belong inside with us, they all have passes." He looked at me like he wanted to help. "Those passes were only good until eleven P.M. It's almost one o'clock," he said, then paused. "Okay, leave one of your boys with me, I'll see what I can do." I left Godfather at the door with him and went inside.

The club was jam-packed. When we hit the stage to perform the crowd went crazy—our first time performing in the Tunnel after all those years of hanging out there!

My Benz was parked outside the front door, and as soon as we stepped outside after popping bottles in VIP, I saw Fakey and his crew looking disappointed because they couldn't get in. Fakey walked up to me and the police told me to move my car. "Meet me around the block so we can talk," I told Fakey.

Around the corner, we got out of our rides to talk on the sidewalk. Fakey told me that Ice's car was stolen while they were trying to get in, and Ice wanted me to pay for it. Ha! "Tell Ice to get out the car and tell me that himself," I said. Fakey got Ice. I knew Ice way better than I know Fakey from partying together in the Tunnel for years while Fakey was locked up. Ice had a dumbass look on his face when he walked up, like he knew he was about to tell me some bullshit and he also knew that I wasn't gonna go for it.

"My car's missing and I don't know if it got stolen or towed," he said.

"That's not my problem," I said. "I'm not paying for it."

"Forget about it, P, it's not your fault," Ice said, and got back in the car.

"Don't even worry about it, niggas is just mad they couldn't get in," Fakey said. "I tried to convince them to let ya'll in but you came too late. I told you the passes were only good till eleven P.M.," I said. "At least you tried," he said. "We're really mad at Havoc because we grew up with him and it seemed like he didn't give a fuck about us. . . ." While Fakey was speaking, somebody got out of the car to take a piss on the corner. I couldn't see who it was from where I was standing. Engaged in conversation, I didn't take notice as the kid snuck around some cars, moving toward me, snuffing me right in my nose. I dropped to the ground, unaware of who or what hit me. As I was getting up, I saw it was the little dirty nigga Worm! He lifted my chain off my neck while I was still in a daze and then he ran to get back inside the car.

"Yo, what the fuck is you doin'!" Fakey screamed as if he was confused, but right away I suspected that these niggas set me up. *Why would they have Worm with them when they're fully aware of all the situations with him and Mobb Deep? They wanna set me up? I'm the one who gave them twelve passes.*

Havoc always told me, "Stop hanging out in QB, don't trust them niggas." But it's not my style to cut everybody off because of a few bad apples in the bunch.

I was one of the only niggas in Queensbridge actively shooting videos and movies, showing love to the up-and-coming artists, and keeping close ties when everybody else stopped coming around. I wasn't trying to be something that I'm not. I didn't let money or fame make me paranoid to the point where I was scared to come to the hood. I didn't have reason to have fear in my heart because I'm genuine. Only liars have fear, because they're scared somebody will catch on to their lies. The only reason I'd stop dealing with a person was if they did something foul to me, and nobody from QB ever did anything foul to me until then.

Worm snatched my chain and ran. I popped open my car's hood to get my gun out to shoot up that piece-of-shit Land Rover that he, Fakey, Spank, Mega, and Ice were in. I looked over at Stobo and he already knew what I was thinking. The only thing that stopped me from punching holes in that Jeep was Ice and Cormega. If they weren't in there, I'd probably be doing murder time right now. Fakey and Worm thought they were so gangsta, but a real gangsta nigga almost put an end to their career as petty crooks that night. I sat in the driver's seat with the gun on my lap itching to show those wanna-be thugs how I got down. But my better judgment caused me to pull off. *I'll catch 'em soon enough.*

Godfather called later that night telling me that Fakey and Worm robbed Noyd in Queensbridge and hit him in the head with a bottle. *Somebody needs to kill one of these bummy-ass clowns.*

At home that night, when KiKi saw my swollen face and asked what happened I broke down crying. Man, it was embarrassing telling her what happened. All the years I'd been in QB, I'd never had problems with people because my hand didn't call for that. I wanted to murder one of these niggas for making me go home to my woman like that.

The following morning I called Fakey and told him to meet me in Queensbridge to give me my chain back. Fakey said he got it from Worm and could meet whenever I was ready. I called Hav to tell him what was going on. "Don't go, P, don't trust them," he kept telling me. "You shouldn't go to QB no more."

"Man, listen, fuck all that," I said. "I'm not scared of these bitch-ass niggas and I'm getting my chain back."

Havoc was just looking out for my safety, but what he was telling me was the total opposite of how my pops raised me. When I got to the projects, I called Fakey and he told me he had to go to the studio with Nas and we could meet by the Hit Factory in Manhattan. Mind you, I was by myself. No army, no gang, no soldiers. Just me and my nine Ruger. Even if I'd wanted a gang I didn't have anybody to turn to, because my gang was telling me, "Don't do it, don't go." The only person who said he would roll with me was Jonathan Lighty, and I didn't even ask him to roll.

When I got to the Hit Factory, Fakey and Cormega met me outside and Fakey put my chain on my neck. It made me feel like a herb, like he was doing me a favor or something.

"You okay?" Mega asked.

"Yeah," I said. My eye was turning black from being punched in the nose. Fakey and Mega looked at me shaking their heads as if feeling sorry for me.

"Wanna come to the Nas session with us?" Fakey asked.

"Fuck it, why not." I wanted to show them I wasn't scared, so we walked into the session. I talked to Fakey and Nas about Worm. Fakey kept telling me he didn't know Worm was going to do that and blah, blah, blah. As long as Fakey gave me my chain back, he wasn't a problem for now. But Worm was definitely going to get dealt with ASAP.

The next morning, KiKi and I decided to move into a hotel until we found a new crib. Loud Records paid for us to stay in a three-bedroom penthouse at the Flatotel in Manhattan, a luxury skyscraper on Fifty-second Street and Broadway, for two months. *Murda Muzik* went platinum within those two months and we were on top of the world.

After the lame setup that Fakey and Worm pulled at the Tunnel, the very next Sunday Worm was walking around the Tunnel and one of my boys from Hempstead cracked his face open with a Moët bottle. Worm didn't know who broke that bottle on his face or why, so just to tell people he'd gotten revenge, the Sunday after that Worm went back to the Tunnel with a gun and opened fire on a random parked car. After shooting half of his gun clip into the car, killing the young man in the driver's seat and wounding the others, Worm tried to run off but three undercover cops jumped out of a car right next to the car Worm shot up, yelling, "*Freeze!* Drop the gun!"

Worm fired shots at the cops while running to his car with the cops chasing and shooting at him. The cops shot up Worm's ride, riddling his body with bullets and almost killing him. Worm got fifty years to life.

"See, P," Twin told me. "When people try to do foul shit, all we gotta do is sit back and wait, 'cause karma's gonna get our revenge for us." Ironically, the random young man who Worm killed that night just so happened to be the boyfriend of KiKi's homegirl.

KiKi and I found a minimansion on a mountaintop in a town called Pomona in Rockland County, forty minutes from Manhattan. I paid five hundred thousand dollars for the house—five bedrooms, three-car garage, and two acres of land. During our first week there, my daughter Tasia took her first steps in our bedroom. She was scared and started crying at first, but I held her hands as we walked together. Then I let go real slowly and she finally did it—she took ten steps on her own.

CHAPTER 8

H.N.I.C.

> I'm being watched by snake eyes
>
> peeped 'em, shed skin plenty times
>
> Surrounded by crash dummies and empty minds
>
> Get ya shit together thun see between the lines
>
> Stay awake to the ways of the wickedest kind
>
> Infamous 'cause of the way I write rhymes
>
> "Genesis"

Soon after *Murda Muzik* went platinum in 1999, we hit the road for two months on the Family Values Tour, our biggest tour yet, with Limp Bizkit, Run-D.M.C., and a bunch of rock acts. Sixty shows across America, thirty thousand people a night. We took Noyd and Stobo along, and Alchemist was our DJ. If we thought we knew something about groupies, we hadn't seen shit until we saw rock-star groupies. Chicks lined up in packs to get inside Limp Bizkit's dressing room after the show.

We were in front of a huge crowd every night, so it was important that we put together a real theatrical performance. There were barbed-wire fences onstage and Alchemist introduced us like we were coming from jail to perform. Security guards walked us onto the stage handcuffed and shackled in orange prison uniforms. The guards uncuffed us, and we went crazy running around with a lot of energy. The white kids in the audience loved us. I didn't know how they would respond to us because most of our past shows were in the hood, but the crowd knew every word to our songs, especially "Quiet Storm" and "Shook Ones."

Man, we had a lot of fun on that tour. After the shows, we chilled with Limp Bizkit in their dressing room and tour bus. Alchemist was cool with their DJ, Lethal, who was House of Pain's DJ and produced their hit "Jump Around." Al met him growing up in Los Angeles through DJ Muggs from Cypress Hill. Lethal had a nice studio setup on their tour bus, so we hung out and made music.

One night, after the show, Limp Bizkit had a dentist backstage with a big tank of happy gas, nitrous oxide, filling up giant balloons and handing them out to get high. One dude took a whole balloon and as he stumbled off, he fell flat on his face. I took a whole balloon to the head—that shit felt crazy! My boy Stobo took one too. We roamed around backstage feeling like we were floating, fucking with the girls. Havoc wouldn't ever try anything like that. But I was like, *Fuck it, you only live once.* I figured, *If this was the stuff that we all got at the dentist office then what harm could it do?* I can't even remember what it felt like. It just made me laugh a lot.

Ja Rule was on the tour for a few weeks and we shared the same dressing room with him one day. I never really liked Ja's music. I understood his female-targeted songs but where I come from, nobody listened to Ja Rule.

A few years earlier, Steve Rifkind invited me and a few of my dudes to some dress-up party in the city. "I'll be there, but I'm coming in my street clothes," I told Steve.

"That's cool," he said, "I just want you there."

We looked real thugged out compared to the rest of the crowd. Then Ja Rule walked into the party in a loosely knitted sweater with his nipples practically popping out of the spaces in the knit. It looked real homosexual. I would pay good money to see the embarrassed look on his face again when he saw us standing there. The dudes I was with didn't have any mercy, laughing right in front of him.

So on tour, we had to share the same dressing room with this dickhead and he was putting on an ice grill, acting like he was tough now and too big to even talk to us. Something had definitely changed.

The tour ended right before the new year. We went home and got our platinum plaques for *Murda Muzik*. The plaques had blood splashes on them just like our album cover. I started hitting the studio every day to finish *H.N.I.C.* and the *Murda Muzik* movie sound track. I asked Delorean and Draws from Havoc's block to help me find some new rappers from QB for the sound track, and they started spreading the word. I showed a lot of niggas love on that sound track and gave a lot of dudes their first check ever, paying people twenty-five hundred dollars for a song or a beat.

Nas was working on an album called *QB's Finest* at the same time. I found out that his QB album stood for "Queensboro." He was getting all the Queens rappers together like LL Cool J, Kool G Rap, Run-D.M.C., the Lost Boyz. But when Nas heard about what I was doing with new rappers from the Bridge, he changed his "Queensboro" into "Queensbridge" because he didn't want me to be the first to get all the new artists from QB together. Nas saw himself as King of Queensbridge, so he had to be the first to pull it off. Nas didn't know that I had people around him who would come tell me everything.

Nas started booking studio sessions in the room right next to me in Soundtrack Studios, so whoever I had coming to do songs he could intercept and have them come over to his session too. Funny-ass nigga.

Ever since I first started coming to Queensbridge with Havoc in 1989, Nas always acted as if he was too good to fuck with Mobb Deep. He started doing songs with us after "Shook Ones" blew up, but Nas treated it like it was strictly business—he never tried to hang out or be cool with us and definitely not me, probably because he thought I was wack at first. That's understandable, I would've acted the same way if I was him. But while we were both working at Soundtrack Studios I learned that Nas was suddenly being managed by Chris Lighty and he started calling my crib like he really wanted to be homies now. KiKi would tell me that Nas called. We were both in shock. Why the sudden drastic change of heart? The only thing I could attribute it to was the platinum success of *Murda Muzik*.

One day, Nas asked me to join his session and spit something for *QB's Finest*. I did a verse on the song "Da Bridge 2001": "*Me and my dogs comin' through, we the grain, go against us, you feel the pain. . . .*"

After I laid my verse, Nas and I kicked it for a few hours for the first time, talking about the rap game. I told him that I thought Jay-Z was taking shots at Mobb Deep in his song "Where I'm From" on *In My Lifetime, Vol. 1*. Jay had a line in that song, "*I'm from the place where you and ya little mans hung out in every verse in ya rhymes.*" The only person in the history of rap music who talked about Marcy projects in a verse was yours truly—me—on *The Infamous*'s song "Trife Life." I rhymed, "*Every angle of the car was smoked out and tinted, so we couldn't tell if the enemy was in it, it might have been TNT, I wasn't tryin' to wait and see, we jetted through Marcy 'cause D's ain't baggin' me.*" Jay was definitely talking about me.

On the song "Money, Cash, Hoes" with DMX, Jay said, "*New York's been soft ever since Snoop came through and crushed the buildings, I'm tryin' to restore the feelings.*" Jay was quieter than a church mouse when the Snoop and Pac, Mobb Deep and Biggie drama was on fire. Jay was nowhere around when all that shit with Pac was poppin' off. But that's how it was in rap—niggas always going at each other, saying slick shit in their rhymes. If you said something slick, I caught it. And best believe I came right back at you.

"Jay wasn't shooting videos in the projects until he saw your video 'Halftime' and our 'Shook Ones' and 'Survival of the Fittest' videos," I pointed out to Nas. "The projects ain't even Jay's style. He was on some speedboat, Versace, champagne-parties-in-the-Bahamas-gettin'-a-tan-type shit." Before his success I had seen Jay at different functions over the years, but mostly at Club Esso, where he threw Cristal parties. Biggie used to come through too. I knew Jay's style because I watched him come up. And now Jay-Z was copying our style. Plus Jay and his little rap protégé Memphis Bleek were dissing Nas on songs without saying Nas's name.

"We should put Jay on blast in our verses for biting our style and taking subliminal shots at us," I told Nas.

"Nah, fuck him," Nas said. "He ain't nobody to be dissin'."

"All right, cool," I replied. "I'm gonna deal with him on my own."

Nas didn't see what I saw. I knew exactly what Jay was doing, taking cheap shots on the low. Fuck that. Jay wanted to take indirect shots; it was my turn to shoot directly at him.

Jay-Z had animosity toward Nas 'cause he wanted Nas to be in his "In My Lifetime" video. Nas refused. Jay even got Nas's phone number from E-Money Bags and called Nas personally but Nas still wouldn't do it. Things were about to boil over.

The next day, I started working at Soundtrack early, aiming to complete four songs per day. Clean and sober again after the Limp Bizkit tour, I didn't allow anyone to smoke in Studio A while I was working. Changing my life for the better eventually helped KiKi to quit the weed and poisonous bullshit just like me.

Cam'ron was in a session with a hot new producer down the hall. Cam introduced me to the producer and asked me to do a song with him for his album. I wrote my rhyme in about twenty minutes and laid it down, then Cam came up with the chorus. The song, "Losing Weight," ended up being a hood classic. Cam asked me about the dragon tattoo on my hand and I explained that our whole Mobb Deep crew had it on our right hands. Cam then showed me a tattoo on the backhand side of his palm: DIPLOMATS written in script.

Before I went back to my own session, Cam'ron told me, "Yo, P, you should come hang out with me and my boys in Harlem one day."

"Who's Cam'ron?" KiKi asked late the following night. "He called for you today." Cam started calling my crib looking for me. "He sounds real cocky on the phone, like I'm supposed to be excited to speak to him," KiKi said. I never called Cam back. Not because I didn't like him—I had nothing against Cam—but because I didn't like new people trying to be too cool with me. I wasn't trying to hang out with him and his crew in Harlem because my mind was in a whole other space at that time. Strictly business.

•　　•　　•

I got word from my man in Queensbridge that Little Lord was home from doing seven years for that carjacking back in '93, the same kid I sold my Acura to back when he was the youngest drug dealer in the hood, running around with Killer Black, getting into shoot-outs. I scooped him from Brooklyn and took him to Soundtrack Studios. He said he was rapping now and went by the name Littles. I was happy that he wanted to change his life around, so I cut him a check and had him put a song on the movie sound track. I even let him lay an eight-bar a cappella on *H.N.I.C.* so he could get his buzz started. Little Lord seemed like a different person now, no longer acting like the cocky ruthless badass—he was acting real humble and happy to be free.

Right after Little Lord came home, Hav's man Free High from QB was also released from prison for murdering a cab driver on Twenty-first Street in Queensbridge. At Soundtrack Studios, Free High—who came home with razor slashes across both sides of his face from a fight in Rikers Island—explained that he beat the murder rap because his lawyer proved that Free High couldn't have killed the man since he was the one who called 911 from the pay phone up the block. Not only did he beat the murder, but Free High also sued the New York Department of Corrections and won forty thousand dollars for getting cut in jail. Free High had turned into a Blood in jail and also turned into a rapper.

Chris Lighty threw a big Violator Records party in South Beach, Miami. Mobb Deep was on the bill to perform with Busta Rhymes, so Havoc and I brought our crew and we all stayed at the Shelbourne Hotel.

I stopped by my mother's apartment to surprise her. She had gotten tired of New York and moved to Miami around '96. I took Alchemist and Gotti along so Moms could meet Al. We talked for about an hour, then hopped back on our scooters and rode around South Beach. Later that afternoon, Alchemist and I jumped into a mini-golf-cart-looking vehicle and drove to sound check at Club Amnesia, where palm trees grew from the dance floor up into the open-ceilinged sky.

Alchemist and I were waiting to check out the sound system when we overheard a conversation between two guys. "Yeah, I hear Mobb Deep is gonna be performing tonight," one of them said. "Those guys think they're so tough and gangster. I don't like them at all." I brushed it off as cheap talk, but during sound check, I noticed that the guy who was talking was the sound man for the show.

The spot was jam-packed later that night as we stood by the bar watching Rah Digga open for Busta with some girls behind her in tacky patent-leather outfits that said FLIPMODE SQUAD all over. Busta is always an extremely hard act to follow. After two songs, our mics started to sound terrible with loud feedback while the music was extra low. "Yo, you better fix this shit!" I screamed at the sound man. "You're fuckin' up our show." But it only got worse. *Wow, this dude really purposely fucked up our show 'cause he don't like us,* I thought, remembering what I overheard him saying earlier. The sound for Busta's set had been perfect. After the fourth song, we had to end our show because it sounded so awful. I found Chris Lighty and told him, "I know this is your party so out of respect I'm coming to you to tell you that I'm about to beat the sound man up."

"Okay, cool," Chris said.

"Are you sure?" I asked. "I'm not playing."

"Come on, I'll help you find him," Chris said. Chris brought me right to the sound man in the booth.

"Excuse me, my man," I said. "Can I ask you a question? Do you have something personal against me or my team? Did we do something to you?"

"No, I don't have a problem with you guys," he said. "I don't know what happened. The sound was just acting up." I pretended like I was turning to walk away while cocking back my arm so I could knock him out. I swung with my right fist, hit him in the mouth with my platinum-diamond ring, knocked out two of his top teeth, then quickly walked to the bathroom to wash the blood off my hand and swap shirts with our security guard, Tim. I gave Tim my royal-blue throwback Braves jersey with white short sleeves and he gave me his mustard-brown striped polo shirt.

The cops had all the club exits blocked off. Luckily I switched shirts, because when we walked out the cops tackled Tim to the ground with guns at his head. While they struggled with Tim on the ground, Chris Lighty's older brother Dave Lighty walked with me in the opposite direction and paid some fool a hundred dollars to give me his scooter so I could zip out quick. Tim got arrested and we bailed him out the next day. He had to go to trial for that case and lost his gun license. I gave Tim some bread for doing that for me, and then like a month or two later the sound man sued me for twenty thousand dollars for his dental bill and won.

Working on music at our Long Island house one day, Hav told me he wanted to throw a Gangsta Party at the crib that weekend. "What's a Gangsta Party?" I asked.

"A sex party, an orgy," Hav said. "We invite like ten females that know what the party is all about, then we invite just a few close friends and get it poppin'. A Gangsta Party!"

"Oh, okay," I said. "Let's do it." Havoc called some strippers and some girls we knew who were down for whatever. We invited Nas, L.E.S., and Little Lord. Gotti, Noyd, Poppa Mobb, Twin, and Ty-Nitty lived at the house so they were automatically invited. Hav also invited a female rapper named Chi-Town who was bisexual, so there'd be lots of females for her to have her fun with.

The night of the party, I picked Little Lord up from Brooklyn, and when we pulled up to the Freeport crib, Havoc had disco lights flashing throughout the whole place. Nas and L.E.S. pulled up at the same time as us. Females were walking all over the house in bikinis or nothing on at all. I poured a cup of Moët and Hav told Nas and me to follow him up to his room where four chicks were waiting for us. They pulled out condoms and started giving all of us top at the same time. The tall, thick, dark-skinned cutie who was giving me head suddenly stopped, pulled me behind her, and got on her hands and knees. So I started hitting her tall ass from the back while she began giving head to the girl who was sucking Nas's dick. We had 'em in all kinds of freaky positions in Hav's room for about forty minutes. Then I bounced downstairs and left Hav and Nas in the room with the girls. I was finished. I poured another cup of Moët and enjoyed the scenery.

Havoc and Nas came downstairs as Chi-Town walked in. Hav grabbed her by the arm and made her sit down on the couch, then Hav had two other females take her pants off. "Stop, what're ya'll doing?" Chi-Town yelled, acting shy because Nas was standing there watching. The two females pulled her panties off and started eating her out. "Stop, come on!" Chi-Town resisted. "What're ya'll doing?" But suddenly she was speechless, pushing the girls' faces deeper into her.

I left early and took my ass back home to KiKi. When she asked me where I'd been, I told her we were working on music. But she ain't stupid.

Women's intuition is powerful. It seemed like KiKi always knew when I was being bad. Shit, what was I supposed to say—I was at Hav's Gangsta Party?

Ron Artest had became a big-time NBA star for the Chicago Bulls, and when he heard about what I was doing with Bars'N'Hooks and the Queensbridge movie, he gave me ninety thousand dollars in start-up money to help with the expenses—studio time, records, stickers, travel expenses, Infamous Records chains for Delorean and Bars, and Infamous Records leathers, jerseys, T-shirts, and bandannas to promote the label. Ron-Ron, as we call him, was a real-ass nigga for looking out like that. To this day, if he asked me for anything I would do it for him.

The new millennium came and the entire world was on pins and needles thinking the end was here. News channels were spreading fear; supermarket shelves were empty from people stocking up on food and water. On New Year's Eve 1999, instead of going to the Tunnel, Justin's, or Cheetah as usual, KiKi and I played it safe and popped champagne while watching the ball drop on TV at home. It was finally 2000, and contrary to what everybody thought, nothing happened. In rural Rockland County, when the ball dropped all we heard was gunfire from machine guns and pistols. I thought a war had started. I forgot that we were up in the mountains with redneck Dukes of Hazzard white people who hunt for deer and bears. KiKi and I made our own porno movie and went to sleep.

I bumped into my boy from LeFrak Shameek's homeboy E-Money Bags on my way to Chung King Studios by the Holland Tunnel in Manhattan. Bags and

I always randomly crossed paths. He loved Mobb Deep. "You the God, P, you killin' these niggas with 'Quiet Storm,'" he said. Bags was a well-known ghetto celeb. The female rapper Foxy Brown even shouted him out on the Firm song "Affirmative Action." Bags and I started hanging out every day after that, talking for hours about the Illuminati, secret societies, the corrupt government, and the history of the Moors. Our appetite for hidden knowledge was the main thing we had in common.

Bags invited me along to visit his homie 50 Cent, a new rapper with a hot single called "How to Rob" who was recovering from multiple gunshot wounds. He said 50 was asking about me. I told Bags that I didn't really know 50 like that and wasn't going to make it. After Killer Black's wake in Queens-bridge and identifying my father's body in Atlanta, I told myself I wouldn't go to any more wakes or funerals. The crew was mad at me for missing our boy Yamit's wake in Brooklyn, but I didn't want to see any more of my people in a casket. So even though 50 was alive, I didn't want to see him hurt up like that.

"Keep It Thoro" was one of the last songs I recorded for *H.N.I.C.* The beat Alchemist made had a horn break that sounded like a natural hook, so I wrote the song without a chorus. Chris Lighty and others kept telling me, "You can't just leave it like that, it needs a chorus with vocals to get radio play." But one of the lines on that song says, *"Heavy airplay all day with no chorus, I keep it thorough, nigga!"* To have no chorus was the whole concept of the song. People liked my music because I didn't follow rules, did and said whatever I wanted.

KiKi kept bugging me to let her rap on the album when I was 95 per-cent finished. Making a good-quality album was more important than letting my wifey spit on a song. The way I saw it, she was just like everybody else who wanted to make a cameo on my album just because they knew me. I only do songs if it makes sense or sounds good. But then Alchemist made the perfect beat that sounded like a ghetto love story. KiKi and I sat up all night in our house in Pomona writing "Trials of Love," about a young couple going through the ups and downs of a music-industry relationship. It was her first time in the mic booth and I had her do the verse over thirty times, but she ended up getting it right. KiKi had writing skills, but I didn't want my woman

ALBERT "PRODIGY" JOHNSON

164

in the same business as me, so I told her that it was just for fun and wasn't going any further than that.

After the Limp Bizkit tour, Mobb Deep did our own club tour across the country. It was nothing compared to those big stadiums, but it was still good money. Bars'N'Hooks came along to get touring experience and I noticed Havoc was keeping his distance from them. You could just tell that he didn't want to work with them. That's how Hav was, all he cared about was Mobb Deep and his own music. Delorean and Bars felt like Havoc was dissing them and took it personally. I realized Bars'N'Hooks were talented musically but mentally they weren't ready to deal with us.

During a three-month break after the tour, I wrapped up *H.N.I.C.* The final song I recorded for it was "You Could Never Feel My Pain," about sickle-cell. I thought it would be interesting to get TLC's T-Boz to sing the chorus because she also had sickle-cell. Steve Rifkind set up a meeting in a studio in Atlanta. I carried the two-inch reels with me on the flight. Two-inch reels are reel-to-reel tapes that we recorded all the music and vocals on before Pro Tools came out.

T-Boz showed up an hour later to the studio with her then-husband, rapper Mack 10. T-Boz and I immediately started talking about how we dealt with sickle-cell. When she heard the track, I wasn't pleased with her response. "It sounds good, but I don't know if my label is going to let me do it," she said when I stopped the music. "I'll find out and get back to you." Right away I knew she didn't want to do it. It's a shame. But she was cool as hell. Steve Rifkind told me the same thing T-Boz did. "Her label doesn't like the idea of her on a song with a gangster rapper."

So I just made a simple hook and my album was done. Steve Rifkind was serious about promoting my album and Loud started running magazine ads for *H.N.I.C.* six months in advance. Since my album was called *Head Nigga in Charge*, I was sitting on a throne in the ads. The idea came from the end of the movie *Conan the Barbarian*, when Conan sat on a throne like he was the king of the world.

"Keep It Thoro" took off and I hit the road again for my *H.N.I.C.* tour. Bars'N'Hooks came along with Delorean's "uncle" Green Eyes. I was training

Green Eyes to be their road manager. His leg was still healing from being shot in the calf muscle by one of Supreme's boys. When Green Eyes came home from doing that fifteen, the first thing he did was step to Supreme about why he hadn't sent money to him or his family while he was doing time. Green Eyes explained to me how he had to whip Supreme's ass. Preme couldn't live with that ass whupping so he had one of his boys shoot Green Eyes in the leg like five minutes after the fight. *Wow.* Green Eyes got up early every morning to walk around the hotels, building the strength back in his leg.

The fans were feeling Bars'N'Hooks. But Delorean kept bothering me about why Havoc didn't like them. "Havoc don't gotta like you, nigga!" I ended up screaming one day. But they still felt offended. Their logic was, "Havoc is from our block. We grew up with Havoc, not you, P. Havoc should be showing us more love." Havoc wasn't obligated to do anything for them, they were signed to my company, not Mobb Deep. Those were some hardheaded little bastards.

We toured the entire East Coast and Midwest, and while we were in Chicago for a performance at our boy Ron Artest's birthday party, an interview I did in *The Source* came out. I picked up a copy in the Chicago airport when we landed. *The Source* put me on the cover. My first magazine cover as a solo artist. In the interview, the writer Shaheem Reid asked about my problem with Jay-Z, referencing an online interview in which they asked if I liked Jay-Z. "No, he's a bitch boy. He talk it and don't live it," I said. I elaborated for *The Source.* "Jay-Z has a quote in the song 'Money Cash Hoes' where he claims: *'New York been soft ever since Snoop came through and crushed the buildings, I'm trying to restore the feelings.'* But Jay was nowhere to be found when that drama popped off between Mobb Deep, Dogg Pound, Pac, and Biggie. That was our little personal beef, not a coastal war. Jay-Z ain't have shit to say when it was on and he was gettin' dissed. Him and Nas. Mobb Deep and Biggie were the only ones from New York active in that situation. So Jay-Z is a bitch-ass nigga for making that quote in his lyrics." Yeah, it was on now.

Ron-Ron and a few of his boys from Queensbridge came to pop Moët with us at the hotel later that night before the party. I'd drink a little champagne or wine occasionally. It's only a problem when you're downing bottles without any discipline. QB was deep in Chi-Town that night. The two-level club was packed, the VIP balcony wrapping around above the dance floor. I bought bottles for my boys with a bunch of fake hundred-dollar bills from my "Keep It Thoro" video that read FOR MOTION PICTURE USE ONLY at the top instead of UNITED STATES OF AMERICA. By the time the club figured it out, they finished the bottles and we couldn't be found in the enormous crowd.

Calls started coming in from industry folks when I arrived back in New York: "Jay-Z is upset because of what you said about him." I was like, "And? Am I supposed to give a fuck? Fuck him." I didn't call him a bitch boy to make him happy, I did it to provoke him to start dissin' me, and I said it because it is the truth. The whole rap world was talking about me calling Jay a bitch—radio, magazines, Web sites and all. It was only a matter of time before Bitch Boy came back at me with something. And that's exactly what I wanted. I knew most of the shooters and live wires from Jay-Z's hood and the other two projects near Marcy—Tompkins and Sumner. So I already knew who Jay-Z would run to. That's my advantage over him. That's how I knew he didn't live what he rapped.

But Jay didn't realize I had those connections. My nigga E-Money Bags went to high school with Jay, and Bags's sister is married to Sauce Money, who was one of Jay's artists. I had connections through the whole borough of Brooklyn, from Red Hook, Cypress, and Pink Houses to Brownsville, Crown Heights, and Bed-Stuy. When I openly expressed my opinion of Jay-Z to the world, it opened up the floodgates on him. Suddenly several different rappers started openly saying the same things about him, from Fat Joe to the Lox and more. Even LL Cool J started firing his shots at Jay. Jay has a line in one of his songs that goes, *First the Fat Boys break up, now every day I wake up somebody got a problem with Hov.* The song is called "Ain't No Love" or some bitch-boy shit like that.

Let me be clear, Jay-Z made excellent music. I really liked a lot of his stuff. But this was not about his music and it had nothing to do with jealousy or envy. This was about the man behind all that. Shawn Carter, aka Bozo the Clown. My situation with that dude wasn't a rap battle; it was personal.

Touching up edits for a clean version of "Y.B.E. (Young Black Entrepreneurs)," featuring B.G. from Cash Money, my son Shaka joined me for a session at

Soundtrack Studios. Shaka was five years old at the time. Mike Delorean and my man Draws from Queensbridge also came along. My engineer Steve Sola told us that Nas was working in Studio B again that night, so we walked over to say what's up. When we walked in, we saw Nas, Jungle, Grand Wiz, Horse and his brother Dula, and some dude we didn't know along with a few females. Delorean noticed some big buds of weed on the countertop plus a few bottles of liquor and a camcorder. Right away Delorean picked up one of the buds to smell and Nas got upset. "Yo, why you touching shit that ain't yours?" Nas asked.

"Damn, I'm just looking at the bud," Delorean said. "I wanted to smell it." Then Delorean picked up the camcorder and started to inspect it to see what kind it was, and Nas barked on him again.

"Yo, what the fuck is wrong with you, son? I told you, stop touching other people's shit!"

"Man, what the fuck is your problem? I'm gonna look at it if I feel like looking at it. What's the big deal?" Delorean said. Nas was clearly a little drunk from the Grey Goose and cranberry juice in his hand and still had sour feelings about that old freestyle Delorean and Cormega put out dissing him. He was also clearly upset that Delorean was talking to him like that now. Nas walked up to Delorean and motioned with the cup in his hand like he was going to toss the red drink in Delorean's face but paused and tossed it on the shoulder of Delorean's white T-shirt. There was a moment of silence, then Delorean grabbed Nas by his throat with his right hand and pushed him up against the wall, choking him.

"Nigga, don't you ever in your life play yourself like that!" Delorean said. "You fucking stupid or something? I'll kill you, you bitch-ass nigga!" All of Nas's boys jumped up but Draws yelled out, "Chill! If they're gonna fight, let them fight one on one. Ain't gonna be no jumping going on in here!" I screamed at Mike Delorean to let Nas go and he did, then we took Delorean back to Studio A. My son Shaka was watching it all in shock.

Back in Studio A, Delorean said, "P, give me the gun! I'm shooting this bird-ass nigga! Give me the gun!" And I replied, "Hell no! You buggin'. You already choked him up against the wall and he didn't try to fight you back, so leave him alone." After about ten minutes of calming him down, I went into the hallway and Nas walked up to me apologizing.

"I'm sorry, man. I had too much to drink," Nas said. "Please forgive me, man."

"It's all good, just forget about it. Ya'll niggas is bugged-out though," I said.

"Nah, I'm really sorry. I'm telling you, I'm just bent right now and I overreacted," Nas said. "I shouldn't have done that. That was foul."

"Don't sweat it, we good," I said. Then we both went back into our studio rooms.

February 27, 2009
Mid-State Correctional Facility
Marcy, New York
10:00 A.M.

"On the rec!" The loud, obnoxious, military-style shout from the CO abruptly woke me from my sleep. He was letting the whole dorm know it was time for recreation. Pulling myself off the steel cot attached to my cell wall, I forced myself to go to the yard. *C'mon, boy, let's go,* I said to myself. *You owe it to your family and to the people who love your music. Now get your ass outside and work out!* It was raining hard so I grabbed my green hoodie and workout gloves and ran to catch up with the other inmates.

Out of thirty inmates in my dorm, only four of us went out to brave the weather. The yard at Mid-State Correctional Facility is the size of a football field and has a large shed with plenty of weight-lifting equipment, pull-up bars, dip bars, and concrete picnic tables. I went out every morning. *You've been in the game seventeen years. What makes you think people are still going to care about you when you get home?* I'd constantly ask myself. My answer was always the same. *Because of my ability to create music. My attitude about life and my physical appearance will all be better than it ever was.*

With all that in mind, I worked out hard for three hours every day. But I worked on my music and attitude more than anything, especially my attitude. My mother always told me, "If you don't have anything nice to say, then don't say anything at all." I didn't fully understand that until I was forced to sit in a cell and think about my whole life. Damn, I had a big mouth. I needed to tone it down. A lot. I enjoyed being a fearless badass, doing and saying things others were scared to. As a teenager, I got my kicks out of doing shit like standing on a long department-store line of white people and their children and reciting the lyrics to N.W.A's "Niggaz 4 Life." *"Why do I call myself a nigga, you ask me? Well, it's because muthafuckers want to blast me. . . ."* Seeing how those lyrics made white people uncomfortable would make my day. My boys laughed hard afterward, saying, "Yo, you crazy, P, what's wrong with you?" It was fun being bad.

We smoked weed and drank big bottles of alcohol in train cars full of passengers, robbed people in front of numerous witnesses, and wreaked havoc throughout the five boroughs. There weren't as many cameras, police, or thousands of tourists roaming the streets of Manhattan. If you were a teenager growing up in the five boroughs during that time, you know why I acted, talked, rapped, and carried myself the way I did. The concrete-jungle education that New York City provided me is priceless. I'm sure it was similar in every inner city on the map, but nothing compares to the every-man-for-himself state of mind that New Yorkers have—you won't find that level of ruthlessness anywhere else in the U.S.

The '80s and '90s were like gladiator school in the streets. My attitude was in sync with my environment. But change is imminent, nothing stays the same. When I think back on all the things I've done in the streets, I realize how blessed I am to still be alive. Sometimes I feel like I'm in one of those movie scenes where everything is moving at light speed around the person in the middle who moves ever so slightly, slowly and calm.

The Tunnel started to die down, so we needed a new church to go to every Sunday, and the Latin Quarter, or L.Q., was it. After one Sunday-night service at L.Q., we went to N.O.R.E.'s crib in West New York, New Jersey, for an after-party with some females. I left early because I wasn't into all that wild after-party stuff anymore.

I didn't make it more than four blocks in my Range Rover before I got pulled over by an NJ squad car for no damn reason. Oh, I forgot, I was black and driving an expensive car. The cops asked for my license and registration. The young Latino officer recognized me. "Prodigy? Is that you?" he asked.

"Yeah, what's up," I said. "What's the problem? Did I do something wrong?"

"No problem, we saw the Georgia plates and wanted to check everything out," the officer said. I'd recently bought the Range from a kid, Loc, in Atlanta who was connected to a tagged-car operation that bought cars off delivery trucks before they reached the dealership. I couldn't resist the dirt-cheap price—ten thousand bucks for a brand-new black-on-black 4.6 Range. The Latino officer's partner shined a flashlight on my window stickers and VIN number tag. "Don't worry, we just need to check your VIN number on your engine to make sure it matches the one on your windshield, because the windshield tag is falling off," he explained. *Damn!* I'd taken the Range to the car wash earlier that day, and while cleaning my windshield and dashboard, they'd knocked the tag loose. "Pop your hood open and then we'll get you out of here." This was about to get bad. An all-black plastic nine-millimeter with a rubber grip and laser sight was in the engine, next to the battery.

Two minutes later, the white cop said the code for "gun" to the Latino. "Step out of the vehicle, please," the Latino cop said. "Turn around with your hands behind your back. I'm sorry, but you have a gun in your engine. We have to arrest you." They read my rights, searched my truck, and found three nickel bags of weed in a jacket one of my boys left in my backseat. *Fuck!* They put me in the squad car and took me to the West New York precinct. The next morning, KiKi and Uncle Lenny bailed me out.

As I was leaving the courthouse, two detectives walked up. "Albert Johnson? We need to talk. Please step into the office." *Shit!* "Where did you get this truck from?" one of the detectives asked after seating me in the office. *Damn, it's over now.*

"I bought it from some guy in Atlanta," I said. "He was selling it, so I bought it."

"Do you know the guy you bought it from?"

"No, it said 'For Sale' on the window, so I negotiated a price."

"Well, this truck is stolen," the detective said. "The tags don't match. Our people checked the engine parts and all the tags match except one. This is the best tagged job we've seen. You know you bought a tagged car, right? Don't lie, we already know."

"Hell no! I make music for a living," I said. "I don't have to buy stolen cars. I've got money." After thirty minutes of interrogation, they grew tired of trying to convince me to snitch, put the cuffs on, and rearrested me. They told KiKi and Uncle Lenny that I was now being charged with grand theft auto and would have to wait till tomorrow to see the judge again.

The next day, the judge hit me with $150,000 bail. I spent a few days in Newark County jail until Steve Rifkind bailed me out. It was my second gun charge and my first stolen-car charge. My lawyer Irv Cohen and I decided to take it to trial. I can't elaborate on the particulars here, but during the trial, Irv approached me in the court hallway.

"Kid, you're a lucky son of a bitch," Irv said after presenting our case to the judge and DA at the trial hearing. "They're dropping the charges to a misdemeanor. You just have to plead guilty to the marijuana and pay a fine." I was relieved and happy as hell. The only problem was, there were about thirty camcorder tapes in the back of the Range including footage of Killer Black, the Scarface Twin, Yamit, remodeling our house in Freeport, classic studio sessions, sex tapes of groupies, and all sorts of rare, priceless memories.

"I need my tapes from the back of the truck," I said.

"Listen, kid," Irv said sternly. "Whatever's in that truck, forget about it. Walk away." It hurt my heart that I lost all that footage.

I gave E-Money Bags $2,500 for a beat he produced for the *Murda Muzik* sound track, which he put toward a silver Navigator. Soundtrack Studios was becoming too expensive, so I made a deal with our engineer Steve Sola and the owner of a cheaper studio in Long Island called Music Palace. I started spending the night at Music Palace because I was working too late to drive upstate to Pomona every night. Green Eyes, Mike Delorean, E-Money Bags, and his homeboy Majesty would swing through.

I bounced over to Queensbridge the following day for the "Y.B.E." video shoot with B.G. from Cash Money. The owner of New York Furs, Irving, lent me fifteen of his best fur coats—chinchillas, minks, and mink hoodies. He looked out for me with the furs because I paid him to make ten butter-soft

Infamous Records leather jackets with leather bandannas to match with some of the money Ron Artest invested in Infamous Records. Although I didn't request it, Loud Records hired a jeweler to come to the set with a bunch of jewelry for me to wear even though I had my own. Baby, Juvenile, B.G., and a bunch of their boys showed up while the video director, Little X, was setting up shots. B.G. pulled me to the side and asked if I could get my hands on some "diesel," which is heroin, so I sent Draws to buy two bundles of dope. B.G. took the bundles straight to the bathroom.

It was the first time a New York rapper did a song and video with Cash Money. A rumor went around that I was robbed outside the video studio for three hundred thousand dollars' worth of jewels, the jewelry that Loud Records had rented for the shoot. The story even made the newspapers. I won't elaborate for legal reasons, but can you believe that the jewelry company thought that I had something to do with the situation? I wonder what would make them think that. Ha!

A week after the video shoot, Green Eyes had a birthday party at a sports bar on the corner of Liberty Avenue next to the Van Wyck Expressway in Jamaica, Queens. I bumped into Bags, who told me that he had drama with some dudes who might show up at the party. He pulled a mini .45-caliber out of his pocket. "I'm gonna lay a nigga down tonight if I see one of them," he said. I had my nine-millimeter on me so if it was going to be something, then somebody would definitely get laid down and out.

The day after Green Eyes's birthday party, I contacted a hot producer named Seven to get beats for Bars'N'Hooks and myself. Seven had well-known hits with Ja Rule and Ashanti. He told me to meet him at the Crack House, a studio owned by Irv Gotti and Ja Rule. When I arrived, I saw Irv Gotti and a couple of his Murder Inc. artists, Cadillac Tah and Black Child. I knew Irv Gotti from seeing him at industry functions but we were never cool. But I knew his R&B singer Ashanti, and her mother, Tina, very well from my grandmother's dance school. When Ashanti was sixteen or seventeen, her mother gave me a copy of Ashanti's demo and wanted me to sign her. She sounded amazing but I wasn't mentally ready to do the label thing. A couple of years later, Irv Gotti and Ja Rule signed her and blew her up.

Irv brought me into the studio, where Seven played me some beats.

I got a call from E-Money Bags so I went into the hallway to talk to him. When I told Bags that I was at Irv's studio, he said, "Tell that nigga Irv that E-Money Bags said what up. He knows me." I told Irv and his face instantly changed, like he was nervous all of a sudden. *What's that about?* I wondered. I made a copy of one of Seven's beats and bounced back to the Music Palace studio to meet Bars'N'Hooks, Green Eyes, and Steve Sola. Late that night, Green Eyes said he needed to talk. He complimented me on Infamous Records and told me to stop hanging out with Bags. He didn't tell me why or by who, just said to stay away because Bags was about to be hit.

Bags was hyped about getting his Navigator. "Come with me to the dealership in Long Island," he said at the studio one afternoon just after Green Eyes told me to stop hanging with him. "They're giving out good deals for luxury cars." We hopped on the Long Island Expressway and headed to Champion Motors. On the way, Bags broke down the whole story about the connection between Irv Gotti, Ja Rule, and Supreme. Bags told me Irv was the neighborhood DJ at park jams and block parties back in the day, and Irv and Ja were just two studio gangsters. "Irv Gotti and Ja Rule, they were the herbs in the hood, and now Supreme's got them under his wing," Bags said.

Before I gave Bags the money for the song he did for my *Murda Muzik* sound track, he was planning to buy a tagged car from this girl named Z who went to my grandmother's dance school and sold tagged cars for Supreme. Capone from QB bought a white buggy-eye Benz from her a few months prior. Bags gave Z a thousand dollars for a down payment, but when he got the $2,500 from me he decided he wanted his money back to get a legit car—a Navigator—instead.

"You've gotta take that up with Preme," Z told him. "Because he told me not to give you anything back." Supreme brushed Bags off like he was a punk. Bags was a member of a Jamaica, Queens, gang in the late eighties called the Young Guns that had a big brawl with another gang from Jamaica, the Lost Boys, at Sunrise Multiplex—somebody was shot in the eye and killed inside the theater. Bags was the shooter. He's the reason why that movie theater has metal detectors to this day.

Bags told me he was coming out of the Coliseum on Jamaica Avenue one day and saw Preme parked in a Land Rover with a dude named Black Jus, another well-known member of the Supreme Team, in the Rover's passenger seat. Bags proceeded to shoot up the Rover with bullets, learning later that he missed Preme and shot Black Jus in his upper inner thigh. Instead of driving Jus to the hospital, Preme drove him ten minutes away to the hood and told somebody else to take him ten minutes back so the D's wouldn't question him. Black Jus bled to death. But if Preme would have dropped him at Mary Immaculate Hospital right around the block from the shooting, Jus might have lived.

50 Cent felt the same way about Irv and Ja, Bags said, and he didn't get along with Preme either. So when 50 first came on the rap scene with songs dissing Irv and Ja, Preme put a hit on 50—and that's why 50 got shot up. Bags knew that Preme put a hit on him, too, for killing Black Jus, but he said he was going to kill Preme first. *Now I understand what Green Eyes was telling me and why Irv Gotti looked like he'd seen a ghost when I told him I was on the phone with Bags, and why Ja Rule was acting tough on that Limp Bizkit tour,* I was thinking as Bags spoke. *He figured he had Preme to protect him.*

E-Money Bags went on to tell me how he was connected with Tupac. Bags's homeboy Majesty and Majesty's brother Big Stretch were blood cousins with Young Noble from Tupac's group the Outlawz, so they all hung out on a regular basis in the early nineties. Tupac was so tight with Big Stretch that he'd given him appearances in two of his movies, *Above the Rim* and *Bullet.*

While he was in New York shooting *Above the Rim,* Tupac had also befriended some dudes from Brooklyn, Jamaican Jackson and Johnny Lynchman, as well as a few other Brooklynites like Biggie Smalls, Little Shawn, and the whole Bad Boy clique. Bags explained that shortly after the filming of *Above the Rim* was complete, Tupac, Jamaican Jackson, and some others went to hang out at a nightclub where they found groupies to bring back to Pac's hotel. One of the females called the cops, claiming that Tupac and his friends raped her, and the judge sentenced him to a year and a half in prison. During the trial, the press questioned Pac outside the courthouse about his codefendants, Jamaican Jackson and others. "I don't know them dudes, they're not my friends," Tupac said. Jamaican Jackson and his friends didn't like that very much.

While Pac was out on bail, he set up a recording session at Quad Recording Studios in Manhattan with rapper Little Shawn. Stretch went with Pac to Quad that night and noticed a man leaning against a street pole reading a newspaper right in front of the studio door as they arrived. Stretch told Bags that when he and Pac walked inside, the man followed them into the lobby, gun drawn, along with two other gunmen. They went straight for Pac's jewelry. Pac had two Glocks tucked into his pants and tried pulling them out but shot himself in the groin. The gunmen opened fire on Pac, grazing him on the head and a few other spots before running off.

Stretch told Bags that he and Pac went up to the studio where Biggie, Puff, and Little Shawn saw Pac bleeding and were all in shock. Bags then told me that they found out who shot Pac in the lobby that night. Bags and Stretch visited Pac on Rikers Island a lot and they told Pac who'd ordered the hit and who took it, so Pac knew exactly what was going on. He knew that Biggie and Puff had nothing to do with it. But when E-Money Bags and Stretch explained what happened, Pac told them that he planned to use the situation to sell a lot of records. Bags explained who was behind it, but Pac said he just wanted to start controversy and that he planned to use Biggie and Puff and turn his gunshot wounds into a marketing and promotion scheme. *Wow.*

As Bags finished the Pac saga, we pulled into the car dealership. Bags ordered a silver Navigator with gray leather interior, TV, and a Sony PlayStation.

In his Navigator the next day, Bags passed me his pager and told me to look at the message. It was from Ja Rule's labelmate Cadillac Tah: *They're over here right now, come get 'em.* Cadillac was referring to Ja and Irv. "You see that, right?" Bags turned to me and said. "Their own man lined them up for me. We just robbed them niggas for their chains."

The year 2000 zoomed by—I turned around and it was 2001. I was in Harlem, rolling down 125th Street on my way to the Triborough Bridge when I slowed down to get a good look at a brand-new 2002 Yukon Denali XL. *I'm buying one of those immediately,* I said to myself. Two months later, I bought an all-white Denali XL with gray leather seats.

My man Gotti from QB and I were sitting in the truck when a new Jay-Z song called "Takeover" came on the radio. The beat was hot so we turned it up and heard Jay dissing Nas and me! I was wondering what was taking Bitch Boy so long. I thought, *Let the game begin!*

Radio station Hot 97 was promoting its annual Summer Jam concert at Nassau Coliseum. Mobb Deep wasn't performing so we paid it no mind. The June day of Summer Jam, Havoc was in the basement in Freeport making beats while the rest of the crew was in the living room playing 007 on PlayStation in the two-player mode. I got a phone call from Illa Ghee, who was at Summer Jam with a bunch of his friends from Brooklyn. "P, this bitch-ass nigga just tried to play you during his show," Ghee said.

"What do you mean?" I asked.

"Jay-Z—I told you that picture was gonna come back to haunt you one day," Ghee said. "Jay had the picture of you when you was a kid dressed like Michael Jackson on the screens onstage." I started laughing. It sounded funny as hell. I had to admit, that was a good joke.

In the song "Takeover," Jay had a line about me: *"You was a ballerina, I got the pictures, I seen ya. Dropped 'Shook Ones,' then you changed your demeanor, we don't believe you, you need more people."* But anybody who went to my grandmother's dance school had seen that picture of me when I was eight years old dressed like Michael Jackson. Jay-Z couldn't confront the issue that started our whole drama, so he diverted the people's attention with a joke. The debate was about Jay not being active in the rap beef with Snoop and Tupac and how he waited years, until Pac and Biggie got murdered, to start running his lips about *"New York' been soft ever since Snoop came and crushed the buildings, I'm tryin' to restore the feelings."*

That's the reality Jay has to deal with when we all get tired of laughing at me in 1982, eight years old, dressed like Mike. But I did like the tactic that Jay used. It was pretty slick.

Nas dropped a song called "Build and Destroy" a few months later and in the lyrics he took shots at me all of a sudden: *"Prodigy used to be my man, through all the robberies. . . . "* At the end of the song, he said something about how he was still cool with me, that I just needed to stop hanging around certain people, those people being Cormega and Bars'N'Hooks. Nas went from playing me close in the studio next door to asking me to be on his QB project to intercepting my artists from Queensbridge—because he didn't know who the new talent was, since he'd stopped going to Queensbridge—to calling my crib trying to befriend me after ten years to playing a part in my movie to "*Prodigy used to be my man.*" What? Was this fool schizo?

People in Queensbridge told me that Nas made that song because he was mad at me for doing a song with Cormega on which Mega took shots at Nas in his verse. Mega didn't like Nas ever since Nas booted him out of the Firm and had started dissing Nas for a living. But I didn't dis him, Mega did. *Why you not confronting Mega?* I wondered of Nas. *You scared? Why didn't you fight Delorean when he choked you up in the studio? You scared? I asked a Braveheart for my chain back? Bullshit. I didn't ask for nothing, I went and got mines back, by myself, when some of my boys from QB told me not to. Why would Nas dis me in that song?*

I didn't realize the answer until months later. Nas was being just as tactical as Jay-Z. After Summer Jam, I started going bonkers on Jay-Z with dis songs, and Nas was actually jealous because my beef with Jay-Z was getting a lot of publicity.

On a Friday night the following winter, Jay-Z went on Funkmaster Flex's Hot 97 radio show freestyling with his new recruits Beanie Sigel, Young Gunz, and Freeway. Bars'N'Hooks, Green Eyes, E-Money Bags, Majesty, and I were at the Music Palace Studio. Jay's boys sounded real good until I heard Beanie take an indirect shot at Mobb Deep, something about "I'll creep on your Quiet Storm." To top it off, Jay had some nigga named H-Money Bags rhyming with them. E-Money Bags started spazzin'. I had a private number to the radio station, and after about eighty rings, somebody picked up.

"Yo, this is Prodigy," I said. "Let me speak to Jay-Z."

"Jay just got on the elevator and left. You just missed him," the person on the phone said.

"Go catch him and tell him Prodigy is on the phone."

"Okay, I'm gonna try, hold on." Five minutes later, Jay got on the phone.

"What's up?" Jay said.

"Yeah, what up nigga," I said. "Hold on, somebody wants to talk to you." Bags was asking for the phone so I handed it over.

"What's up, this is E-Money Bags. How you got some dude with you using my name? You know me, nigga. Who the fuck is H-Money Bags?"

"So what're you trying to say?" Jay asked.

"What I'm trying to say? You know what it is with me, nigga. Don't try to act like you don't know how I rock," Bags said. Bags went to high school with Jay and they knew each other well.

"This is what you called me for?" Jay replied.

"Oh, now you acting tough?" Bags said. "You tough now? You know I'm gonna see you now, right?"

"Say no more then," Jay said.

"Say no more? A'ight, so when I see you, you know what it is."

"Say no more," Jay said.

The following Friday I called Funk Flex and asked if E-Money Bags, N.O.R.E., myself, and Nas could come to the station later that night and do a freestyle session just like Jay and his team did. We wanted revenge. Flex agreed. Bags called Nas to come with us and Nas said he would.

While we were on our way to the station, we called Flex and he put us live on the air. As we crossed the 59th Street Bridge, Nas e-mailed Bags, backing out: *Yo, I ain't coming. Just go up there and tell everybody who the real king of New York is.* Bags read the message to me while I was driving. Maybe Nas was scared we were going to do something to him because he'd just dissed me on his song, but we weren't.

The real king of New York?

N.O.R.E. met us in front of the station and we linked with Flex in the lobby. "Thanks for coming up, but my boss just called and told me to cancel the show," Flex said. "I can't let ya'll up because they think this is gonna cause some beef." No matter what we said, Flex kept saying that he "can't do it" or he'd "get in trouble."

Outside, a Lincoln Town Car pulled up and five dudes with plastic cups of Hennessy in their hands hopped out, screaming, "Yo, what's up!" I grabbed the hammer on my waist. "We're from Far Rockaway, we heard you on the radio saying ya'll were coming to the station, so we came to hold you down." I told them that Flex wouldn't let us on the air. "Fuck them Roc-A-Fella faggots! We came up here to wait outside and creep up on anybody trying to creep on ya'll. We're from Far Rockaway, P, Far Rock got your back."

Soon after the disappointment at Hot 97, the co-owners of *The Source*, Dave Mays and Ray Benzino, told me that the new Source Awards were about to take place in California. "Look, you know this clown Jay-Z is running around frontin' like shit is sweet," I told Benzino. "If ya'll want us to perform at the awards show, then I need you to hook us up with thirty passes and seats for my boys. I promise we won't hurt Jay inside the venue or ruin your show. I just want to show this clown and everybody else what kind of power Mobb Deep has. Please do this for me." Benzino paused for a moment, then said okay.

The whole 12th Street crew got on a plane to Los Angeles—Havoc, Twin, Nitty, Godfather, Gotti, Free High, Little Lord, Y.G., Kiko, Derrick from the Bronx, Mike Delorean, Mr. Bars, Green Eyes, Larry the movie director, Fly, Prince God, me, and like fourteen others. It was the first time on a plane for a lot of them. We stayed at a hotel across the street from the House of Blues on Sunset Boulevard. While we were stopped at a red light on our way back to the hotel from dinner, I looked over at a pay phone on the sidewalk to my right and couldn't believe my eyes—it was our homeboy Draws from Queensbridge! What the hell was Draws doing in California on a random pay phone? I rolled down the van window and yelled, "Draws! Gets your ass in the van!"

"Yo thun, I came out here with thun and them dudes left me stranded," Draws, who only spoke Thun Language, explained. "Thun, this is crazy I bumped into ya'll like this, thuuun!" He was saying that he came to Cali with Nas and Nas had left him. Draws was wild—the nerves in his hands were damaged from being shot, so his palms were always sweaty and he carried a washcloth everywhere.

Back at the hotel, Draws told me how he was calling his man Rain at the pay phone. "You need to meet my thun Rain," Draws said. "Thun got crazy connects in the music industry. I can even get us some guns out here. Thun got a lot of ties in L.A." When he said guns, that sparked my interest. After about an hour, Draws told me his man 40 Glocc was outside the hotel and Rain had arranged for him to bring us the hammers.

In front of the hotel on Sunset Strip, a dude with cornrows introduced himself. "What up cuz, I'm 40 Glocc, these my little homies," he said, motioning to his boys. 40 was cool. I could tell he was Crip because of how he spoke and he and his homies had on blue.

40 Glocc and his people met us at the Shrine Auditorium for the Source Awards the following day. We all had on custom-made football jerseys with Hennessy, E&J, Seagram's, Thug Passion, Bacardi, and other liquor names embroidered on the front and our names on the back so our crew would stand out in the crowd. Lil' Kim flew out to perform the "Quiet Storm" remix with us and brought the whole Junior M.A.F.I.A. crew. Our dressing room was connected to Lil' Kim's so my crew drank and smoked with them until taking our seats two rows from the front of the stage at showtime. Tupac's group the Outlawz were seated directly in front of us. It was our first time seeing each other since the beef, and because so many of my boys were there I didn't want to make the Outlawz uncomfortable. So I made small talk with them to let them know it was all good now.

The famous Polo model Tyson Beckford was also seated in front of us and he pulled a gallon of Hennessy from under his seat, then showed it to Havoc and me. We told him to pass the bottle back and thugged the whole gallon. I didn't drink that hard-core shit anymore but I had to take care of my boys. When the Houston rapper Scarface, seated in the row to our left, saw my team drinking, he was like, "What's up, man?" as if he wanted a cup. So we poured him one. By the time I gave Tyson Beckford back his bottle it was mostly gone.

Mobb Deep was the final act of the night. Smoke filled the stage with the thunder from the "Quiet Storm" intro while Havoc slowly drove a Caddy truck onstage and hopped out when his verse began. The crowd erupted. I hopped out along with Noyd, who was holding a gallon of Seagram's gin, jumping around as it spilled all over. After Havoc's verse, Noyd opened the back door of the truck and assisted the Queen B Lil' Kim out while she spit her verse. "Ayo Prodigy, tell 'em what it is, dun," Kim concluded, and I screamed,

"*Yo, it's the real!*" Our boys in the crowd were wildin' like we were inside the Tunnel back in NYC and the Shrine went nuts.

After my verse, a gang of Death Row Bloods came storming through the entrance and charging down the aisle from both sides. They ran to the stage while we were chanting the last few words of our chorus, chasing Snoop Dogg and Dr. Dre. Snoop, who was with his crew Tha Eastsidaz, ran out the back exit while his boy Tray-Dee stayed and fought a handful of Death Row dudes, whippin' their asses all by himself. The Shrine Auditorium turned into pandemonium with small fights breaking out in the crowd.

Heading back to the hotel on Sunset, I thought, *I wonder if Lil' Kim and them are okay.* I called Kim. She said that I should come hang out at her hotel later. Twin, Delorean, Mr. Bars, Free High, Draws, Gotti, and I hopped into a van to the Swiss Hotel by the Beverly Center mall where Kim and her friends were drinking frozen apple martinis in the penthouse suite. In her room were D-Roc, Gutter, Cease, Banger, and other Junior M.A.F.I.A. members plus five of Kim's female friends. Her hotel room was crowded, so Free High got one of her girlfriends' numbers and then we left. On our way out of the lobby downstairs, Kim's hairstylist ran out of the elevator calling my name. "P! Kim wants you to come back upstairs!" I told my boys to bounce and send a van back to pick me up later.

Back inside Kim's room, I noticed that the Junior M.A.F.I.A. was gone and it was just Kim and her girlfriends plus the hairstylist. Kim poured me another apple martini and we stepped onto the balcony to talk privately. I grabbed Kim by the waist and started kissing her on her neck. I thought about Mary J. Blige and decided to play this situation differently. "Stop, not right now," Kim said. "There are too many people up here." I understood what she meant but I kept trying to sex her right there on the balcony. After five minutes of us feeling on each other, I fell back because it was obvious that she wasn't trying to let me hit right then and there. But the things she told me let me know for sure that I could get with her at some other time.

KiKi always thought Kim and I were sexing, but it never happened. When KiKi first heard the "Quiet Storm" remix featuring Kim, out of jealousy she told me, "That song is wack."

•   •   •

My moms assembled our family lineage and pieced together the branches of our family tree.

Grandmoms teaching a student ballet at the Bernice
Johnson Dance School in Jamaica, Queens

Grandpops *(far right)* playing sax

Grandmoms on crutches onstage at her Lincoln Center comeback concert
with Ben Vereen, as Kerri Edge hands her flowers

In a final letter to his wife, "Budd" summarized his feelings about his return to Kansas City:

"Most of the apartments and all of the black hotels where we stayed are torn down. All gone. It was a strange feeling. I thought about life which does the same thing. We are torn down and something new comes along and takes our place on earth."

A CELEBRATION FOR BUDD

Grandpops's funeral "celebration" program

*** A Celebration for BUDD JOHNSON ***

December 14, 1910 - October 20, 1984

Thursday, October 25, 1984   7:30 P.M.

at

Saint Peter's Church
54th St. & Lexington Avenue,
New York, New York 10022

P R O G R A M

INVOCATION	John Garcia Gensel, Minister to the Jazz Community
MUSICAL TRIBUTE	Clark Terry and Small Ensemble
OPENING REMARKS	Budd Johnson, Jr.
MUSICAL TRIBUTES	"Body And Soul" Frank Foster/Billy Taylor
	"We'll Be Together Again" Jon Hendricks
THE BUDD I KNEW	Billy Eckstine
MORE MUSICAL TRIBUTES	Friends of Budd's
EULOGY	Jon Hendricks and Frank Foster
BENEDICTION	John Garcia Gensel

O B I T U A R Y

Albert Jackson Johnson, III, was born on December 14, 1910 in Dallas, Texas, the second of three children to Kate and Albert Johnson, II. He exhibited an early interest in music, playing his father's horn and taking piano lessons from Mr. Walton and Madame Pratt. He and his brother "Keg" and friends formed a group called the Moonlight Melody Six and played local gigs. At the age of 18, he left Texas for Kansas City, thus beginning an illustrious career which was to span over five decades. During this time, "Budd" played with such other jazz greats as Lionel Hampton, Louis Armstrong, John Coltrane, Duke Ellington, Lester Young, Charlie Parker, Count Basie, Earl "Fatha" Hines, Benny Goodman, Miles Davis, Dizzy Gillespie, Quincy Jones and Al Sears.

In addition, Budd pioneered the early days of Bop by organizing and arranging for several important small groups. He acted as the musical director for Billy Eckstine's Orchestra and also arranged for Woody Herman, Buddy Rich and Atlantic Records. "Budd" played the Newport Jazz Festival and every major festival around the world, receiving many honors and awards. He was a visiting professor at Queens and York Colleges.

While pursuing his musical career, "Budd" met and married Bernice Milbrey. One son, Albert Jackson Johnson IV, was born of this loving union.

On Saturday, October 20, 1984, Albert "Budd" Johnson passed away while on a nostalgic return to his musical beginnings. He leaves to mourn a wife, Bernice; a son, Albert; a grandson, Tchaka; a granddaughter, Kim; a sister, Ruth and a host of other loving relatives and friends.

(more)

THE NEW YORK TIMES, TUESDAY, OCTOBER 23, 1984

Budd Johnson, 73;
A Jazz Saxophonist
From Swing to Bop

By JOHN S. WILSON

Budd Johnson, a versatile saxophonist and arranger who was a catalytic figure in the movement of jazz from swing to be-bop during the 1930's and 40's, died of a heart attack on Saturday in Kansas City, Mo. He was 73 years old.

Mr. Johnson, who lived in Hempstead, L.I., was in Kansas City for a performance.

The career of Mr. Johnson, who was born Albert Johnson in Dallas on Dec. 14, 1910, spanned 60 years, starting in 1924 when he was the drummer in a teen-age band. He soon switched to saxophone and in 1933 was leading a group jointly with the pianist Teddy Wilson when they both joined Louis Armstrong's Orchestra.

The following year he joined the Earl Hines Orchestra and for the next eight years he was Mr. Hines' musical director. He brought the then little-known be-bop musicians Dizzy Gillespie and Charlie Parker into the Hines band in 1942.

Arranger for Big Bands

He wrote arrangements for the early bop-oriented big bands led by Billy Eckstine, Boyd Raeburn, Woody Herman and Mr. Gillespie and in 1944 was a member with Mr. Gillespie of the first be-bop group to play on 52d Street in New York. Shortly later he organized the first be-bop recording date, released under Coleman Hawkins' name on the Apollo label.

In the 1950's and 60's, Mr. Johnson played with the orchestras of Count Basie, Quincy Jones and Benny Goodman and toured the Soviet Union with Mr. Hines. For several years he was co-leader with Oliver Jackson and Bill Pemberton of the JPJ Quartet and was active as a lecturer and conductor of music clinics at colleges.

Mr. Johnson is survived by his wife, Bernice; a son, Albert Jr., of Hempstead; a sister, Ruth Hickman of Dallas, and a grandson. A funeral service will be held on Thursday at 7:30 P.M. at St. Peter's Church, Lexington Avenue at 54th Street.

The *New York Times* obituary for my grandfather, Budd Johnson

Nana and me by the Christmas tree at her apartment in Ravenswood, Queens. I'm like ten years old.

Moms reciting poetry and Pops playing a drum in the park in 1971

Pops was the baddest muthafucker I ever knew. Check out his gangsta lean in 1977.

Moms onstage with the Crystals on a British television show, 1964

Me on my brother Greg's lap at Washington Square Park on the day of Moms's graduation from NYU, 1976

THE CRYSTALS (1960'S)

To my chaka I love you, Mom

FEATURING LEFT TO RIGHT: LALA, BARBARA, FRANCES AND DEEDEE

Me on Pops's lap with Moms and Greg at Flushing Meadows Park, Queens, 1977

Pops in federal prison in Georgia. He told me they gave him the nickname "New York" while he was there.

TCHAKA JOHNSON
T.J. your future is coming, but only you can decide where it's going.
Always remember there is no such word as can't.
You may not know how at the moment, but you can
if you want to—and you "will" succeed in all your endeavors
Love always, Your Family

Age eight, dressed like Michael Jackson
at Grandmoms's dance school. Jay-Z
tried to dis me at Summer Jam 2001
by showing this photo and calling me a
ballerina during "Takeover," but I was just
trying to look like Mike.

Rockin' Adidas in
Grandmoms's dance
concert program

LORD TEE / The Golden Child

Lord Tee is a fifteen year old student at the H.S. of Art and Design,
N.Y.C.. He has been rapping since he was eleven years old and it's
one of his favorite things to do along with drawing, designing T
shirts and attempting to expand his cultural and social self. He
writes and produces his own Rap material.

Lord Tee is the grandson of Jazz great Budd Johnson(saxophonist and
arranger) and legendary dance teacher, Bernice Johnson. His parents
were both doo wop singers in the sixties. His father sang with The
Chanters and his mother sang with The Crystals.

Lord Tee's D.J. is childhood friend Chosen One (Shaun Rodriguez) who
has D.J.'ed private parties for years.

Management: Fatima Johnson
(212)306-2876

Carey and me at Shirt Kings in
the Coliseum Mall, Jamaica, Queens,
at the end of the summer in 1989.
Every finger on my right hand had a gold
ring. I thought I was Slick Rick.

Original bio my moms made for me

Original Jive Records
demo deal

Havoc and me in the lunchroom at
Art and Design High School. Taken the day
after I broke my hand on a kid's forehead
while robbing him for his Polo jacket

prodigy

havoc

POETICAL PROPHETS
contact: fatima j. management   (201) 435-6872

Havoc and me, Poetical Prophets

Fake ID from the 42nd Street ID spot.
I was still fifteen in this photo,
getting into clubs when I was
way too young.

Me with the Gucci link at
the end of my first year of
high school while visiting
Pops in California

Carey, his friend Ali, and me
on 125th Street in Harlem on
Thanksgiving. I'm seventeen.

Havoc and me around the time we signed with
4th & Broadway/Island Records in Soho, NYC, 1993

The Twins outside a hotel
room in Virginia after a show
promoting *The Infamous* album

Mobb Deep, Nas, and Raekwon after recording "Eye for an Eye (Your Beef Is Mines)" at Platinum Island Studio in Manhattan, 1995

Mobb Deep and Biggie Smalls in a locker room backstage during the Big Mack tour, 1995

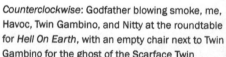

Clockwise, from left: Miller Don, Money No, me, unknown, Twin Gambino, Nitty, Riley a.k.a. Dark Brother, Scarface Twin, and KiKo outside the venue in Philadelphia

Counterclockwise: Godfather blowing smoke, me, Havoc, Twin Gambino, and Nitty at the roundtable for *Hell On Earth*, with an empty chair next to Twin Gambino for the ghost of the Scarface Twin

Me in the backyard of the Pomona crib in Rockland County—
five bedrooms, three-car garage, and two acres of land

From left: Nitty, Killer Black, Twin, and me at Loud Records in the lounge area, 1996, right before *Hell on Earth* dropped

Counterclockwise, from right: Me, Noyd, Derrick, and Gotti at a late-night pit stop at the Waffle House in North Carolina during the *Amerikaz Nightmare* tour

Murda Muzik DVD cover, the first movie I made, shot on 16mm film

The Queensbridge crew at the Tunnel on the Sunday that Fakey came home (*counter-clockwise from left*): Godfather, Fakey in the fisherman's hat, Cormega, 40 from Queensbridge, Money No, Twin, Mr. Buttface, Stobo in the shades, Mr. Chalice, me, and Rueben

At the Tunnel during the *Hell on Earth* era in 1996 (*clockwise, from far left*): Money No, me, Karate Joe, Havoc, Godfather, the Twins, Ice, Ahmed from Brooklyn (*with braids*), and Nitty (*with his head down in front of me*)

Alchemist and Havoc during the "Keep it Thoro" video shoot in Queensbridge

Mobb Deep with Cash Money's Baby and B.G.

Mobb Deep signing Jive deal with Jive president Barry Weiss (*behind me*), the Jive staff, Londell McMillan (*bottom left*) and Chris Lighty (*bottom right*). You can see from my facial expression that it was hard for me to sign that deal—I wanted to stay independent.

Left: On the ice throne for an *H.N.I.C.* ad. *Right:* Illa Ghee and me in the Apollo basement at Justo's Mixtape Awards celebrating just after he came home from jail in 2003

Mobb Deep backstage with Cormega at BB King Blues Club in NYC during my last show before turning myself in for my prison bid

50 Cent and me on the couch at *106 & Park* when 50's *Curtis* album dropped. They told 50 not to bring anyone along but he said, "Fuck that, come up there with me."

Tony Yayo, me, 50, and 40 Glocc
in the G-Unit office in 2006

Havoc and me on
a visit at Mid-State
Correctional Facility

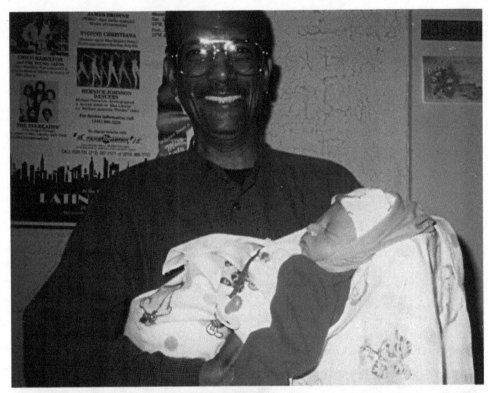

Pops happily holding Shaka,
the first and last time he'd
see his grandson

Shaka and Tasia at Shaka's graduation in
Rockland County

After an *H.N.I.C.* promo tour throughout the Tri-State Area and down the East Coast, in October 2001 I took a bunch of my boys to Puffy's restaurant Justin's on Twenty-first Street in Manhattan, down the block from Soundtrack Studios. Drinking champagne while checking out the scene, the rapper Queen Pen spotted me and asked me to dance. More the type to lurk in the cut watching my surroundings, I wasn't big on dancing, but for Queen Pen I made an exception. While we were grindin' on each other, she started sucking and tongue-kissing my ear. I was a bit shocked. We'd done a song together a year or two earlier and it was strictly professional. After she molested my ear, the DJ made an announcement. "Big shout out to Jay-Z and Jermaine Dupri up in the spot. I see ya'll!"

I walked over to my people. "Where's Jay-Z?" I asked, surveying the shadows of Justin's. "I don't see him." So we lined the front door of Justin's on both sides. We weren't going to let Jay-Z leave without dealing with us first. "P, we're gonna beat the lips off Jay's face as soon as we see him," Godfather, Nitty, and Nitty's cousin Kiko all assured me. Kiko had a gun and he wanted to shoot Jay.

"No! It's not that serious," I said. "We're just gonna beat him up. Don't pull that gun out." Through the crowd, I saw Jay and Jermaine walking with three bodyguards toward us. Jermaine Dupri was aware of my beef with Jay and visibly shook, started speed-walking with his bodyguard when he saw me. He quickly hightailed it out the door. Jay-Z spotted us lined up at the door waiting for him. Then from about two yards away, he extended his hand to shake mine.

"It ain't no beef," Jay said. "It's just music, man. No drama."

"Oh yeah?" I said, shaking his hand.

"I just wish you would've spoken to me before you said those things about me in *The Source*," he said. "But it ain't no beef, all right?"

"Yeah, okay, cool," I said, and let him walk out of the club. Keep in mind that I *let* him walk out. Queen Pen is my witness. I could have changed Jay's future that night, but I chose not to. Jay put up the white flag and his cop-out made me instantly realize that he wasn't a threat. He's just a big ol' stuffed animal, a camel to be exact. I got serious beef with real gangsters. Jay's just a waste of my time.

•   •   •

A few days later I heard that Mike Delorean and his boys from QB had broken into Havoc's crib and stole his sampler, keyboard, PlayStation, and even a framed portrait of Havoc hanging in the living room that Hav later found under the porch. Then they walked around Queensbridge asking people if they wanted to buy Hav's stuff. How stupid could you be?

A week after the break-in, I saw Delorean sitting in a brand-new black Excursion. "I traded in the blue Benz you gave me for this," he told me. I asked him if it was an even trade. "No," he said. "I still owe fifteen thousand." The blue Benz—with a TV inside and twenty-inch rims—that I gave them as a signing advance was totally paid for. Then I looked at his neck and saw that the Infamous Records chain I got him with Ron Artest's investment money was missing. "I sold the chain 'cause I had to put money down to get the truck," he said.

"So, you sold the chain and the Benz to get a truck that you can't afford and you robbed Havoc's crib?" I said. "What's wrong with you, man? You just fucked everything up for us."

I severed my ties with Bars'N'Hooks. How stupid could you be?

At the end of 2001, I received my certified-gold-album plaque for *H.N.I.C.* Havoc only produced two songs on *H.N.I.C.* but not because I only wanted two beats. I was forced to find other producers because Havoc wasn't showing any excitement or enthusiasm about my solo project. I wish Hav would've done my whole album.

Shortly after I got my gold plaque, Bags and I went to check Havoc in Freeport. After the break-in, Hav's uncle Lameik gave Havoc two pit bulls, Black and Blaze, that ran loose in the yard and barked at all who passed by, especially mailmen and delivery people. We walked up to the gate surrounding the house and the dogs went bananas as if they wanted to kill Bags. They looked crazy, hate and fury filled their faces, barking like never before. Bags couldn't come inside the gate because I couldn't control them, and when Havoc came out, he couldn't either. Hav had never met Bags before so he came to my truck and made small talk. We were in the area and I wanted to introduce them.

Bags and I drove back to Queens. Parked in front of Majesty's crib in Hollis, we sat in Bags's Navigator and played PlayStation for a while. "I'm gonna come get you early tomorrow so we can start working on a mix CD together," I said.

"Cool," he said. "Call me when you get up." I hopped out of the Navi and into my truck and went home early for a change.

The next morning, I called Bags around eleven to see if he was up and ready. Somebody else picked up his phone.

"E?" I asked, confused.

"No, this isn't E. Who is this?"

"It's P, let me talk to Bags."

"This is Detective [Can't Remember]. You'll hear about what happened to E soon." I hung up quick. *Oh shit, did they kill Bags like Green Eyes said?* I wondered. *No, maybe he got locked up for something.* I couldn't reach Majesty on his phone, so I went to his crib later that evening.

Majesty and a few others were sitting on the steps at his front door with a big bottle of Hennessy and plastic cups. Maj explained that his family was having a cookout earlier that day in his backyard. Bags had parked his new Navigator next to the house as usual and they took a smoke break in the Navi because they didn't want to burn the weed in front of the kids in the yard. Maj ran back to the house to get a plate of food before it was all gone, and while he was filling up his plate, four masked gunmen ran up on the Navigator from behind and opened fire. Bags's truck and body were riddled with bullets. Stray bullets went flying through Majesty's house and almost hit the little kids in the yard. Bags died with his gun in his hand. He must've seen them coming but it was too late.

I didn't want to cry, but it was hard not to. I couldn't control it.

"P, I wanna show you something," Majesty said. He went into the house and came back with an eighty-page spiral notebook and handed it to me.

"What's this?" I asked.

"It's one of Tupac's notebooks," he said. "He left it here when he used to hang with my brother. You need to read that." I opened it and saw Pac's notes and poems, plans, scribble-scrabble, and chicken scratch. It was amazing to have Tupac's notebook in my hands. "I wanted you to see this 'cause you need to know how similar ya'll niggas is," Maj said, pointing out pages outlining Pac's plan to unite OGs, community leaders, rappers, and street hustlers from every hood across America to help create more positive and peaceful communities. He had it all mapped out.

Reading his notebook gave me a newfound respect for Tupac. I knew about Pac's Black Panther and activist upbringing, but now I got a glimpse of the real him. Tupac envisioned similar plans for everything that I used to speak with E-Money Bags and Majesty about, but his plan was more precise and made more sense. When I was done reading, I was at a loss for words.

Looking at Maj, I felt pain for him. He lost his brother Stretch, who was murdered in Hollis in the late '90s right after Tupac was killed. Somebody shot up his MPV minivan and Stretch crashed into a tree. And now he lost his best friend, Bags. On the way home, I thought about how Hav's dogs went crazy when they saw Bags the day before. *Could it be they sensed something? Maybe E had an eerie energy that the dogs could feel.* R.I.P., my nigga.

After Bags got killed, I was upset but had to stay focused. I had a beautiful woman and kids, money, cars, jewelry, fashion, fame, power—and since I wasn't abusing drugs and alcohol, I had my health. I felt unstoppable.

I finally learned how to defeat my sickle-cell pain and was living proof that sickle-cell could be controlled with a proper diet and healthy lifestyle. It took a lot of discipline and self-control but I was now living pain free. It felt like a natural high. Anybody who experienced the destructive lifestyle I'd been living and then made that 360 change will know exactly what I mean.

I called Queen Pen and asked her to play a part in my *Murda Muzik* movie. During a scene where she got out of a Range Rover and pistol-whipped a dude for selling drugs on her block, Queen Pen stepped onto the curb the wrong way in her high-heeled shoes and broke her ankle. In show business there's a saying, "Break a leg." Queen Pen must have taken that shit seriously. Ha! Just kidding, Q.P. The foul part was, we didn't even use the scenes that she broke her foot filming.

Half of the movie was complete when my director, Larry, pulled some bullshit. Our verbal agreement was that I would play a small part in his film *Statistic* and in return he would help direct and film *Murda Muzik* for 5 percent of the profit. My lawyer drafted a contract for Larry to sign and we met in

Manhattan to look over the agreement. Larry took the contract for his lawyer to check out and suddenly stopped picking up my phone calls for several weeks, which turned into months after I had already spent about three hundred thousand dollars of my own money on the project.

"I deserve more money and credit than this!" Larry insisted when he finally got back to me. He said if he didn't get what he wanted, he wouldn't finish filming, and he had all the film that we'd shot. It turned into a big legal battle. I felt like kicking myself in the ass, not to mention Larry.

The movie was delayed for a year and I was so furious with Larry, and more so with myself, that I became self-destructive. Three hundred thousand of my own money and this dude was refusing to finish filming and withholding my film reels until I agreed to his terms or at least came close. I asked Hav for a cigarette. That was the beginning of my downward spiral, into the old poisonous lifestyle that took me so long to shake.

At around one A.M., I went to my bedroom, turned my stereo to the *Quiet Storm* radio show on WBLS—old-school R&B slow jams—and turned off the lights. The only light in my room was the dim glow from the stereo-system equalizer and tuner. As I lay relaxing to the old-school sounds, I saw a black, shadowlike figure walk across my room. It looked like the black Spider-Man— no face, no features, ghostlike, all black. Scared, I pulled the sheet over my head and forced myself to sleep.

When I couldn't control the way the film was going, I lost my mind. It seemed like that shadow was all the negativity that I had flushed out of my mind, body, and soul just waiting for an opportunity to jump back inside me. And it did. The next morning, I woke up with sickle-cell pain. That one cigarette turned into packs and that occasional drink turned into bottles of Hennessy and more weed than a Western town. The evil, nasty, disrespectful bastard was officially back in full swing.

CHAPTER 9

I'm a young rich ass nigga who love to

show you how a nigga get his lights blew

teach you the mystery of God and murk you

"Pray for Me"

After recording a bunch of new music, Havoc and I got Loud Records to open a new budget for our next album in March 2002. KiKi came up with the title. Relaxing at home in Rockland, she was flipping through the dictionary and told me, "Ya'll should name the next album *Infamy*!" I knew it was the perfect name and when I told Havoc, he agreed.

All the drinking and cigarette and weed smoking that I started doing again I hid from KiKi. She had cleaned her body of all that poison along with me, and I didn't want her to start back up just because I had. Plus I was embarrassed. I wanted her to be proud of me. If she found out, she'd have been disgusted. But my sickle-cell pain started to surface every now and then so she probably knew something wasn't right.

Havoc made this beat in the crib one day that reminded me of "Quiet Storm" because of the house-music-style drum pattern. Hav didn't like it, but luckily I was there before he had a chance to erase it. "This is another 'Quiet Storm,' son!" I said. "The drums are similar."

"Yeah, I know, but it ain't all that," he said.

"Give me an hour to write to the beat and I bet you'll change your mind," I said.

One hour later we had "Hey Luv (Anything)." Although the beat reminded me of "Quiet Storm," this guitar-riff sample over the drums and bass line reminded me of romancing a woman while her man was close by so I had to whisper in her ear on the down low. When Hav heard my verse, he followed suit and wrote a similar verse minus the talking-in-her-ear thing. Now all we needed was an R&B chorus. We decided to try to get Puffy's group 112, ran the rough version by Chris Lighty, and he agreed to get them for us. 112 listened to our lyrics and came up with the perfect chorus. We were done with the bulk of the album, played it for Steve Rifkind, and he set up the photo shoot for the album artwork plus a video shoot for the 112 single.

A few days later we came up with a new song that was more hood, with an up-tempo beat that sounded like some Beach Boys surfer hip-hop. We put Noyd on it and called it "Burn." Havoc had the idea to feature the female rapper Vida on the chorus. Vida had just signed to Irv Gotti and Ja Rule's label Murder Inc., so I was surprised she agreed. It was so hot we stopped the presses on "Hey Luv" and put out "Burn" first. We wanted to satisfy our core audience, and "Hey Luv" had a crossover radio sound. Loud agreed. "Hey Luv" targeted a female audience even though the lyrics were still hood— especially my verse, because I'm talking about robbing a dude's woman. If that ain't grimy then what is?

This was our first album since the Jay-Z vs. Prodigy beef, so people were waiting to see how we, and especially I, would retaliate. They heard me dissing Jay on mix CDs after Summer Jam, but this was the new Infamous Mobb Deep album, so people wanted to see what was going to happen. Jay-Z told me, "It ain't no beef; it's just music." So I gave Jay some "Just Music" to listen to on "Burn." *"Just pain, just sufferin', and worse than that, you let me get my hands on you so I'm takin' advantage, and that shit that you pulled ain't do me no damage, you don't know me, but we 'bout to change that shit. . . . "*

We leaked the song to Funkmaster Flex, who played it on Hot 97, and DJs across the country started doing the same. Mobb Deep was back once again. A lot of people thought Jay-Z ruined my and Mobb Deep's career, but there's no evidence of that. We were still in our own position of power, as was Jay. Jay just made it look better because he had so much money from Roc-A-Fella Records and he was selling more albums than us. But we weren't selling any less than our past albums. Jay must have been pissed that radio was playing our dis record because Vida backed out of the video shoot. Well, when Vida had come to the studio to record her part on the song, I had kicked it with her and got her phone number. So I called and asked her what happened.

"P, you know I love ya'll and I want to do the video," Vida said. "But Jay called Irv and told him not to let me do the video. Irv said I couldn't do it. I'm mad as hell because it would be good exposure."

"It's all good, love," I told Vida. "Too bad though." Wow. *Wow.* What was Jay so worried about that he had to tell Irv Gotti *"Don't let her do that video"*? Oh well.

A thought struck me after I got off the phone with Vida. *Oh shit, that's how he got it!* I said to myself. When Vida told me that Jay-Z called Irv Gotti like a little girl, it hit me that Ashanti must have showed Irv my grandmother's concert program book with my Michael Jackson picture in it. Irv must have given it to Jay-Z. Irv Gotti probably didn't like me because of E-Money Bags and didn't let Vida do our video. Ha! Two bird-ass bitch boys. Jay-Z and Irv Gotti. I laughed thinking about them plotting with that picture like they had some information to destroy me. Ha!

Scott Storch produced the last three songs for our album. Scott was a ghost producer for Dr. Dre, meaning Scott made the beats but Dr. Dre took the credit, Scott told me in the studio. When a big-time producer like Dre takes a young, up-and-coming producer under his wing, the big-time producer lets the young one learn a lot of his tricks and helps the young one get his beats out there. The young producer usually gets little to no production credit, but after a while he may become as big as his mentor. Scott Storch became the hot new shit on the scene when people discovered he'd been making most of Dre's bangers.

We were the first to grab Scott, buy tracks, and give him full credit. On *Infamy* he produced "I Won't Fall," plus "Kill or Be Killed" featuring Ronald Isley from the Isley Brothers. I wrote the bridge for Ron Isley to sing. Let me tell you, Ron Isley was a player for real. He came through the studio with two fly young ladies who were singers. Ron and the ladies sang the bridge together. I was open. *I wrote R&B lyrics for Ron Isley.*

At the very last minute, Havoc got in touch with R&B singer Lil' Mo and they made a song called "Pray for Me." When they played it for me, Havoc did this new style of rapping where he was cutting words in half, like "in-fa-mous" and "mur-da," pausing between syllables. It was unique—nobody had ever rapped like that before. Hav left the first sixteen bars open for me and I copied his flow. The album was done.

We received bad news right before we handed in the finished product. Steve Rifkind sold Loud Records to Sony for about eighty million dollars, and Sony dropped most of the Loud artists, keeping only the most profitable. Luckily, we were one of those profitable groups.

So now we were forced to be on Sony Records. Steve had hinted that he was going to do this when *H.N.I.C.* came out. He said, "I'm about to start getting into Southern rap music and I'm not signing New York artists anymore." Steve didn't give us any warning about the sale of the label to Sony, though. He basically used us as a bargaining chip because he knew that if we found out about it, we would have fought to get off Loud—and without Mobb Deep, Steve would have gotten less money from the sale. Sony's not a bad company; it's a major record label, while Loud was just an independent. We were only upset because Sony's a huge company and we were used to being the center of attention at Loud. At Sony, we were little goldfish in an ocean of sharks. We played it smooth and let our album get its numbers, but we were quietly scheming to get off Sony.

For the time being, we had to make sure *Infamy* did well, and it was doing just that. "Burn" created so much hype that we started getting calls for tour dates.

We toured overseas and it always amazed me how much they loved Mobb Deep. Alchemist became our official tour DJ and an honorary Mobb Deep member. On tour we turned the boy Alchemist out—aka the Rare White Vulture or Rare Bird. He learned how to be a vulture quick, because on the road we moved with that old New York–minute mentality with food, alcohol, females, whatever. Move fast or get left out. Alchemist caught on fast.

The new album dropped while we were on tour. We shot the "Hey Luv" featuring 112 video in Atlanta. Little X was the director. The video-production team wanted me to pick my love interest from a pile of models' pictures, but I told them that I was going to use my baby's mother KiKi instead. And why not? She looks just as good as any video model, if not better, and she'd get paid for it. KiKi was open and flew to Atlanta with me. We're kissing in the video and when it came out, people were saying, "Oh shit, P turned into a sucka for love. He's kissing some chick in his new video!" Nah, sorry, that's my woman for real.

People were saying, "Mobb Deep is soft now. They're doing radio love songs." But "Hey Luv" is far from soft. It got more radio spins than "Quiet Storm" and gave us a gang of new female fans. We loved it. The ladies would be lined up in the front row and I'd find the best-looking one and spit my whole verse looking her straight in the eyes. So despite Jay-Z and his fans' attempt to make us look as if we lost a battle with him, *Infamy* sold over eight hundred thousand copies, proving that our power and position hadn't changed.

I must admit that my lyrics had become very lazy and sloppy. I was messing up spiritually and healthwise, back on drugs and alcohol. My decision making was terrible, and it was evident in my music. My mind, body, and soul were clouded and polluted. People who paid close attention to my lyrics were saying, "You're slippin'. You're not rapping the same." And I thought they were crazy. I was arrogant, acting as if whatever I wrote to a beat was hot. I was feeling myself—or playing myself, rather—but I couldn't see it at that time. Even though I put my all into making good songs, my negative behavior was showing up in the form of lyrics that didn't grab people as tightly as they once did. My grip was slipping.

After getting our gold plaque for *Infamy*, we did a concert at the Nassau Coliseum in Long Island. Several other acts were performing that night. Backstage was packed. Walking to the stage, somebody next to me said, "Yo P, what's up?" When I turned to look, it was 50 Cent. I didn't really know 50 but it was good to see him healthy. It took him a while to recover from those nine gunshot wounds in 2000. I gave him a handshake, then got onstage to perform. 50 stood on the side of the stage watching, or should I say scheming, because nobody knew yet that he was about to take the music industry by sheer force.

A week after the concert, Havoc and I met L. Londell McMillan, a young black entertainment attorney from Bed-Stuy, Brooklyn, who had his own firm and several big celebrity clients, including Prince, Stevie Wonder, Michael Jackson, and Spike Lee. He was the lawyer who got rappers the Lox and R&B group Total off Bad Boy Records, so we figured he was the perfect person to get us off Sony.

It took a few months of negotiation, but finally, after eight years of being slaves to record companies, we were free! *Infamy* was damn near platinum and we were free. That's unheard of in this business. You don't let an artist out of a contract whose album's on the verge of going platinum. It gave us power to do anything we wanted.

Londell promoted artist empowerment, and he and I became close. "I want to get a distribution deal and stay independent now that we're free," I told him at his office, seeking his thoughts on how Mobb Deep should proceed. He agreed 100 percent.

"You guys are in an incredible position right now—you all need a distribution deal," Londell said, offering to assist in securing the right deal. "You're going to get five times the amount of money." I was all for it.

Havoc found a fully equipped studio for sale right off the Van Wyck Expressway in Jamaica, Queens, and decided to sell the Freeport house, move into a condo in New Rochelle, and make the new studio our official headquarters. Before selling the Infamous minimansion, our friend, a police officer from the neighborhood, threw a pajama party at his house and invited us. I didn't like the idea of being cool with a cop, but the guy was a big Mobb Deep fan: He gave us a bunch of plastic police PBA cards that saved you from catching tickets. Havoc, Gotti, Poppa Mobb, Free High, Noyd, Fly, and I wore boxers, white tees, and Timberlands to the party. There were ladies with barely anything on all over the house.

As we were getting ready to leave the party a few hours later, Free High was standing next to me in the living room. "I love you, P!" he exclaimed out of nowhere, biting my neck.

"*Yooo!* What the fuck is you doing?" I screamed while his drunken ass laughed. "You're buggin' out, what's wrong with you?" I was ready to punch him but Poppa Mobb calmed me down.

Free High started acting real strange. Poppa Mobb and I were watching TV in Freeport when Free High stopped by, going on and on about his new girlfriend, Lil' Kim's homegirl whom he met in Lil' Kim's hotel room after the Source Awards. He told me how he pistol-whipped the dude who he caught the girl cheating on him with. Havoc told me he'd heard that Free High killed the dude and shot the girl too. It was hard to believe. Then when we were out of town for a show, this old-timer walked up to me while I was walking to a store by the hotel. "Are you Prodigy from Mobb Deep?" the old-timer asked.

"Yeah, what's up?"

"You know this nigga named Free High?"

"Yeah, that's my nigga," I said. "What's up?"

"Yeah," the old-timer said. "That nigga killed my niece. I'm looking for him."

Oh shit. "What? Damn, I ain't seen him in a long time," I said. But I'd just been with Free High two weeks before. I had no idea what to think.

A month or two later, Free High was arrested for making a direct sale to an undercover cop in Queensbridge. At his trial at the courthouse on Queens Boulevard, the judge sentenced Free High to five years. He'd just come home three years earlier after beating the cab-driver murder rap. Free High laughed, grabbed the court officer's gun, and shot at the judge. They tackled him to the floor and the judge hit that fool with all kinds of time. The crew was all at the Freeport crib the morning Free High shot at the judge, watching the story on the NY1 news channel. "What an idiot," we all agreed. Free High's probably never coming home.

Havoc finally sold our house and moved into his new spot in Westchester County. Our new studio in Queens was official, on a nice quiet block. We hung up all our gold and platinum plaques on the control-room and mic-booth walls. Our friend Fly learned how to work Pro Tools and became our engineer. A lot of hits were about to be made.

CHAPTER 10

FREE AGENTS

Sittin' back plottin on ways

How we can get this money, we need us a payday

Dig in my pocket, it's nothin' but change

I dig deeper, but still comin' up with change

So we called our lawyers to fix this shit

He said it's aight, we 'bout to be free agents

Have patience, we can't though, we need paper

"Paid in Full"

Settled into our new studio and freed from being slaves to any record company, we felt refreshed and had a boost of musical energy like never before. We celebrated by recording a mix CD called *Free Agents* to let the entire music industry know we were free to make a new deal.

I didn't want to do another regular record deal and become slaves to somebody else's company after we'd fought so hard to become free. With a regular deal, we'd only be profiting around ninety cents per album sold. With a distribution deal, our profits would be more like four or five dollars per album. But Havoc didn't agree.

"If we go independent, then we won't sell as many albums as we would on a major," he said. His logic was that we would have to do all the promotion, radio, and marketing work ourselves. "I don't want to focus on business, I just want to make music," he said. Some people aren't built for wearing both hats. I told Havoc we were a team and I was capable of being creative as well as handling our business, so I would make sure Mobb Deep was straight on both sides. But he didn't agree and we argued.

My passion was to own and operate my own business. I observed how all the older artists did it—Wu-Tang, Puff, Jay-Z, Master P, Cash Money. Chris Lighty would try to discourage us, saying, "Everybody thinks they can do it like Cash Money Records now. It's not that easy." But it *was* that easy. My grandmother raised me to own and operate, so I was built for it like a brick mansion.

I was angry that Havoc didn't want to take advantage of this stellar opportunity and started to realize the true downside of having a partner—we had to agree or the partnership would collapse. Londell tried to talk sense into Havoc but it didn't work.

"Look, why don't we just keep Mobb Deep on a major label and put out solo albums independently?" Havoc said. "People are used to seeing our product pushed by a major machine. If we do it ourselves now, it's gonna make us look small and ruin our reputation." Havoc had a point and I decided to go with his plan. The songs we recorded for *Free Agents* were some of our best, and it ate me up inside that we were going to let somebody else live lavishly off our hard work and talent. But for the love of Mobb Deep and Havoc, I kept my mouth shut.

It took two months to complete *Free Agents*. 50 Cent was going hard to get back in the game and get signed again, releasing a bunch of mix CDs, including *Guess Who's Back* through Bob Perry at Landspeed Records. We set up a meeting with Bob Perry, who ran Landspeed, a small but successful label. Havoc called 50 to record some songs with us right before our meeting with Bob. Havoc, Noyd, and 50 did a song called "Bump That" that I used for the *Murda Muzik* movie sound track. Havoc and 50 did another song called "Pop Those Things" that I had a verse on—we put it on the side because it was so hot we wanted to save it.

We explained our plan for the project to Bob. We wanted a healthy six figures up front for *Free Agents*, didn't want our faces on the album cover or any advertisement for the project—no radio, videos, or interviews; we just wanted the industry to know we were free. Bob agreed to the terms, and we put it in contracts and signed a deal to get 50 percent of all profits.

Right before *Free Agents* dropped, KiKi and I were at the supermarket when I got a call from the Violator Management office. "I have 50 Cent on the phone for you," Chris Lighty's assistant said. 50 got on the line.

"What up, P?" he said. "I heard ya'll are doing a deal with Bob Perry at Landspeed. I'm calling to let you know that I don't think you should do the deal because if Bob fucks up the project it's going to make Mobb Deep look bad. You guys are in a great position right now to do something big." I fully agreed with 50 and wanted to tell him how I really felt about being independent, but Havoc and I had already come to a compromise. I couldn't explain it all to 50 because that would show a sign of weakness, as if Mobb Deep didn't have our business or partnership in order.

"Yeah, we already did the deal," I told him. "It's all good, it's just a mix CD to let the industry know we're taking meetings for a new deal. The way we structured the deal with Bob, we can't lose."

That was my first real conversation with 50. Chris Lighty was managing him, he had a tremendous buzz, and he'd been going hard at Ja Rule, Murder Inc., and Supreme. 50 was just as cool as E-Money Bags told me. Hearing the fire in his voice on his mix CDs, I could tell he was about to blow up huge.

A couple weeks later, *Free Agents* was released and sold four hundred thousand copies, quicker than expected. Calls started coming from Universal, Warner Bros., Jive, and others. A few years earlier Dr. Dre had signed this new white rapper named Eminem, who'd become the biggest-selling artist in the game. He made an autobiographical film called *8 Mile* and used two songs from *The Infamous* in the movie, "Shook Ones" and "Survival of the Fittest." We didn't know he was going to be rapping to our beats in the actual film and we were happy as hell. Eminem showed Mobb Deep extra love in his movie and we loved him for it.

Eminem's manager, Paul Rosenberg, started managing Alchemist. I asked Alchemist to pass the word to Paul that we were interested in doing a deal with Eminem's Shady Records. Al said he'd try.

Havoc and I took a meeting with Warner Bros. They offered us a fifty-fifty profit-split deal. Warner Bros. had just signed a new female R&B singer named D'Mello, and the A&R asked if we would do a feature on her first single, "Best Love Story." Soon after we shot the video, we found out that Eminem had just signed 50 Cent to Shady Records. 50 put out his first major hit, "Wanksta." The world was in a 50 Cent frenzy.

Our next meeting was with Universal Records president Kedar Massenburg, who happened to be the nephew of Dr. York, whose books I'd been reading for years. He offered the same fifty-fifty profit deal. Chris Lighty had become the head of Jive's Urban Music Division, so we met with Jive president Barry Weiss, who was interested in giving us the same fifty-fifty split.

Havoc and I discussed the pros and cons and decided to go with Jive, since our manager Chris would be handling our project. After about a month of negotiations, we inked the contract and had a small signing party at the office with the whole Jive staff. In the Jive–Mobb Deep signing photo, I'm the only one not smiling. All that was going through my mind was, *We just signed away our power and our grandkids' power once again.*

We went to work on our new album. I came up with the title *Amerikaz Nightmare* because we were rebellious and against the grain and corporate America fears that.

Londell McMillan helped me complete the deal with my *Murda Muzik* movie director, Larry. I cut Larry a small check and kept all the rights, then we shot the last few scenes and began the long, tedious editing process. I hand-picked every cut, like putting a puzzle together. I edited all day and recorded songs at night. After three weeks, we had a rough version of the film with a score by Alchemist. "I know you're upset with me, but you're going to thank me because I've taught you a lot about the movie business," Larry said. "If you think the music industry is foul, the film industry is way worse. These people are sharks."

The film was finally done—thank the Most High! It took three years and a lot of money to complete: My friends would joke that I must have been making *Titanic*. *Murda Muzik* was shot on 16mm film. Nowadays you can make a good movie using professional-quality digital cameras, but any real moviemaker will tell you that there's nothing like the look that film will give you.

I started shopping for a company to release my film. The first meeting I took was with Lionsgate, but I wanted more offers. There was a black film festival in Acapulco, Mexico, and all-access passes were like eight hundred dollars, but it was worth the bread. I wanted to rub shoulders with others in the film industry. I brought KiKi so we could enjoy Acapulco while we weren't handling business. This was only our second trip together outside the Tri-State Area and our first out of the country. Gotti and my man Derrick from high school took turns watching the kids while we were gone.

When we landed in Acapulco, we rented a Jeep Suzuki drop-top so we could move around town. Driving along the beautiful oceanside, far away from dirty New York buildings, it felt great to be with KiKi.

Most celebrities were staying at the same hotel, so I saw a lot of familiar faces like Mekhi Phifer, Bill Duke, LisaRaye, and Master P and his wife. I attended seminars and learned about film editing, directing, and distribution. On the last night of the festival, I bumped into my cousin Eric Daniels, who had become a writer and producer for Disney movies. Remember when my pops kidnapped me and took me to Detroit? Eric was Pops's cousin Beverly's son; now he was a grown man at the festival with his wife. It was a great surprise to see him.

Biz Markie was DJing at a club across from the hotel, so KiKi and I decided to go. We argued a lot in Mexico over other women, but I promised I would leave all that kind of stuff for her book. KiKi and I had another argument at the Biz Mark party and went back to our room to have angry, drunk sex.

The next morning we flew back to New York, back to the normal hustle. Jive pressed up our "Gangsta Roll" singles to get the buzz going for *Amerikaz Nightmare*. We had a hot song with 50 Cent called "Pop Those Things" in the stash but I told Havoc it wasn't a good idea to put it on our album. 50 was too hot at the time and I wanted to avoid anyone saying, "Oh, Mobb Deep is only hot now because of 50." I already had a 50 Cent collaboration on the *Murda Muzik* sound track called "Bump That." DJs only played

50's verse from "Bump That" on the radio then would switch to another 50 song, like our verses didn't even matter. Wow. That didn't feel good. It made me want to go hunt for the DJs who did that.

50 would make new songs out of other rappers' and R&B singers' tracks. This had a lot of rappers upset because 50 would turn their singles into his singles. Havoc and I decided to do what 50 was doing, taking his "Magic Stick" beat and making our own version called "Matic Clips," about guns instead of sex. It worked.

Ja Rule from Murder Inc. was upset that 50 was dissing him on his "Wanksta" single. The whole song was clowning him, so Ja retaliated by making a song called "New York." I'm not a Ja Rule fan. He was always corny to me. Plus my man E-Money Bags didn't like his whole Murder Inc. and Supreme Team crew, so Ja Rule was the enemy.

"Ja Rule is shooting his video today and he wants us to be in it," Havoc said in the studio one day.

"So what," I said, looking at Hav, puzzled. "Fuck Ja Rule. I don't want to be in that nigga's video."

"Come on, I'm going," Hav said. "Come with me."

"Nah, I'm good. Fuck Ja and his video."

"You ain't gotta be in it if you don't want to," Hav said. "Just come with me so I ain't gotta go by myself. There's gonna be mad bitches there."

"Okay, I'll meet you over there," I said, though I had no intentions of showing up. "Send me the location."

That night I went to Alchemist's crib in Manhattan to bring him a copy of the *Murda Muzik* movie. I'd started bringing my camcorder everywhere and filmed us in Alchemist's apartment working on a song for his album called "Hold You Down." Alchemist's brother Neil had 50 Cent's DVD *The New Breed*, so we watched 50's DVD and *Murda Muzik* and smoked a few blunts.

At our Queens studio the following day, Havoc was mad that I stood him up, telling me that I missed out on seeing all the females and rappers that were in Ja's "New York" video featuring Fat Joe and Jadakiss. *So what*, I said to myself. *I don't give a fuck who was there.* All I cared about was Mobb Deep and *Amerikaz Nightmare*. We proceeded to work on the album. Fuck everybody else, especially Irv Gotti and Ja Rule.

CHAPTER 11

AMERIKAZ NIGHTMARE

P, yeah you heard of him, big ignorant chains and sports cars

Gallons of Bacardi, bent at the awards

I need a bitch like Christina Aguiler-y for a broad

I know I can splack that, she dyin' for a thug

And she heard of me, she know about my Infamous life

Shootouts in New York with various types

Fast money, faster guns, we party every night

"When U Hear The"

Alchemist played a new beat for me at his crib as we were putting the finishing touches on *Amerikaz Nightmare*. He sampled the eighties hit "She Blinded Me with Science," transforming it into a hard-core club banger. The beat was so hot that we played it for Havoc and immediately wrote a song called "Got It Twisted" to add to the album at the last minute. We always came up with the hottest songs for our albums at the last minute.

As soon as Chris Lighty and Jive heard "Got It Twisted," they wanted to shoot a video and use it as the official first single. Jive wasted no time. Director Benny Boom shot the video in Los Angeles. When the video came out, we got a call to do a small tour in Europe, including a festival in Sweden with all rock'n'roll acts: Mobb Deep and Busta Rhymes were the only rappers. Havoc and I released a mix CD, *The West Coast Mixtape* hosted by DJ Big Mike, featuring us rapping over Tupac, Snoop Dogg, Mack 10, Ice Cube, Suga Free, and other West Coast rappers' tracks.

As soon as we arrived at the hotel in Sweden, swarms of kids were waiting for us. Alchemist and I went for a stroll to check out the scene. Two little blond kids, no more than eight years old, walked up and started rapping. I didn't realize it at first but when I listened, I realized they were reciting my rhymes from the West Coast mix CD that we released no more than a week before.

"Yo, do you hear what they're saying?" Alchemist said. "That's from the West Coast CD!"

"Yeah, I know!"

"How do you know those lyrics, shorty?" Alchemist asked.

"My brother got it off the Internet," one of them said. "Do you want to meet my brother and his friends? They've got a lot of girls they can hook you up with."

We laughed and told him to get his brother. That was the first time I realized the power of the Internet. Within a week, this little eight-year-old Swedish kid knew a verse, by heart, word for word, that I'd just written and recorded. It was amazing.

Seeing the people in Sweden for the first time was also amazing—nothing but blond-haired, blue-eyed females all over the place. Five minutes later, the two little kids came back with a crew of dudes in their early twenties. When they saw Alchemist and me, they started excitedly repeating more of my lyrics and some rhymes of their own. We posed for pictures with them on their camera phones, then Alchemist and I walked around to check out more of Sweden.

At around eleven that night, we took the stage after Busta Rhymes. An hour into our performance, I saw something unbelievable. The sun started shining and it slowly became daytime all over again shortly after midnight! From midnight until eight o'clock the next night, there was full sunshine. I felt disoriented like I was on drugs.

In the hotel lobby after the show, Alchemist and I saw the two little kids again. It was two A.M. but the sun was shining bright.

"Hey, do you want to see something crazy?" the chubbier blond kid asked.

"What?" I asked. *I guess these kids' parents let them stay out because it still looks like day time.* "And what are ya'll still doing out?" They ignored the question and led us into the hotel business lounge, where there were complimentary computers and faxes for guests.

"Watch this," the skinnier blond kid said as he started quickly typing on a computer keyboard. Suddenly, the power went out throughout the entire hotel. *Yo! This little bastard's some type of computer hacker!*

"I just shut them down, *ha ha!*" he said, laughing. "It will take them a long time to figure out what happened."

"Ya'll some li'l troublemaking muthafuckers, huh?" I said. "Let's get out of here before we get blamed for this."

"I'm going to hire you guys to be our Swedish street team," Alchemist told the kids, taking their phone numbers in the lobby. They were happy.

After Sweden we toured Switzerland, Norway, and Poland, and our last stop was Amsterdam, Holland, home of the world-famous Red Light District and legal marijuana. I filmed everything on camcorder for our *Infamous Allegiance* DVD. Walking through the Red Light District, Derrick, our man from high school, was filming all the prostitutes in their windows, who closed the curtains when they saw the camera. One prostitute saw Derrick filming and ran out of the glass door trying to hit Derrick, calling him "nigger." Ha!

•   •   •

Back in New York, I went to the Violator Management office while making my usual rounds in Manhattan. 50 Cent arrived five minutes later and Busta Rhymes was also there; we kicked it for a few minutes. Mona Scott, one of Chris Lighty's partners, called me into her office and asked me to consider costarring in a straight-to-DVD film called *Full Clip* along with Busta Rhymes, Xzibit, Bobb'e J. Thompson, and Tiny Lister, better known as Deebo from the movie *Friday*.

The script was basically a rewrite of *Bucktown*, the old seventies film starring Fred Williamson, of whom I was a big fan, so I signed on to the project. Filming would begin in a few months, so I had time to memorize my lines.

50 Cent's *Get Rich or Die Tryin'* debut studio album was selling like crack, over ten million copies. He became the biggest-selling rap artist next to Eminem and Nelly from St. Louis. Atlanta rappers were also on the rise. OutKast had sold millions of albums, T.I. was on the come-up, while Ludacris and Lil Jon were popular across the country at that time because they offered a new energy.

50 took full advantage of how hot he was by hooking up with Jay-Z, who plugged him in with Reebok to create a G-Unit sneaker. 50 also started a label imprint, G-Unit Records, signed West Coast rapper the Game, and planned to release a G-Unit crew album with his artists Lloyd Banks, Tony Yayo, and Young Buck. He created G-Unit Clothing with Marc Ecko. He was doing all the things that we should have done as soon as we became famous, except we were too young and foolish. In life, you have a small window to take advantage of opportunities, and if you're slow to move, the window will close.

But Havoc and I are a rare breed. Our position as the Most Infamous is permanent, and Mobb Deep will forever be hot no matter what. All we have to do is do what we do. We pay close attention to the music industry but we don't get caught up about anybody's success. Be yourself to the best of your ability and your possibilities will be infinite.

I finally released the *Murda Muzik* DVD through Koch Films. It felt like a huge mission accomplished to see it on shelves. My *Titanic* was on the market.

•   •   •

Havoc and I had a huge album-release party on the night that *Amerikaz Nightmare* was released. Hundreds of people were lined up outside because the spot was at capacity and the fire department threatened to shut us down. The Game, the Lox, Black Thought from the Roots, Treach from Naughty by Nature, Raekwon from Wu-Tang, M.O.P, and many actors, comedians, and rappers showed up. There was a freestyle cipher onstage before our special performance. We were popping so much champagne and Hennessy that when it was time to perform, I was twisted. When "Survival of the Fittest" came on, I spit the lyrics for "Shook Ones." Ron Artest was onstage with us and Havoc was looking at me like I was crazy. Despite that error, the turnout confirmed that the world was still hungry for that Mobb Deep sound.

Jadakiss, Styles P, and Sheek Louch from the Lox squeezed through VIP after the show to show us love. It was extremely crowded, so Havoc and I stood on the couch to get some breathing room. Havoc spotted a video vixen he used to mess with named Erica, a good-looking Latina female who rode in the passenger seat of Fabolous's GT Bentley in his "Breathe" video. Hav pulled her onto the couch where we were standing when he spotted another one of his chicks.

"Keep an eye on Erica," he told me as he headed toward the other woman.

"Okay, cool," I said. Erica was just as twisted as I was. Havoc was gone for a long time so I grabbed her in front of me, my arms wrapped around her waist, my hands at the front of her black cocktail dress.

"What's really good, ma?" I whispered in her ear.

"Whatever," she said. I put my hand up the front of her dress and started fingering her right there on the couch in front of everybody. She had no panties on.

"You coming with me," I said. "Let's go."

"Cool, I'm with you," she said. I took her hand and led her to the exit. As we were walking to the parking lot, Havoc rolled up in his G-Wagen Benz. "Erica! Get over here!" he shouted.

"Chill, son! We'll see you later on!" I yelled, but Havoc demanded that she get into his truck. Erica let go of my hand and bounced with Havoc. Wow, the vultures were out that night.

I took my ass home and went to sleep. I know KiKi's reading this, saying, "Ahhh, good for you!"

After a couple of months of preparing and rehearsing my lines, I flew to Los Angeles to film *Full Clip* with Busta Rhymes, Xzibit, and Tiny Lister. The production people set me up in a room at Le Meridien in West Hollywood for two weeks. I played an ex-marine sniper called into town by Xzibit, who also played an ex-marine, to take over a small town alongside Tiny Lister and Busta Rhymes's hype man Spliff Star. I learned a lot from an on-set acting coach as well as Tiny Lister, who schooled me on inside information about Hollywood.

The entire movie, which was very low budget, was shot in an old hotel in downtown Los Angeles, with tons of homeless people in makeshift tents and cardboard refrigerator boxes on the sidewalk. On set, Tiny flipped out on the production crew if they made him wait more than five minutes to shoot his parts. He acted just like Deebo from *Friday*.

"That's how you gotta do these fools, Prodigy," Tiny pulled me to the side and said. "You gotta remind them that you're a professional. Look at them. I bet they won't ever call me out of my trailer again unless they're sure they're ready." And they didn't.

Across the street from the hotel, the production crew rented a parking lot with five trailers for the main actors. Busta Rhymes and Xzibit's trailers were the biggest and most modern, with a queen-sized bed, full bathroom, kitchen, dining area, dressing room, and a living room with TV, stereo, and games. Mine was a small trailer with a three-seater couch, makeup mirror, and bathroom. Spliff Star's was right next to mine. We'd smoke and talk in each other's trailers and became real cool. There's a scene where he and I get into an argument while playing pool and Tiny Lister breaks us up before we start fighting. We had to act serious but kept busting out laughing.

After the first day of filming, I called KiKi. She said she wanted to fly out to spend a week with me. She'd never been to California. The next day on set, I saw this kid Sean, one of the best tap dancers at my grandmother's dance school, whom I hadn't seen since I was thirteen. He'd become an actor and was playing a cop in the movie.

Alchemist and Twin were in town and we were chillin' in Xzibit's trailer after wrapping for the day. Xzibit said he was taking acting seriously and had a lot of scripts coming his way. He'd just gotten a script for another movie called *Gridiron Gang* starring the Rock. Xzibit was our Loud labelmate for years, so we'd hung out on several occasions. He invited us to his crib. Alchemist had somewhere to go, but Twin and I hopped into Xzibit's Hummer to his modern, multilevel house in the hills.

We played video games in the living room and met Xzibit's son and his woman. Busta Rhymes showed up an hour later along with Paul Rosenberg, Alchemist, and Eminem's manager. Xzibit, who was the host of MTV's *Pimp My Ride*, took us into his garage and showed us his '64 Impala lowrider.

The next day, I strolled around the Beverly Center mall with 40 Glocc and his boys, buying white tees and sneakers and checking out ladies. A petite light-skinned female with blond hair, a sun visor, and a tennis skirt so short you could see her panties was going up the escalator. I left the group of twelve dudes I was with and went up behind her. When we got to the top, I asked her name.

"Keyshia," she said. Keyshia was beautiful. While I was typing her number into my phone, 40 Glocc and all the homies walked up. Keyshia got nervous, but then she realized they were with me and calmed down. I called Keyshia as soon as we got back to the room. 40 Glocc kept saying that I should have brought her back with me.

"What's up, it's P. Where you at?"

"On my way back to the studio," Keyshia said. "I've got a session today."

"Do you rap or something? What do you do?" I asked.

"I sing. I'm doing a song for the *Barbershop 2* sound track. You should come hang out with me over here."

"Oh, word? We just did a song for that sound track. I got a group called Mobb Deep."

"Yeah, I know who you are," she said. "Come to my studio session so you can hear my songs."

"Damn, I can't 'cause I'm doing a movie out here and I've gotta breeze by the set soon. Why don't you stop by my hotel so we can kick it before your session?"

"I can't. I'm late. Why don't you stop by before you go to the movie set?" We went back and forth on the phone a few times that day, but that was all.

After the first week of filming, I flew in my lady KiKi to be with me. KiKi got out of the cab from the airport and walked through the trailer parking lot in a tight jogging suit that you could almost see through. Spliff Star and others were trying to talk to her because they didn't know she was coming to see me. She knocked on the trailer door and we hugged and kissed. She told me right away about everybody who tried to talk to her on her way in. KiKi always told me when people I knew tried talking to her. It didn't bother me at all because KiKi's so beautiful that every man alive would try if he had enough heart. I enjoyed it. It meant I was doing something right.

I knew KiKi probably had her little things on the side but she was serious only about me. The other fools were just for play. Even though I messed around with a lot of other women while I was with my boys, I'd turn down the baddest female to stay with my woman because I loved her. Those other females were meaningless.

KiKi watched me on the set that day, then we took it back to the hotel. The next morning, after room-service breakfast, I saw Spliff Star in the lobby. He told me the front desk had been robbed the night before. Two dudes with shotguns rushed the hotel office and stole a few thousand dollars. After sharing that story, Spliff told me that Cam'ron was out front.

Cam'ron was standing outside with his man Jim Jones. I hadn't seen Cam since we did "Losing Weight" together. I was wearing a white-and-pink-striped Polo shirt that I bought from my man Keith's store in Harlem, white shorts, white Filas, and my Infamous Records forty-inch chain. Cam introduced me to Jim and told me that he saw my movie *Murda Muzik* and liked it. I didn't want to leave KiKi by herself for too long so we talked briefly, I said peace to Cam and Jim, and I went back upstairs.

It seemed like after Cam'ron saw me rocking my pink-striped Polo shirt, he went pink crazy. I was known to throw on pink Polo shirts every now and then since 1989. I went to high school in Manhattan with a lot of

Brooklyn dudes who were in gangs like Decepticons and Lo-Lifes and that's where the trend of hood niggas rocking pink started. Brooklyn dudes wore pink Polo sweaters, purple, orange, yellow. Brooklyn muthafuckers loved Polo when I was in high school. I just kept the trend going in 2003. Maybe it's just a coincidence, but I never saw Cam'ron wear pink before that day in L.A.

A few days after KiKi left to get back to our kids, we finished filming. Alchemist, Twin, and I drove to Las Vegas to chill for a few days before flying back to New York. But before we hit the highway for Vegas, we stopped at Alchemist's homeboy Mr. Cartoon's tattoo and car shop to get my first Mr. Cartoon tatt. "I want a half angel, half demon on the back of my neck," I told him.

On our way to Vegas, we drove through the Death Valley desert, where the average temperature's over 100 degrees Fahrenheit. But as we drove through, we saw snow all across the desert. Yes, snow! It was extremely rare for it to snow in Death Valley. I took it as a sign that major changes in all our lives were about to take place.

We checked into the Hilton Hotel and Casino. Alchemist was a crap-table junky. He taught me how to play. I'm not a gambler because I don't like giving away my money, but sometimes I blow a few thousand hoping to win. Not on that trip. I turned three hundred dollars into eight hundred playing the dollar slots, kept gambling, and ended up with $280.

Alchemist was another story. That boy stood at the crap table for eight hours straight. Winning and losing, losing and winning with a crazed zombie look on his face.

Back home, our new album was doing well but Jive suddenly didn't want to give us control of the marketing and promotion budget. I had a list of promotional items that I wanted to give away at our concerts and other events, but the marketing team didn't seem excited about the album anymore. *Amerikaz Nightmare* sold roughly four hundred thousand copies and was creeping its way to gold, so it was strange to see that Jive was losing interest so fast. But Jive was used to selling millions of albums with Britney Spears, R. Kelly, 'N Sync, and others. Mobb Deep was small-time sales compared to their major-selling artists.

I was really upset with Jive and Chris Lighty because I had the know-how to help *Amerikaz Nightmare* sell triple the amount that it sold. All I needed was my marketing and promotion plan approved and for Jive to cut the check. This was a clear sign that the deal wouldn't last long. I missed Loud Records and Steve Rifkind. Steve understood the power of street promo. Not corporate promo, street promo. Together we understood our core audience and exactly how to reach them. Oh well. We had to make the best of the hand we were dealt.

It was three A.M. and I'd just made the forty-minute drive home from our Queens studio to Rockland. KiKi and the kids were fast asleep and I was tired but couldn't fall asleep. I hooked up my son's PlayStation to my bedroom TV and played *Freedom Fighters* until heaviness crept under my eyelids at four thirty A.M. It was a crisp, clear night, so I could see the stars and moon from the large window next to our bed that looked down on the whole block. Our mountaintop home was the highest on our block, so we didn't have curtains or blinds covering that window because nobody could see in. But we could see out.

Suddenly, all the power went out. I looked out the window and saw that the whole block was blacked out, so I decided to go to bed. As I lay down next to KiKi, a bright white light beamed into the bedroom window. It looked like a police helicopter's searchlight, except it was silent. *Oh shit, are the police looking for somebody over here?*

"KiKi, get up!" I reached over to wake KiKi. "Look at this shit!" The bright white beam began changing colors—red, yellow, green, blue, orange—repeating randomly. "Do you see this shit?" I asked.

"What the fuck is that?" KiKi said.

"Do you see this shit?"

"Yes, go look out the window and see what that is!" she said.

"I'm not going near that window."

I knew what it was. A UFO was hovering over our crib, shining light beams into our bedroom. *Holy shit.* After three or four minutes, the night sky turned black again. I was happy that KiKi was with me so I had a witness this time. When the sky turned black again, a feeling of fear took over. *Something is in our house.* The power came back on.

I peeked down at the other houses on our block and all the power was back on. KiKi must have had the same feeling that I had. "Go check on the kids," she said.

"I'm not going to check on shit," I replied. I was shook.

"Nigga, go check on the kids!" she barked.

"You go!" I said. But I got the shotgun from the closet, woke the kids up, and brought them to our room.

"What's going on?" the kids asked, half asleep.

"Mommy and I just saw a UFO," I told them.

"Where?" Tasia said. "I wanna see it too!"

"It's gone now," KiKi said. "Get in our bed."

I sat on the edge of the bed with the shotgun in my hands as my family slept, still in shock. Maybe my fear was just guilt because I wasn't living right and subconsciously thought I was in trouble. Or maybe it was all the movies I'd seen. At six A.M., as the sun started shining, I went to sleep.

I had been begging and praying for another sign from the Most High and for a witness to see it with me. After KiKi and I had that extremely close encounter, I was convinced that the ancient Egyptian teachings that Dr. York revealed in his books were facts beyond a shadow of a doubt. I knew the truth about many of life's mysteries but I was stuck smoking, drinking, and not walking the straight line I was taught to follow when I knew better. I felt like a fallen angel.

The UFO came to my house to show me the light, as if to say, "Wake up, nigga! Snap out of it! We are real and you are important to us! Okay, we gotta go for now, hope you're ready when we come back!"

I'm not talking about little green Martians and all that science-fiction crap, so save the Prodigy-believes-in-green-men-from-Mars routine. It's much deeper than you know. I only deal with the truth and facts that have been concealed from humans of all races because discovering these facts would collapse the mountain of lies and corruption. A mind-boggling amount of misinformation is released through movies, books, religion, education, and news to confuse us.

Every race of people has its own truth, history, and origin. Black people's ancient ancestors didn't share the same mental, physical, or spiritual composition as us; they were far more advanced. But they created us in their likeness and we carried on their traits, many of which were cut off or watered down due to our own foolish ways, crossbreeding with other races (melanin has powerful physical and spiritual properties), and the mental enslavement and brainwashing that we were put through. When people like myself discover the truth and attempt to share it with others, some will say, "Prodigy is a racist conspiracy theorist. . . . He watches too much science fiction. . . . He's a wacko."

I was receiving the gift of enlightenment from my ancient black ancestors, the Most High, and the universe. But as much as I thought I knew, I had a lot to learn about self-control. I was acting like a late baby, too comfortable in Mommy's warm dark stomach to come out and deal with reality. It was way beyond nine months and I was refusing to be born.

Back in Fantasyland, home of the dumb, deaf, blind, and blissfully ignorant, Mobb Deep booked a concert in a small town near Albany called Cohoes. Havoc, Alchemist, Twin, Noyd, Derrick, this tall security guard with dreads, and I were driven in a Turtle Top van outfitted with a TV, DVD player, and a PlayStation four hours upstate. Derrick was acting as our road manager and went to collect payment from the venue before we walked in. Ten minutes later, he said the promoter didn't have all our bread yet because they were still collecting money at the door. So we found a parking spot in the cut and waited in the van until they were ready. Alchemist lit a blunt in the meantime.

Twenty minutes later, a cop knocked on the passenger window where our security guard was seated. "Oh shit! Put the weed out!" we said, scrambling. Twin lit a cigarette to hide the smell. The security guard rolled down the window.

"What are you doing over here?" the cop asked.

"We're performing at the club, just waiting for the promoter to pay us before we head inside," the security guard explained.

"Oh yeah, so why do I smell marijuana?" the cop said.

"No, that's just cigarette smoke. No marijuana over here," the security guard replied. "We're just waiting to do our concert."

"Yeah? I smell marijuana," the cop said. "We'll see when the K-9 gets here. Turn the vehicle off!" He called the K-9 unit, the police dogs that sniff for drugs. *Ahh man!* I had a .25-caliber gun in my jacket pocket, my usual gun for clubs, shows, or out of town. I quickly put the gun in my Timberland boot, under my right foot.

Squad cars rolled up within a few minutes. Alchemist pulled a big bag of weed—an ounce of Kush—from his jacket. "Yo, take this for me, son," he said to Twin, seated beside him. "Hold this."

Twin looked at the size of the bag and said, "I'm not going down for all that. I'm not taking that shit. You buggin', son." Twin and Alchemist quietly argued over who should take the weed. In the past, Twin told Alchemist that if they were ever in a situation like this, Twin would take the weight. But Twin meant a twenty or fifty bag, not the Ziploc pillow that Alchemist pulled out.

"Why would you bring that much anyway?" Twin asked. "It's not like we're going away for a week."

"Fuck it. Forget it." Alchemist said, putting the pillow back in his pocket. A cop approached the van shining his flashlight. "Everybody step out the van," he ordered. "One at a time."

Alchemist got out first. The cop pulled the Ziploc weed pillow from Al's pocket and held it in the air for the other cops to see. I was relieved that the cop didn't ask Al to take off his sneakers. I got out next. The cop frisked me, searched my pockets, and was done. *That was a close call*, I thought.

"What are those, Timberlands?" he said, looking down at my boots.

"Yeah."

"Take off your boots."

Damn! I took off my Tims and prepared myself mentally. "He's got a gun in his boot!" the cop alerted the other police. They pulled out their guns and made us lie on the ground, dragged everybody else out of the van, cuffed us, and searched the vehicle. The security guard with the dreads started sobbing uncontrollably. "I can't go to jail, man, please. I got kids," he pleaded. "I didn't do anything." Twin, Noyd, and I laughed. It was funny to see a six-foot-ten, three-hundred-pound fool cry.

The driver, an unassuming older black man, had a duffel bag in the back of the van. The cops searched the bag and found crack cocaine and a box of nine-millimeter bullets. We looked at each other, like, *Crack? Bullets?*

That's why that dude was speeding so fast the entire drive upstate. He was high on crack! The cops must have been happy as hell.

At the precinct, Hav, Noyd, Twin, Derrick, and the security guard were released and they kept Alchemist, the driver, and me. Twin agreed to call KiKi to contact my lawyer, Bob Kalina. I fell asleep on a hardwood bench attached to the cell wall.

The judge let Alchemist go without bail and the next morning hit me with twenty thousand dollars' bail. Until I could get the money, I was transferred to the Albany County jail twenty minutes away from the precinct. After I was processed, they handed me a jumpsuit, jail shoes (that looked like Vans skateboard sneakers), sheets, a blanket, mug, toothbrush, toothpaste, and rule book and directed me to my tier. "Yo, that's Prodigy!" a few inmates yelled out. "No, that's Havoc, nigga! Mobb Deep!"

As I walked to my cell, I noticed the van driver a few cells down from mine, sweating bullets like he was going through withdrawal from his crack habit. He looked scared. "Are you okay?" I asked, stopping at his cell gate.

"Ye . . . yeah, I'm all right," he said, looking at me as if he didn't recognize me.

"I'm about to put my shit in my cell then use the jack," I said, meaning the phone. "You want me to make a call for you?"

"Yeah, please," he said. He told me he didn't have anything to write with, so I asked one of the inmates to borrow a pencil and wrote down his number.

I called KiKi. She cursed me out for getting locked up again and told me that she and Havoc were putting my bail together. Then I called Mr. Crackman's number but nobody picked up. Oh well. I told him to be easy and try to calm his nerves, gave homeboy his pencil back, and locked in. Hours later, the chow wagon came around with dinner and an officer called my name, saying I was bailed out. *Yes!*

Back in the city, I stopped in the Bronx to see Derrick, who'd driven the van back from Albany and parked it in a lot a few blocks from his apartment building. Derrick and I walked over to the lot so I could get some CDs and DVDs that I left in the van. We looked at each other and couldn't resist the temptation. Yes, we took everything of value out of that vehicle. We gutted it out—the TV, PlayStation, DVD player, stereo, speakers, and navigation system. Thank you, good-bye.

A few days later I called Bob Kalina. "I'm sitting here looking at your address and guess what?" Bob said. "You live around the corner from me! I live in Pomona too! My guy in Albany is trying to work out a deal because it's looking like an illegal search. We'll see. I'll pick you up and we'll drive to the courthouse together, if you want."

"Sounds good," I said. He told me the court date would be in two weeks.

When I finished my call with Bob Kalina, I got a call from my mother. "T'Chaka! I just read on the Internet that you got arrested with a gun and crack. You're smoking crack?"

"What? Hell no, ma!" I said. "The driver had crack in his bag, not me."

"Oh, thank God!"

Whoa. The media was making it seem like I was smoking crack. Ha!

The next morning, KiKi asked me to go to the supermarket. My Denali needed gas so I pulled into Exxon on Route 59, two minutes from our house. While I was pumping gas, a black BMW X5 truck with tinted windows pulled into the station and stopped suddenly while it was headed toward the pumps, backed up, then pulled up next to the driver's side of my truck. I opened my passenger door and discreetly put my nine-millimeter Ruger on my waist. Yes, I was still carrying guns after I just got arrested for one a few days before—.22s, nines, .25- and .45-calibers. *My life doesn't stop just because I got arrested—the drama doesn't stop*, I reminded myself. *Wherever and whenever, never get caught slippin'.*

A dark-skinned dude with dreads hopped out of the X5. "Yo, Prodigy! What's up, man?" He walked toward me. "My name is Ronnie. I've seen you around the town. I'm from Spring Valley. I'm working on a knockout DVD, a lot of hood fights and shit like that. I've got my camera in my truck if you don't mind doing a drop for me."

Knockout DVD? Is he gonna try and knock me out on camera? This is why I've got a gun on my waist, for fools like this, I thought to myself. "No problem," I replied. "Get your camera. What's the name of your DVD?"

"*Paper Chase*," he said, camera in hand.

"What's up, this is the Head Nigga in Charge, Prodigy from the Infamous Mobb Deep. You are now watching the *Paper Chase* DVD. Peace." After recording the drop, Ronnie gave me one of his DVDs and I got in my truck and bounced.

Two weeks later, my Albany case was dropped to a misdemeanor and dismissed. I was ordered to pay a fine and stay out of trouble for two years. I don't know how Bob Kalina and his Albany lawyer friend pulled it off.

"Your luck is gonna run out," KiKi said. "You need to stop getting arrested with those guns." Even Twin would say, "You got bagged with mad hammers and stay beating the cases. Niggas gonna think you snitchin' soon, son." Snitch? Never. But my luck was damn sure about to run out. When you build an extensive criminal record, after a while the judge and prosecutor can hit you based on your history. My criminal-history cup was about to spill over.

We booked a show in Connecticut with 50 Cent. Mobb Deep and G-Unit's first performance together—I was real excited. The promoter rented a Turtle Top van, as usual, and a driver. I decided to drive my white Yukon Denali. I wasn't bringing a gun but I was leery about hired drivers since our last one had crack and bullets in the van.

The whole crew bought navy-blue T-shirts and bandannas to wear for the show. No gang significance—we just wanted to look in sync since this was an important show. Little Lord, Havoc, Ron-Doo, Fly, and Derrick rode in the van. Illa Ghee, Alchemist, and I took my truck. We left Manhattan at ten P.M. and got to the club at midnight. It was packed.

In the dressing room upstairs, Havoc, Alchemist, and I discussed our set list while eating sandwiches and drinking beers. Alchemist set up and brought us our mics. Showtime. My favorite song to perform from *Amerikaz Nightmare* was "When U Hear The," produced by Alchemist, because it sounds incredible banging through concert speakers. I suggested that Al should make a beat out of the score music from the movie *Scarface*. Every time Al Pacino's character Tony Montana got angry, this crazy keyboard sound came on. I always wanted to make a beat out of that, so Alchemist finally did.

Fly, Ron-Doo, and Derrick were waiting in the dressing room after the show with some real pretty Puerto Rican ladies they found in the crowd who wanted to meet us. We took pictures, then Havoc and I sat down to catch our breath and cool off. I always ended up out of breath and soaking wet from sweating while performing, feeding off the crowd's energy, so I had to rest for twenty minutes after shows. None of us had seen 50 Cent in concert before, so we went downstairs to watch.

Last to leave the dressing room, I approached the staircase—one flight down, U-turn to the right, then another flight down. The G-Unit entourage was on their way up and kept to my left as the Mobb Deep entourage headed down on my right. As I started my descent down the right side of the stairs, a big white security guard in a G-Unit T-shirt put his arm across my path and held on to the staircase railing so I couldn't go past him. "You can't come down," he said. "G-Unit is coming up."

What? All my boys just walked down past him and he decided to stop me? I looked at him like he'd lost his mind. "My people are going downstairs," I said. "Excuse me." He stiffened his grip on the railing.

"You have to wait, G-Unit is coming up," he said, stopping the stair-well traffic. I was wearing my big platinum Infamous Records chain, flooded with diamonds. *This fool can't recognize me?* "Man, get out of my way," I said, flung his arm out of my way, and continued down the steps. He made some disrespectful comment as I shoved past him, so I turned and shouted, "Man, shut the fuck up!" Someone was tapping my shoulder.

It was 50. He was trying to say what's up and give me a pound but I didn't notice because I was arguing with that fool. "What's up, man, my bad," I said. "This bitch-ass nigga tried to stop me from coming down!"

"What up, P? You good?" 50 said.

"Yeah, we about to watch you perform." I proceeded to catch up with my boys.

As I went down the last flight, I tried to calm down but the security guard reached through the railing, grabbed my arm, and yanked it hard as if he was trying to pull it out of the socket. "I'll fuck your punk ass up!" I shouted but he walked into the dressing room upstairs.

We found a spot in the corner with a good view of the stage. It took ten minutes to get my mind off what had just happened. I didn't calm down until DJ Whoo Kid started 50's show with "What Up Gangsta" and 50 and his boys ran onstage. We were just as hyped as the fans in the crowd. After the song, some idiot from the front row threw a drink in a plastic cup at 50 and hit him in the chest. 50 took off his G-Unit spinning chain, handed it to one of his boys, jumped into the front row, and started beating on the culprit, then jumped back onstage and continued his show. The crowd went nuts.

Surveying my surroundings as the next song started, I saw the big white security guard in the crowd to my right. I couldn't resist. "Ayo, do you know who I am?" I asked.

"Look, I'm sorry, it was a misunderstanding," he said.

"What the fuck is your problem? You stupid or something?"

"It's just a misunderstanding," he said. "I apologize, man."

Just get over it and enjoy the show. Forget about it, I told myself, though I was pissed. *This dude tried to rip my arm off.* I lightly pushed his chest as I went to turn back to the show. He grabbed my arm again and yanked it the same way.

Without delay, Little Lord punched him in the mouth and Ron-Doo hit him with a left and a right to the face. I put my rose-gold Rolex and chain in my pocket and waited for an opening so I could get my punches in too. But my boys beat him into the corner next to Fly and then Fly treated his face like a punching bag. Fly, Little Lord, and Ron-Doo stepped back to see if he'd fall or fight—the opening I was looking for. I hit him with an uppercut left to his mouth and his tooth dug into my knuckle. Then I hit him with an overhand right to the side of his jaw and dropped him. His G-Unit shirt was hanging off him and his pants were around his knees. We ran out the exit door to avoid getting locked up because we'd just beat up one of the club security guards.

From the corner of my left eye as we were running out, I saw the G-Unit crew jump off the stage. Illa Ghee and I jumped into my truck, Illa took the wheel, and the others hopped into the Turtle Top van. My left knuckle felt broken and was dripping blood. As I looked out the window to the right, about ten G-Unit crew members ran outside. "Where they at? Who was it?" they shouted. One looked at me through the truck window while I was shaking my hand in pain. "Who was it? It was Prodigy?" he asked his boys. I would soon learn his name was Haleem. "Come on. Forget it," he said. "It was Prodigy."

I then realized that the guard we beat up was G-Unit's security. A police squad car idled at the parking-lot exit waiting for traffic to move to pull out, so we had to wait. Ten G-Unit dudes, some of whom wanted to retaliate, stood scattered around our cars. The squad car pulled out and some of the G-Unit dudes were in the way of the Turtle Top van. Little Lord opened the double doors and shouted, "Get the fuck from in front of this van before I start layin' niggas down!" He was bluffing like he had a gun, but none of us had guns that night. Lord's bluff worked.

We hit the highway heading home, my hand throbbing. I called DJ Whoo Kid to apologize to 50 for beating up his security guard. I didn't know the guy was with them. I thought he worked for the club. I should've guessed from his G-Unit T-shirt. Whoo Kid connected me with 50. "What up?" 50 said. "What happened?"

"Yo, first off, I didn't know he was working for you. I thought he was the club's security," I said. "You saw me arguing with him on the stairs. He put his hands on me so we beat him up. You guys would've done the same thing if somebody put their hands on you."

"No doubt. Don't even worry about it, P. It's all good," 50 said. "You're okay, right?"

"Yeah, I'm good."

"All right, cool. I'll speak to you later." And that was that.

My hand swelled like a Mickey Mouse glove the next morning and kept bleeding slightly. The swelling didn't go down and after a few days my hand took on a greenish tint. I went to the emergency room and the doctor told me that it wasn't broken but it was infected. She said that the human mouth had more germs than a dog's mouth and if I had waited any longer, they might have had to cut my hand off. That dirty-mouthed security guard almost cost me my hand. Back to normal after a week of antibiotics, I decided from that point on to aim for the nose instead of the mouth.

New York radio station Hot 97 was promoting a free Nas concert in Central Park. *Wow,* I thought when I heard the ad, *this is gonna be a major event.* The only major Central Park concert I could remember was when my grandmother did the Diana Ross show and I was too scared to go onstage. The next thing that popped into my mind was, *Mobb Deep needs to be a part of that concert.*

Nas and I were beefing at that time because of his "Build & Destroy" song—he was trying to discredit me and I was defending myself. I never had anything against Nas. In fact, I loved him like a friend and mentor until he showed his true jealous, envious, and greedy colors. Then I had to flip on him. I still loved him. But when I heard about the Central Park event, my business mind kicked in. "Let's holler at son and tell him we want to perform," I told Havoc.

"After you shitted on him? He probably won't do it," Havoc said. I reminded Havoc that Nas took shots at me first and I only did what I was supposed to do in retaliation. Plus it was petty. I told Little Lord to reach out to Nas's boy, Tim Lord, and find out what was up. Little Lord said the same thing Havoc said. "Okay, I'll try," he said. "I doubt it though."

A week later Tim Lord called back and said Nas agreed.

Fourth of July weekend 2004, I was drinking Incredible Hulks with Illa Ghee and his boys Black-M and Ant at Brooklyn Drinks in Bed-Stuy, a bar where we were regulars, down the block from Woodhull Hospital. It was great to have Illa back home from his five-year bid in Virginia when he got caught in that house raid.

After Brooklyn Drinks, we drove to Alchemist's crib in Manhattan to link with Twin, Al, and Al's brother Neil Diamonds to celebrate Illa being free and Independence Day. Alchemist made a deal with Koch Records to release an album, *First Infantry*, and had just received his advance, so he splurged on the new Porsche SUV. Al drove his Porsche, and I took my Denali XL to Club Chaos on Avenue A in the Lower East Side.

The bouncers let us in with no problem and it was packed inside. DJ Cutmaster C from Queens was spinning. We went straight to the bar and ordered a round of drinks. Cutmaster C walked from the DJ booth over to us. "What's up, P? I want to introduce you to my man," he said. A little light-skinned dude beside him said, "Yeah, I was locked up with your mans Little Lord from Queensbridge." He started name-dropping people from QB. "My name is Web. Yo, why can't you do a song with my artist Joe Budden?"

Why can't I do a song with Joe Budden? The way he said it turned me off. Nobody ever asked me to do a song with him. Who said I "can't" do a song with him? I looked at that clown like he had four heads. "Your man right here knows how to get at me if ya'll need a song," I said, pointing to Cutmaster C. Then I gave both of them my back. I hadn't even gotten to take a sip of my drink yet.

There were some good-looking ladies in the spot and a few of them started to creep their way over to us. Just as I was about to reach out and grab the hand of one who was standing in arm's reach, somebody slapped my drink out of my hand. When I turned, it was Web, being held back by his boys. I took off my thick necklace and wrapped it around my fist like brass knuckles. Security ran over and jumped between us. They pushed Web and his boys toward the exit. "Let's go outside and handle these clowns," I told Illa and Twin.

Illa was on parole and didn't want to violate and I didn't blame him. "You know my situation. But if you wanna go get them I'm with you," Illa said.

"Let's go right now," I said.

Outside, they were nowhere to be found. I figured they were still in the club and walked to the corner to get my nickel-plated .25 automatic from my truck. My man Black-M saw me and said, "Nah, gimme that. You ain't shooting nobody. That's my job. You rap, I'll shoot."

We waited across the street from the club for ten minutes when these fools came stumbling out the front door. Security body-slammed one of them on the sidewalk. Twin ran across the street and snatched the necklace off the neck of the kid lying on the concrete and Illa Ghee grabbed a forty-ounce beer bottle from the garbage and threw it like a football at one of the others, hitting him in the face. Black-M grabbed Web, trying to snatch his chain, but got a handful of shirt instead. Black-M put the gun to Web's stomach and squeezed two shots. Web spun around to free himself and avoided both shots. He and his boys ran away at top speed. We hopped into the trucks and peeled off. Wow, Club Chaos was chaos for real and the fireworks exploded that Fourth of July.

The following night, I had a copy of a popular DVD street magazine called *Smack DVD* at the studio featuring an interview with an up-and-coming rapper from Spring Valley, New York, named Saigon. Alchemist made a couple of tracks for Saigon, but I hadn't heard any music from him that grabbed my attention. But while Havoc, Little Lord, Fly, and I were watching his *Smack DVD* interview, Saigon did something that grabbed all our attention. Pulling out an *Amerikaz Nightmare* CD, Saigon said, "I'm tired of washed-up rappers like these niggas right here," holding up our album cover so the camera could get a good view. "All these old-ass rap muthafuckers need to give it up and make room for the new artists. I'm tired of this same old bullshit!" Saigon sparked a lighter, set our album cover on fire, dropped it on the ground along with the actual CD, and stomped it with his boot.

Wow. We were in shock. We never did anything to Saigon—that clown wasn't even on our radar. He was obviously just trying to make a name for himself. It became Saigon hunting season.

A few days after seeing the *Smack DVD*, Alchemist's brother Neil had a small birthday party in downtown Manhattan's Tribeca neighborhood. Ron-Doo from Queensbridge, Godfather, Gotti, Twin, Alchemist, and I were drinking Coronas in the back of the bar when Saigon walked into the spot. *Ah man, here we go.* The nine-millimeter Ruger on my hip was concealed under my shirt and leather jacket. "Look who just walked in," I tapped Ron-Doo and told him. "It's Saigon."

Godfather walked over and told me the same thing. Saigon spotted us staring at him so he walked straight up to me. "Yo P, I wanna apologize to you about that *Smack DVD*. I know you must have heard about it by now," he said, looking like a scared puppy with its tail between its legs. "I'm a big fan of Mobb Deep and I don't know what was wrong with me. I said some shit I shouldn't have said."

"That was some real disrespectful shit you did, man. What's up with you, man?" I said.

"Yo, I swear I'm a fan of your shit. I love Mobb Deep," he replied. "Please forgive me, P. I fucked up."

I could step on this clown like a roach if I wanted to, I thought. If he'd spoken with the slightest bit of aggression in his voice, I would've snapped on Saigon. But that clown was chirping away like the bird-ass nigga he was, singing sweet songs of "forgive me." Being the intelligent, compassionate person that I am, I told him, "You know what? Forget about it. We all say things we regret sometimes. Don't sweat it. We're good."

"Listen, I just want you to know that I really love Mobb Deep. Ask Alchemist, I'm ya'll biggest fan," Saigon chirped.

"All right, man, don't sweat it," I said. "It's a small thing to a giant."

"I really am a fan, no bullshit. I felt stupid when I saw that DVD. I don't have no problems with ya'll."

"You ain't gotta explain all that. It's over," I said. "We're good."

"I'm a fan, P," he kept chirping. "I'm just a big fan." Ron-Doo sipped his beer, staring at Saigon as he said it again. "I grew up on your music, I love Mobb—"

Ron-Doo cut him off. "Man, shut the fuck up and get away from us before we hurt you, nigga!"

There was a long silence. Saigon looked at Ron-Doo, looked at me, then turned and walked out of the bar. We all laughed. "Come on, we can't let him walk outside after that," I told Ron-Doo. "Let's make sure he doesn't try to ambush us."

A foolish, cocky person would have laughed and continued partying because Saigon looked like a coward. But I knew better than to beef with a person and then let him go outside without following. That person could be hiding outside with a gun, waiting. So we walked outside behind him.

"Yo, these niggas is frontin', son!" Saigon was running his motor-mouth to his boys. He turned and saw Ron-Doo and continued his tough-guy act because his boys were watching.

Ron-Doo stood in front of Saigon, looking down at him. "What's up, nigga? What you wanna do?" Doo asked. "You pussy."

"Yo, I ain't got no beef with ya'll niggas. Back up off me. I'm trying to leave," he said with bass in his tone. Saigon's boys pulled him away, but Ron-Doo was in his face calling him pussy. "I ain't got no beef with you, P, but I'm gonna see your boy right here," Saigon said, motioning to Ron-Doo with his finger. Ron-Doo was seconds away from punching Saigon.

"Come on, let's bounce or I'm gonna end up clappin' one of these niggas," I told Ron-Doo. "They're not built like that. Let's go." I'm not into fighting, I'm a gun man. I'm guaranteed to shoot somebody if I've got my gun. A very ignorant, negative mentality, but that's just how I was. So I tried my best to avoid shit like that.

"I'm gonna see you, nigga!" Saigon screamed as we walked to my truck. "I'm gonna see you again!"

"You soft, nigga! Shut your mouth before you get hurt!" Godfather shouted back. Saigon started walking slowly toward us. I walked back over to him. "Go home, man. I told you it was all good but you kept talking," I said. "You're making it a problem."

"Your boy tried to play me. If he wants to fight then we can fight," Saigon said.

"Niggas ain't tryin' to fight, son," I said, grabbing Saigon's left hand and tapping it on the gun on my hip. "Just go home, nigga. You buggin' right now." Saigon finally shut up.

It was drizzling rain on the day of the Central Park concert. Slowly, our crew of seven—Hav, Fly, Ron-Doo, Little Lord, his two homeboys from Marcy projects, and I—made our way through three crowded police-barricaded checkpoints. Security guards led us to Nas's trailer. I knocked on the door while the rest of the crew stood outside. Nas's woman Kelis was sitting on a counter with a camcorder in her hand filming me as I walked in. Nas, his boy from Queensbridge Super Ed, and Fakey were sitting around talking.

"What up, nigga?" I greeted Nas.

"You don't love me no more," Nas said.

"Why do you think we came here? I miss doing songs with you, nigga."

"Yeah right, you don't love me no more," he said, playing around.

"Okay, whatever, man," I said. Fakey walked over and said, "P, we need to talk. . . ." A security guard knocked on the door and opened it. "It's showtime!" Nas and Kelis walked ahead of us so he could hurry to the stage. Walking behind them, Fakey said again, "P, we need to talk," putting his arm around my shoulder for privacy. "What's up with you making songs dissin' Worm and all of us?"

"You already know what's up with all that. Ya'll did what ya'll did and I did what I did. What, you thought I wasn't gonna say nothing back?" I said.

After "Build and Destroy" and "Ether," Nas and Fakey started saying slick shit about me on songs and being disrespectful, so naturally I did the same to them. Now that clown Fakey was confronting me about it. Ha! Little Lord walked over. "Don't talk to that bitch-ass nigga. Fuck him. You ain't got nothing to say to him," he told me.

Fakey looked over at Little Lord, then looked back at me and said, "Your man here is about to get you into some shit. See, I don't got no problem with you, P, but your man here is about to cause a problem."

Then Fakey stepped away from me and he and Little started arguing. "What you say, nigga?" Fakey said. "What you wanna do?"

Nas and Kelis were way ahead of us now, heading toward the backstage gate. Fakey quickly reached in his pocket and pulled out his Nextel walkie-talkie phone and started chirping people backstage. "Son, these niggas think they gangstas, get everybody together and meet me at the gate right now," he said. *Ha! Nigga please.* Fakey chirped again. "Hurry up and tell niggas to come to the gate now!" He looked at us and said, "We gonna see who tough now. When we get backstage we'll see."

Little Lord said, "Cool. Let's see."

Nas and Kelis were already inside the twelve-foot-tall white gate leading backstage. When the security guard opened the gate for us, twenty dudes were waiting for us to walk in. Assuming that they were the dudes that Fakey was chirping, Little Lord and his two boys from Brooklyn punched the closest ones in the face, then another, then another. Everybody started brawling. Somebody slammed the gate shut behind us, locking Havoc and Fly outside. It was just five of us against twenty.

Fakey walked in before all of us and then disappeared in all the commotion. I noticed that for some strange reason, the twenty dudes and Fakey were all wearing dark-green promotional T-shirts for Shyne's album, *Godfather Buried Alive.* Shyne was in prison serving ten years for a shooting inside a Manhattan club with Puff Daddy.

Fakey must have been helping promote Shyne's album, so anybody with a Shyne T-shirt was immediately considered an enemy and target. As Ron-Doo and I pushed and punched our way farther inside the backstage area, Ron-Doo looked at me, grabbed my arm, and pushed me to the side, out of harm's way, shoving me right into Nas, who was watching the fight. My first instinct was to break his face, but instead I asked him, "Yo, what's up with all this? You set us up?"

Nas acted as if he couldn't hear me. Kelis sat on the edge of the stage secretly filming the fight. I looked around for Fakey but didn't see him anywhere. Suddenly, all the Shyne T-shirts started scampering away. Little Lord's two Brooklyn boys had knives out, blood dripping from them. "Come on! Where ya'll going!" they taunted the Shyne dudes, some of whom were taking their Shyne T-shirts off and pressing them to their stomachs, chests, and heads to stop the bleeding. "Come on!"

I spotted Fakey hiding behind the staircase leading to the stage. Ha! Just as the fighting stopped, Tim Lord handed Nas a microphone and Nas began his show with "New York State of Mind." Little Lord and Ron-Doo walked over and asked if I was okay. "Yeah," I said. "Look at Fakey hiding behind the stairs."

"You pussy!" they barked at him. "What's up now?" Fakey stayed quiet behind the stairs and just looked at us. Tim Lord walked over and gave me a microphone. He told me to wait on the staircase to get cued in. Halfway up the stairs, I yelled at Ron-Doo, "Yo, where's Havoc? Get Hav!"

Five plainclothes police officers ran backstage. One of the cops grabbed a big closed umbrella from a picnic table and started swinging it between my people and Fakey's in an attempt to keep them separated. Little Lord's boys from Brooklyn still had their knives out in front of the cops and the cops looked scared and didn't do anything about it. Kelis kept filming the action backstage, then turning the camera toward Nas performing. Havoc and Fly made their way to the steps where I was sitting. Busta Rhymes and Q-Tip were standing off to the side during the whole fight. Busta walked up to me and said, "Ya'll niggas is crazy, man! Why ya'll fighting each other? I saw the whole shit."

"Hey, shit happens," I said.

"Ya'll Queensbridge niggas is crazy," Busta said. Q-Tip just shook his head, gave us a pound, then ran onstage to perform the song "One Love" with Nas. Tim Lord gave Havoc a mic and told us we were up after Q-Tip. The only thing on my mind was, *What if these niggas try some bullshit while we're performing?*

The music stopped. "I wanna bring out some very special guests," Nas announced as his DJ, L.E.S., dropped the beat for "Eye for an Eye." The crowd went crazy. That was the first time we ever performed that song together live, though we were missing Raekwon from Wu-Tang Clan. After we performed our single "Got It Twisted" from *Amerikaz Nightmare*, Nas stood between Havoc and me with his arms around our shoulders, kissed us both on the cheek, and told the crowd, "I love Mobb Deep! These are my niggas!"

We regrouped with our boys backstage. "We've gotta pay attention walking out of the park because these niggas might try to ambush us," Little Lord said. But nothing happened.

Later that night, as I told KiKi about what happened, I wondered, *Did Nas set that whole shit up? Or was it just Fakey? Why was Kelis taping it all?* Fakey better hope Nas never released that footage because it would be proof that he's a bird—that couldn't back it up when real niggas called his bluff.

Soon after that Central Park concert, we took a few of our boys to a big DJ convention in Puerto Rico. The night we arrived, we bumped into Styles P and Jadakiss from the Lox and Pharrell from the Neptunes. Fabolous stepped out of a limo with a large entourage and a good-looking female in a long white mink coat. He also had that kid Web, whom we almost shot on the Fourth of July, with him.

The woman in the mink, Gloria Velez, the famous video vixen and the baby mother of Aaron Hall from Guy, kept peeking over at me while standing with Fabolous, who was doing an on-camera interview. I motioned for her to come over and she did. I asked her name, as if I didn't know, and we exchanged numbers. I'd never met Gloria before but called her over to show Web that I didn't give a fuck that she was with them. Web was watching through the large lobby window.

Fabolous finished his interview and was waiting for Gloria to come back. So I kept talking to her a little longer just to fuck with him. I didn't have anything against Fabolous. I liked him and his music. I wanted to piss Web off for that bullshit he pulled at Club Chaos.

While Havoc and I were being interviewed in a hotel conference room later that day, Little Lord spotted Web in the room and approached him about the situation. Little Lord called me over after the interview and Web apologized. "Yo, man, I'm sorry for that night. I was real drunk and fucked up," he said. "I was in the wrong."

"No problem," I said. "We good." And that was that. I went over to show Fabolous some love.

Back in New York, I got some bad news. A letter from the IRS came to my house saying that I owed over three hundred thousand dollars in unpaid back taxes that had accumulated from 1996 to 2003. I wanted to blame our accountant Arty Erk, but it was my own fault. Foolish spending. Ever since we signed with Loud Records and our career took off, I would get checks from publishing, advances, budgets, and all kinds of outlets—fifty thousand here, ten thousand there that I didn't take to our accountant. Instead I deposited them in my account or cashed them and went on shopping sprees—cars, jewels, clothes, drugs, alcohol, and partying. Man, that shit caught up with me.

For too many years, I made terrible financial decisions. I set up a meeting with an IRS agent to figure out a way to pay it off. The best option was to sell my house and pay the bill from my profit. A lot of that tax bill came from financing my own movie and paying for most of its production in cash instead of checks. I did that because I was getting cheaper prices with cash, but now I was really going to pay for it in the end.

Then I found out that KiKi was messing with a few dudes behind my back. I was devastated, crying like a little punk when I found the e-mails in her phone and she confessed to me. I'd never cried over a female before. I felt like a chump.

I had the wrong attitude about our relationship. I was hardly ever home, hardly ever called, and acted as if the material possessions I gave her were enough for her to overlook all those shortcomings. I felt like a certified loser. "You know you just made me worse now," I said out of humiliation. "You think I was a coldhearted muthafucker before? Now you're gonna see cold." I couldn't help it. That's how I really felt. I had no right to be upset, I was out there doing the same thing.

KiKi apologized and I knew in my heart and mind that she wasn't going anywhere. I knew the rules in the game of love very well. KiKi used to tell me, "You know that whatever you're out there doing, remember that I'm doing the same thing."

"What d'you mean by that?" I asked, knowing damn well what she meant.

"If you're being faithful, then I'm doing the same thing," KiKi said. "If you're cheating, then I'm cheating."

Being the revenge-driven, selfish asshole that I was in our relationship, I got my vengeance by doing more of the foolishness that brought her to cheating in the first place. I was a dumbass jerk with a lot to learn.

We sold the house and made a decent profit. Eighty percent of the money went to the IRS, so we didn't have enough to buy a new house—we rented a two-bedroom apartment from KiKi's aunt in Bridgeport, Connecticut. Bridgeport, a poverty-stricken town, was about two hours from New York City, and traveling back and forth was stressful, but we had to tough it out until I got my money in order. Alchemist let me stay at his crib in the city a lot. And whenever I wasn't working, I was with KiKi and the kids.

The Bridgeport schools had no money, so the textbooks were old and the teaching was mediocre. I felt horrible about subjecting my family to those conditions. My kids deserved the best, and I promised that we wouldn't live out there for long.

Financial problems, relationship problems—and then, to make matters worse, Jive dropped Mobb Deep. We knew something was wrong when Jive wasn't showing enthusiasm about promoting *Amerikaz Nightmare* any further. The album was almost gold at the time they dropped us, so our selling power was the same.

The only thing that being dropped from Jive hurt was our pride and ego. But why would we want to be aligned with a company that wasn't excited about us? We were free agents once again. We booked a few shows, rented a tour bus, and set up our studio equipment in the back. Havoc didn't want to stop making beats just because we were on the road.

On the bus we had some deep conversations about the music industry and our position in the game. "This is crazy," I told Alchemist and Havoc. "We've got some of the best music in the industry, you guys are two of the best producers, we sell nothing less than gold or platinum—I don't under-stand why these company owners don't snatch us up and take full advantage of our power."

"It definitely feels like niggas are hating on us or something," Havoc said.

"Eminem, Dr. Dre, and these other niggas need to sign Mobb Deep," I said. "We need people that got money and know our worth. I'm tired of hop-ping from label to label."

Headed home from the brief tour a few days later, Alchemist got a phone call from his manager Paul saying that Eminem wanted Al to be his offi-cial tour DJ. Alchemist was thrilled. DJ Green Lantern, who had been Eminem's DJ since the beginning of Em's career, had made a bad move.

Jadakiss did a segment on a street DVD called *On the Come Up* rid-ing in the back of a car talking to DJ Green Lantern on speakerphone. Ever since Ja Rule dissed 50 Cent on "New York" featuring Jadakiss and Fat Joe, 50 saw it as disrespectful for Jadakiss and Fat Joe to be a part of Ja Rule's dis record. 50 started taking shots at whoever was on the song. Jadakiss started talking about his new beef with 50. "Yeah, you gotta go in on these niggas, son," Green Lantern said to Jadakiss, not knowing that Jadakiss was filming the conversation. "Tear they ass up now." When Eminem and 50 saw the DVD, they fired Green Lantern and hired Alchemist.

Now Alchemist was in with the most successful camp in the game. I felt confident that Mobb Deep would be next to get pulled into the winner's circle where the big money was at. Alchemist flew to Detroit to meet with Eminem and left me with his apartment for a while. Havoc and I set up a meeting with Jimmy Iovine, president of Interscope Records, home to some of the biggest names in hip hop, including Death Row, Aftermath, Shady, and G-Unit. He was interested in doing a deal with us. We were surprised that we were even on Jimmy's radar and immediately booked a flight to Los Angeles to meet him.

Right before we left for Los Angeles, 50 Cent released "Piggy Bank," taking shots at Ja Rule, Fat Joe, Jadakiss, and Shyne, and he even threw a jab at Mobb Deep: *"I'll do ya little ass like Jay did Mobb Deep."* I was baffled. *Damn, now I gotta deal with this fool,* I thought to myself. *I like 50 Cent but I* guess this is what my life is gonna be about. Rap beef and street drama. Why did he do that?

And then it hit me. Havoc! Havoc's appearance in that faggot-ass Ja Rule video!

Then Havoc told me that he was informed that if Londell McMillan represented us, Interscope wouldn't deal with us. "Certain labels had bad dealings with Londell in the past," Hav said.

"Nah, don't you see that these labels and their legal personnel are just hating on Londell because they know he's gonna get the best deal possible for us?" I said. "They can't tell us which lawyer we can or cannot use." But Havoc wanted to fire Londell and hire a new lawyer so we wouldn't ruin our chances of getting signed.

"That's illegal. You can use any lawyer that you want," Londell told me at a meeting in his office. "These label lawyers don't like me because I know how to negotiate, and these companies want to make slaves out of artists. What do you want to do?"

"Sorry, man. I think you're the best there is, but I gotta move with my partner."

My nigga Havoc . . . I felt like choking myself for being so loyal to him sometimes. When Jive dropped us, I was ready to walk away from Mobb Deep for a little while, fed up and ready for a brand-new start. I wanted to establish my own indie label and get a distribution deal, focus on my solo career until further notice. House money was okay, but I needed Manhattan building money. I needed great-grandchildren money.

A day later, Havoc set up a meeting with an attorney named Theo Sedlmayr, who used to be partners at a firm with Alchemist's manager, Paul Rosenberg. Theo was now 50 Cent and Eminem's lawyer, and I could tell from his words and attitude that, in Theo's mind, Mobb Deep was a thing of the past. His assistant brought over retainer agreements for us to sign giving Theo permission to do business on our behalf. It was painful for me to sign that paper. I felt like I was disrespecting Londell. The vibe I got from Theo was that he didn't seem genuinely concerned with our career. But Havoc and I had to be on the same page, so to make our lives easier we moved together on things.

We lit cigars as if this was a celebration. "So, Interscope is showing some interest?" Theo said.

"Yeah, but we would rather fuck with Eminem. Isn't that your client?" I asked. "Wouldn't he be interested in signing Mobb Deep?"

"No, Eminem is looking to get away from signing hard-core acts. He wants conscious rap now, like Pharoahe Monch and Mos Def."

This man actually wanted me to believe that Eminem wouldn't be interested in signing Mobb Deep after what Eminem did for us in his movie? It sounded like bullshit to me. "What's up with 50 Cent? Isn't he your client too?" I asked. "You should get him on the phone and see if he's interested."

"No, 50 isn't looking to sign anybody right now. He's got too much on his plate already. Let's just see how it goes with Interscope and take it from there."

Why would you represent a client who you don't believe in 100 percent? It seemed like Theo was only in it for the payday and to add another name to his roster.

Havoc and I flew to L.A. to meet with Jimmy Iovine at the Interscope office. Those meetings with labels made me sick to my stomach because it felt like I was begging to be signed by executives who had no idea about what's hot in the street. I knew our music was powerful enough for us to be independent. I hated it with every molecule in my body but tried to be as humble as possible and not show any signs of disgust in my face. I'm a boss, not an employee.

"Mobb Deep, it's nice to finally meet you guys," Jimmy said after greeting us in his office. "I know a lot about your music and history. So you're looking for a new label to call home, huh?"

"Yeah, we seem to outlive all our labels. We're looking for a company that understands our music and audience and can push our albums to the maximum without dropping the ball," I said.

"I know you guys are veterans. You're like a classic car that just needs a fresh coat of paint," Jimmy said. "I wouldn't want to sign you guys directly to Interscope, I'd rather bring you in through Aftermath, Shady, or G-Unit because they know more about how to promote your style of music. So let me run this by Dre and Eminem and see if they're interested. We'll do it like that, okay?"

"That sounds good," Havoc and I agreed. The way Jimmy spoke made me feel more at ease. He seemed genuinely interested and somewhat knowledgeable. Our first pick would be to sign with Dr. Dre. Shady was our second choice. Since 50 Cent just dissed us, we knew he probably wasn't interested. We flew to New York and I stayed at Alchemist's apartment for a few days to be alone with my thoughts.

Back in Bridgeport during breakfast with my family, Havoc called. "P, where you at? I've gotta tell you something," he said, sounding excited.

"I'm in Connecticut. What's up?"

"You ain't gonna believe this shit. I just got a call from 50. He said he heard that Jive dropped us and he's interested in signing us. He wants to have a meeting right away."

"What? That's crazy! The nigga just tried dissing us on his song and now he want to sign us? He might be trying to set us up, son," I said. *This nigga 50 is trying to make us look stupid or something*, I thought. *Trying to pull a chess move like Nas.*

"Just come to the studio early tomorrow so we can talk," Hav said. "He wants to meet us tomorrow afternoon."

June 30, 2009
Mid-State Correctional Facility
Marcy, New York
1:00 A.M.

Prison is for losers and dumb fucks. The intelligent winners are out in the street with their freedom. Ain't nothin' cool or glorifying about being locked up—whoever thinks this shit gives you street credibility is a fool. All prison does is screw up your life for a short, long, or permanent period of time. My time was short. I don't care if you say you're innocent and got set up or if you feel your crime was justifiable, you still made some type of mistake, wrong move, did something you shouldn't have done, or went someplace you shouldn't have gone. Basically, you did some dumb shit and got caught slippin'. I'm not shittin' on inmates, there are plenty of good brothers and sisters trapped in the system. I just want to make it very clear, especially for young kids, that prison is nothing to be proud of.

I'd been to five different facilities during my bid—Rikers Island (one month), Downstate (two months), Gouverneur (one month), Oneida (a few days), and my final stop on my New York State prison tour, Mid-State Correctional Facility (two years, eight months). Inmates and COs from all over New York, from old-timers to young bloods, showed me and Mobb Deep crazy love. It gave me a crazy boost of inspiration.

I'd never been away from the studio for so long in my life. I ordered a few instrumental mix tapes from the prison catalog to write songs to, but I can't write to the best of my ability to another artist's music. I needed original, never-heard-before production from my home team to write hits.

It was like trying to get a Muslim to eat pork, getting a beat cassette in Mid-State. They allowed only screwless cassettes shrink-wrapped in plastic with an invoice from a music distributor. First, I had to order screwless mix tapes or albums from the prison catalog, which only mailed goods to jails. KiKi sent Alchemist the cassettes to record over, then Alchemist sent them back to KiKi, who mailed them to my *H.N.I.C. Pt. 2* distributor to be re-shrink-wrapped and shipped with an invoice. It took about six months to get a beat tape in my hands.

When I finally got my beat tapes, I turned into a songwriting tsunami in that eight-by-ten steel box. All my producer homeboys started sending me hot shit—Alchemist, Havoc, Sid Roams, S.C., and my dude Stevie J who used to produce for Bad Boy. I wrote seven albums with the first few cassettes. I gave thanks to the Most High for blessing me with that amount of creativity. I didn't mark notches on my walls for every day that went by like they did in jail movies. I never paid the calendar any attention at all; watching the days made them seem slower. I went without knowing the date or trying to find out. Then the next thing I knew, three months would fly by.

Letters were coming in from all over the world—Serbia, Russia, England, France, Germany, Hong Kong, and all around the U.S., but the letter

I wanted and waited for most never came—Havoc's letter. I'd written Havoc twice from Downstate, once from Gouverneur, then once from Mid-State. He hadn't responded. Hav never even contacted KiKi to check on my family.

KiKi e-mailed, texted, and called Hav on my behalf on several occasions and he responded twice out of twenty tries. "Stop reaching out to him if he doesn't want to respond," KiKi said. "Maybe he's trying to tell you something. Maybe he doesn't wanna do Mobb Deep anymore."

"No, keep trying," I insisted. "That's my partner. If he doesn't wanna be my friend, we still gotta handle our business."

"If you come home and you're still dealing with dudes like that, who don't give a fuck about you, then I'm not fuckin' with you no more," KiKi said.

My man Tyson from Queens started making the four-hour drive from Jamaica in his messed-up hooptie to see me. I would ask him about Havoc but Tyson said he didn't know what was up with him. I told Tyson to put Havoc in the car and just bring him. "I'm gonna put him in the car and tell him we going to the liquor store," Tyson said. "Then come straight to you!" Ha! That sounded funny, but this wasn't a joke.

My partner wasn't communicating with me, and there were things we needed to discuss. Even though I was locked up, there were still plenty of ways to keep our money coming. But without communication, it just didn't work. I wasn't concerned only with business, I was concerned with Hav's well-being. He was more than just a music partner, he was my friend.

If there's one thing you learn from prison, it's patience. So I decided to be patient with Havoc. *He'll come around eventually.* I needed to focus on my number-one priority: me. I wanted to build a powerful vocabulary. Besides Dr. York's books, the only books I'd ever read in my life were *The Autobiography of Malcolm X* and *Who Moved My Cheese?* I was missing out on a world full of literature and put it in my mind that I would be like a Tibetan monk locked up in the mountains for three years of study and research. By the time I was released, I would come home a mastermind.

I started receiving books in the mail from KiKi and my friend Laura Checkoway, who is also the editor of this autobiography. Laura sent me some random books that she thought I would be interested in and she was 200 percent correct with her choices. She sent *Target Zero: A Life in*

Writing, the autobiography of Eldridge Cleaver, one of the most infamous Black Panthers. I tore through the book in a week. She also sent *Medical Apartheid* by Harriet A. Washington, an incredible book about the history of medical experiments on black people. My wife sent Assata Shakur's autobiography. Foxy Brown told me she read it right before she went home from her bid on Rikers. Assata Shakur was also a Black Panther, and her story was amazing. I also read *Long Walk to Freedom*, the autobiography of Nelson Mandela.

Not only did reading build my vocabulary, it also allowed me to see life from different points of view. It made me more enthused about life, love, family, God, and my career. It's funny how the right book can do that to you. I see it like this: Knowledge is food for the brain. You can fill up on junk food (fiction) that will cloud your brain with all kinds of pollution, or you can fill up on health food (facts) that will turn your brain into a strong, intelligent muscle.

When I spoke to friends and family over the phone and during visits, they all told me they could see in my eyes and hear in my voice that I had a fresh new energy. I was taken away from my family and recording studio, the two things I loved. It gave me a brand-new appreciation for them. It's true when they say that you don't know what you've got until it's gone.

There were four inmates I was cool with in my dorm: Young from Poughkeepsie; Alex from Hunt's Point in the Bronx; Leggz Diamond from the Bronx; and Brandon from South Jamaica, Queens. Whenever we hung out in the day room and watched shows like *106th & Park*, MTV and VH1 videos, and music-awards shows, I'd get frustrated watching all the artists performing and promoting their new product. It inspired me and made me fiend for a studio like a dope addict. Whenever I got that frustrated feeling, I'd tell my boys, "A'ight, I'm out. I'm going to the studio." And they knew that meant I was locking in my cell to write songs with my Walkman.

CHAPTER 12

BLOOD MONEY

Now homie if I go to hell and you make it to the pearly gates

Tell that nigga God we got beef

And tell that nigga Jesus I'ma see him when I see him

And when I see him I'ma beat him like the movie

For leaving us out to dry in straight poverty

For not showing me no signs he watching over me

"Pearly Gates"

Twelve noon, Harlem: Riding up the West Side Highway in the backseat of Havoc's black 2005 4.6 Range Rover with black rims, aka the Black Jellybean, I was extremely anxious to see how this monumental meeting was going to turn out. 50 was having a Reebok photo shoot underneath the trestle on 125th Street and the West Side Highway. I had a gun on my waist, as always, but when we pulled up to the spot, I left it in the car. I didn't know if I could trust 50 after he took that shot at us on "Piggy Bank," but I decided to give him my trust, so I put the sixteen-shooter under the car mat and stepped out of the truck.

Chris Lighty, our former manager who we'd parted ways with shortly after the Jive deal, greeted Havoc, Fly, and me with his devilish baby-face grin, then walked into a trailer. 50 came from the back of the trailer and got right down to business. He told us the amount of respect he had for us, saying that he was our biggest fan and that Mobb Deep motivated him to be a rapper. He gave us all kinds of compliments and said that he wanted to see us on his level of success selling multimillion units. It was weird hearing that from someone who sold over ten million and didn't have to give us the time of day. He said he would send us a deal memo—a rough draft of a contract to start the negotiation process—ASAP.

Back at the studio, Havoc and I discussed the offer for hours. It felt like we hit the lottery, like a miracle. Now we could relax and create dope music without stressing money or label problems, just as Havoc wanted. I could move my family out of Bridgeport. Finally somebody with power recognized our power.

We were going to need a new lawyer because Theo would be a conflict of interest since he represented 50. And he said 50 wouldn't be interested. Ha! I told Havoc that we should ask for two million dollars to sign. I wasn't expecting two million, but when you do business, you start high and the number works its way down. Havoc didn't understand that concept. He thought asking for that much would turn 50 off and we'd lose the deal. But I believed if 50 was serious about all the things he told us, then he should pay the price. I knew how ill we were and how much we were worth.

Driving to Connecticut to chill with KiKi and the kids that night, all kinds of thoughts were running through my head about my next move. I was wrapping up *H.N.I.C. Pt. 2* and planning to release it independently under my own label, but that call from 50 might change my plan if all went well. Since the Jive deal soured, I wanted to stop doing Mobb Deep for a little while and start focusing on Prodigy. I was beginning to see very clearly that Havoc and I were completely different. I knew it all along, but reality was hitting harder than ever. To tell you the truth, I didn't want to do the deal with 50. I felt as

ALBERT "PRODIGY" JOHNSON
240

though I wasn't being a man by doing the deal. That's why I wanted so much money to sell him a few Mobb Deep albums.

The following morning I told KiKi the news but she never got excited about anything related to rap music, so 50 Cent didn't mean shit to her. She just wanted to get the hell out of Connecticut. I wrote down the pros and cons of the deal. When I did the math, it made more sense to do it. I e-mailed 50's lawyer Theo saying that it was nice meeting with 50 and we were excited to do business, but that we needed an advance of two million dollars upon signing. I CC'd Havoc and 50's assistant Pretty Sha so they all got the message at the same time. Havoc immediately hit me back with an e-mail barking on me for sending the message. He called me foolish and said he was tired of my antics. *He's mad because I'm trying to get us paid?* KiKi and I laughed at his angry e-mails. Pretty Sha hit me back and said he would get the message to 50.

I was talking about the new deal while smoking with Alchemist at his apartment later that day when 50 called asking for my e-mail address to send a song for Hav and me to check out. Twenty minutes later, Al and I listened to the first of thirty Mobb Deep featuring 50 Cent tracks. I burned it to a CD and rushed back to Queens to link with Hav, excited to show 50 how fast we worked. We knocked it out within an hour. We didn't have Internet at our studio in Queens so I jetted back to Alchemist's crib to send it. That back-and-forth process became my daily routine for the next three weeks.

After three weeks we had thirty songs done. 50 called one day when I was at the ATM around the corner from our Queens studio saying he was impressed by how fast we worked and how good the songs were turning out. Anytime he called, I stopped everything to speak with him. If I was driving, I pulled the car over to concentrate on our conversation. 50 said he had a surprise that he couldn't hold in, but not to tell Havoc so at least Hav could be surprised. "I'm buying you two Porsches as a bonus," 50 said, since we had knocked out so much music before even inking the deal. He wanted people to see us with the cars and know we were signing to G-Unit. I didn't know what to say—50 was giving us two Porsches! I just said thanks.

As soon as I got off the phone with him, I raced back to the studio to tell Havoc what 50 told me not to tell him. Just like 50, I couldn't hold it in.

Hav was hyped. The one-of-a-kind special-order Porsches would be delivered in a week.

"Do you know how to drive stick shift?" 50 asked.

"No," I said, but I would damn sure learn fast.

I practiced in a Honda Prelude before picking up my keys and insurance card from 50's accountant right next to Long Island Jewish Hospital. I drove my brand-spanking-new silver 911 Turbo S series with black leather interior to the studio to see Hav's white GT3 and compare the two. Hav's Porsche was very rare—only one hundred made in America. My car was making so many females stop and look that I called the turbo holes on each side pussy holes. I was in love with my Porsche with the pussy holes.

The next morning I woke up to the sounds of Alchemist making beats. I felt weird living with Al because I didn't want to be a burden, so I swept the floor and kept things as neat as possible. After cleaning, I searched the Web for information about the Illuminati, secret government UFOs, and the origins of races and religions. I became a real Internet junkie staying with Al. Eventually I forced myself to turn off the computer and drove to the Queens studio. Fly, Hav, and Nyce were there when I arrived. Nyce was a rapper from Southside Jamaica, Queens, who'd been renting our studio whenever we weren't using it. Hav took a liking to him and wanted to sign him. It took me a while to get used to new people and Hav kept new faces popping up.

That Monday, Mobb Deep's new lawyer, Evan Friefeld, called saying he got the deal memo from 50's lawyer. The contract was a two-album deal with a little over one-million-dollar advance for Hav and me to split and a merchandising deal for clothing, 70 percent for us, 30 percent for G-Unit. It was a regular artist deal, meaning we got nineteen points for each album sold. That's about eighty-nine cents to one dollar per album. If we signed the deal, we would be going on two back-to-back major tours, Eminem's Anger Management and 50 Cent's Massacre tour. Plus we would be on the movie sound track for 50's flick *Get Rich or Die Tryin'*, going to premieres around the world. We signed on the dotted line real fast.

A few weeks later, 50 threw a big party at his crib in Connecticut. My cousin JM, 40 Glocc, Majesty, E-Money Bags's younger brother Reem, and I took the two-hour drive, smoking six blunts along the way. Hav followed a few hours later. 50's driver, Bruce, let us in. *Wow*. 50 had transformed Mike Tyson's crib into a palace with like six living rooms, six kitchens, seventeen bedrooms, a club, strip club, pool tables, racquetball court, indoor and outdoor basketball courts, indoor and outdoor pools and Jacuzzis, lake, waterfall, dirtbike and four-wheeler track, and a studio, gym, sauna, movie theater, elevator, and shooting range. 50 told me I could have any bedroom I wanted, except his of course, and that I could stay there whenever I wanted.

50's personal chef came over to me. "50 told me to tell you this house is yours," he said. "Anything you want, I'll cook it for you. Anything you need."

We partied all night and kicked it with our new label mates Tony Yayo, Lloyd Banks, and Young Buck. They embraced us like family. Then we took the long drive back home.

50 called the next morning and told me to get ready for the U.S. run of Eminem's Anger Management tour, which would be followed by his Massacre tour. He then told me that he would be at the G-Unit office later. Alchemist's crib was a block away from the G-Unit office, so I walked over there all the time. People at the office must have been like, "Damn, P's here a lot." Havoc only made special guest appearances every blue moon.

"Where's Hav?" Yayo and 50 always asked. "What's up with Hav?"

"Making beats," I said, and I wasn't lying. Havoc was in the studio like a lab rat twenty-four hours a day. Otherwise, he had somebody's chick drinking Hennessy and putting her legs behind her head.

I was trying to stay close with our new crimies, the Unit. I didn't want to miss a beat. Diamond District jewelers came to the office offering 50 gifts he didn't even want. When he brushed them off, Yayo and I befriended them and got free shit. I brought jewelry and clothes to Havoc at the studio in Queens. He'd ask how did I get it all and I told him he needed to come to the office more often. He needed to be in the mix in order to reap the benefits.

50 announced to the public that along with Mobb Deep, he was signing another hard-core rap duo, M.O.P, the Mash Out Posse from Brownsville, Brooklyn. Mobb Deep and M.O.P started our careers at the same time, both signing to Island/4th & Broadway back when we put out *Juvenile Hell*. When Loud Records briefly merged with Relativity Records in 2002, Mobb Deep and

M.O.P were label mates. We had a hit record with "Hey Luv" featuring 112 from *Infamy*, and M.O.P had their hit "Ante Up" from their album *Warriors*. Now here we were, together again in 2005 on G-Unit Records.

The week before we went on tour, we shot the video for "Outta Control," a remix to a song produced by Dr. Dre originally on 50's *Massacre* album. It was our first Dr. Dre beat. M.O.P made a cameo appearance in the video. 50 made a bunch of T-shirts that read MOBB DEEP/G-UNIT/GAME OVER; G-Unit reminded me of Mobb Deep because of how hard they worked in the studio making quality music. Tupac also reminded me of our work ethic; it seemed like he had an endless amount of songs. Anybody can push themselves and make one million songs, but are they good songs? Most people make one million pieces of shit. Our music, our songs, are works of art. Not fast food. Our shit is home cooking.

The day we left for the world tour, I couldn't wait to get onstage and felt the crowd's response on opening night, July 11, in Chicago. I hadn't been nervous before getting onstage in a long time, but this was major. Mobb Deep, M.O.P, Eminem, Lloyd Banks, Yayo, Young Buck, and 50 all had our own buses, each bus wrapped with pictures of our faces on them— Yayo, Banks, M.O.P, Olivia, Mobb Deep. I noticed 50's face wasn't on there; he was really using his power to promote his artists. I think Olivia rode in 50's bus. I wondered, *Why is 50 wasting money on Olivia?* She was garbage and not very good-looking. Sorry, O. She never had a hit record, so what was the purpose? 50 could have had any R&B female he wanted but for whatever reason he chose her. Strange.

But I paid it no mind. I figured 50 would realize sooner or later who's pulling weight and who's not.

A few of our people joined us on the road—Twin, 40 Glocc, Nyce, and Hav's uncle La. Alchemist was Eminem's DJ, so he had a bus with a few of Em's boys. Often Eminem and 50 flew in private jets to the next state. Sold-out arenas every night. We stayed at the Ritz-Carlton in every state, top-of-the-line. We were on a strict schedule. The road manager would call and we had to be in the lobby on time or get left. 50, Yayo, and Banks had their own bulletproof trucks with drivers who met us in the next state or followed the tour buses, which drove from city to city in a pack. *I gotta get me one of them armored trucks*, I thought.

At the arena, we'd be in the G-Unit dressing room blasting music, flooding the room with weed smoke, and drowning in Hennessy. 50 didn't smoke or drink, so he needed his own separate room. He had a private chef and a catering service. The best food, of course, was in 50's dressing room. I made my way to his room for a nice steak dinner every chance I got. He never minded me coming over to grub with him. Stylists outfitted us in tons of clothes—fitted hats, sneakers, boots, tees, socks, and drawers, all G-Unit brand.

"Ya'll know the Infamous Mobb Deep, right?" 50 introduced us onstage every night, the crowd screaming. Mobb Deep did three songs in the middle of 50's set—"Shook Ones," "Quiet Storm," and "Outta Control." I worried I might bust my ass coming down the steps from the tall scaffolding as we took the stage. I held on tight to the railing while walking down a spiral staircase every night. After our work was done, Twin, Nyce, 40 Glocc, and I would walk into the crowd to fuck with the fans and the females, signing autographs and posing for pictures.

Alchemist would be upset that while we were in the crowd getting all the girls to bring backstage, he was setting up to get onstage with Eminem. So Al started going in early. He'd be in the crowd while we were onstage with 50. Alchemist brought our boy Ron Gotti from Queensbridge to help assist with equipment. It felt good to have all of us together on such a big tour— Hav, Twin, Gotti, Alchemist, Nyce, 40 Glocc, and me.

Our crew was veterans when it came to touring and swooping up the ladies to come backstage or to the hotel, with twelve years of seasoned game under our belts. We knew exactly what to say and do and called ourselves Vultures. The G-Unit crew was animals just like us, so we came up with a name for them, Hyenas. Some nights we bumped heads going after the same females. "It's the Vultures versus the Hyenas," Twin said one night, and I fell on the floor laughing.

You know the Vultures won, 'cause we fly! Ha! Nah, but when the Hyenas felt like they might lose a girl to the Vultures, they would use their secret weapon, five words: "50 wants to see you." It was over after that. We called that cheating. 50 didn't want to see shit, they just said that to get them to the room. It's all good. We had a lot of fun all over the United States in every major city on the map.

A crew of six females in Florida got on our tour bus and followed us halfway across America, hopping off in Texas somewhere after we had our fun with them. They didn't know how they were getting back home and didn't care. We damn sure didn't either.

A couple of dudes, whom I won't name, would pay for groupies to fly or bus back home. We called them Care Bear Thugs. If I named them they would get their Vulture wings or Hyena tails clipped. If the G-Unit crew caught one of their Hyenas being a Care Bear, they would subpoena him to Hood Court and he would have to stand trial in front of everybody, then get judged by a jury of Hyenas.

At the hotel after the show, instead of fucking with chicks, I would often go to the studio truck where 50 was always working on the *Get Rich or Die Tryin'* movie sound track. 50 never fucked with chicks after the shows. He's strictly business. It took a real bad chick to get his attention.

50, Yayo, Banks, Buck, and I put in the most work in the studio truck, along with Spider Loc, an L.A. Crip who joined Young Buck for his fifteen-minute set every night. It's crazy that G-Unit had an L.A. Crip down with them and Mobb Deep had an L.A. Crip also, 40 Glocc.

One night at the hotel, 50 told me that he was going to sign Mase and bring him on tour. Mase was dope when he first came out as Murda Mase on songs with DMX and Cam'ron, but now? Personally, I wasn't feeling the idea but I figured 50 knew something I didn't. I felt 50 was watering down the power we would have if it was just Mobb Deep and G-Unit—powerful Queens hood music, consistent and invincible.

After about fifteen shows, we went to New York for a weeklong break. 50 had his eight-year-old son Marquise with him on tour, so I figured I would bring my nine-year-old son Shaka with me when the break was over. Shaka was open when I told him he was coming with me.

The "Outta Control" remix was getting a lot of video and radio play, but I was starting to hear a lot of hatred because Mobb Deep signed with G-Unit. Fans approached me in the streets, asking, "Why did ya'll sign to G-Unit? Ya'll Mobb Deep, ya'll don't need 50." I read similar comments on the Internet and in magazines. But true Mobb Deep fans should've been happy that their favorite group was still active after fifteen years, making big deals, writing rhymes, and crafting beats that were timeless.

I don't care if it's on G-Unit, B-Unit, 3-Unit, Loud, Sony, Koch, or Nuts in Ya Mouth Records. We do what we do, wherever we decide to do it.

I understood how the fans felt. They wanted to see us as independent label owners, not employees. I felt the same way. But Havoc didn't want that and I was being loyal to my partner. We were making a lot of money and doing what we loved so, hey, there was really nothing to complain about.

After the one-week break, our crew met on Twenty-seventh Street and Eleventh Avenue and got back on the tour bus. KiKi's fifteen-year-old cousin Man-Man came along so that he could keep an eye on Shaka while we went to the after-parties.

Man-Man and Shaka had never been on a tour bus before, so I taught them the number-one rule: No shitting in the bus bathroom! You also had to sleep on the bunk with your head to the back of the bus because if you faced front, you might break your neck if the bus stopped short. The kids usually stayed up front watching movies or playing PlayStation. At the Ritz, I taught the kids their next lesson: No food from the minibar, no ten-buck candy bars. When we got to the arena, I introduced Shaka and Man-Man to 50. 50's son wasn't on the tour anymore—he'd gone home for a few weeks. Afterward, 50 told me that my son walked up to him and said, "My dad said we were gonna be rich one day and now I believe him."

Mase joined the tour. Mase hung out in 50's room doing push-ups and sit-ups. 50 tended to have that effect on people. At showtime, I brought Shaka to the side of the stage to get a good look. I instructed Shaka and Man-Man to hold their ears during the explosion in the beginning. When it was Mobb Deep's turn, Shaka was damn near onstage with us, watching in the background. This was his first time seeing me perform, and there were like forty thousand people screaming and singing his father's songs. I was happy he got to see that.

After we finished, Mase came out shimmying, doing his famous dance. It looked like Puffy was going to hop up out of nowhere, saying, "Take that, take that!" The crowd loved it, but the Vultures and Hyenas were backstage mimicking it. "Take that, take that!" I felt like walking up to 50 and asking, "Why?" but I didn't. I was happy to have a great position and enjoy it with my son and my friends.

Man-Man and Shaka started roaming around the arena with the sons of Lil' Fame and Fox from M.O.P. They were hopping gates and disrespecting the security and arena personnel. When people told them to stop running around before they hurt themselves, they'd say, "This is my dad's show," and keep wilding. After roaming around in the crowd, I caught up with the little terrors and saw them jumping over a three-foot gate without using their hands. "Don't buss your face open and ruin yourself," I warned Shaka. "Your tour will be over after that." That made him relax.

50 told me he would watch my son at the hotel while we went to the after-parties. I didn't want to impose on his privacy but he said it wasn't a problem; he never went to the after-parties anyway. Everybody in G-Unit liked my son. Shaka's a good kid with a fun personality, always joking and play fighting.

DJ Whoo Kid would DJ the after-parties for extra money and promoters gave us free bottles of everything while we acted a damn fool standing on all the chairs and tables going crazy to our music and enjoying the women. Our job was to leave an impression in every state. Make people say, "Them Mobb Deep/G-Unit boys is wild."

When I walked into 50's room at the hotel to get Shaka after an after-party, I smelled something burning. This little fool was cooking the complimentary fruit on the coffeepot hot plate! 50 didn't know what was going on because he was knocked out sleeping. At four A.M., this little boy was starting a damn fruit fire. I cleaned up the mess and took Shaka back to our room, where Man-Man was knocked out. Shaka's crazy. He must've been tired and delirious doing that crazy shit.

50 had a tattoo artist on the tour who would tatt people up every day. I decided to get G-UNIT on my hand like Yayo, Banks, Buck, 50, and the team. 50 made me feel real comfortable like I was a brother. I felt like part of the family. When I showed Havoc, he was buggin' like, "Wow." I didn't show anybody else.

Backstage before the show the next night, 50 looked at my hand and did a double take. "P, let me see your hand," he said. "Oh, shit. Okay."

Later that night after the show, everybody had chicks at the hotel except for me. I was wandering around the hotel looking for everybody but they were all "busy" in their rooms. I took a walk to the studio truck but only the engineer was there. So I walked over to a tour bus with a light shining through the windows and climbed inside and what I saw shocked the hell out of me.

50 was getting a tattoo. I stepped in to get a closer look. MOBB DEEP enclosed in a semicircle—our logo—inked in black on his wrist. I was stunned. I didn't know what to say. I chilled there for five minutes then went back to my room. As I lay in bed trying to drift off, I thought about how glad I was that I got the G-Unit tattoo first without telling anyone. It was an official gesture of loyalty, and 50 did the same. The next day Havoc got a G-Unit tattoo when I told him that 50 got Mobb Deep.

A lot of so-called fans said that I was sucking 50 for getting a G-Unit tattoo. They shut up when they found out he got Mobb Deep. A lot of people wanted Mobb Deep to be fraudulent so bad. Sorry to disappoint you, but the Infamous Mobb Deep are some of the realest in rap. We create while other rappers steal, acting as if we don't exist so you won't discover where they got it. I call 'em "closet fans."

Our next stop on tour was Virginia Beach. The clear, sunny skies felt like the tropics when we arrived, and we had plenty of time to kill before the show. I took the boys for a walk on the boardwalk to enjoy the scenery and weather. I noticed my son and Man-Man checking out girls their age around the hotel and started giving them pointers on how to approach females and start a conversation. Then I would test them. I hadn't had the official birds-and-bees convo with Shaka yet, but I could see that it was time.

There was a pretty little girl checking into the hotel with her parents, so I told Shaka to try his skills on her. I saw a purple flower in a small landscaping pot and I told him to pick it out and give it to her. To my surprise, Shaka wasn't scared at all. He stepped right to his business and started talking to the girl. Shaka walked back to where I was standing, cheesing.

I gave Man-Man a couple of condoms and told him to practice safe sex, if it happened to come down to that. Better safe than sorry.

I had a radio interview with 50 so I left Man-Man with the spare room key and told them to be safe. In the hotel hallway after the radio show, I saw Shaka and Man-Man strolling in the complimentary hotel robes and slippers talking about, "What's up, player," like they were two Hugh Hefners in the Playboy Mansion. I asked them where they were coming from and they said they were working out in the hotel gym with Mase. I asked them if Mase spoke to them and they said, "No, he didn't say much." They said they were running on the treadmill and stationary bike, then they hit the pool and Jacuzzi.

Some of the G-Unit crew told me that Shaka and Man-Man had a couple of young groupies in the room. The kids told me nothing happened, though. That night at the show, Man-Man and Shaka were signing autographs for young girls on their pant legs and back pockets of their jeans. These little dudes thought they were superstars! Shaka was telling people that Man-Man was his security guard. Ha! Man-Man looked older than his age so it was believable.

We were having the time of our lives, six-star hotels, cream-of-the-crop groupies, flights in G-5 private jets, a traveling professional studio, radio and TV shows, the best food, weed, and no sleep—maybe a little. It seemed like every day we had thirty magazine interviews, four radio shows, and twenty video interviews. Havoc always hated doing press—getting him to do interviews was like pulling wisdom teeth—so I did a lot by myself. I loved doing press, although constantly being asked the same questions and repeating the same answers did become annoying. I tried to just have fun with it.

After Virginia Beach came Atlanta, Orlando, Minneapolis, Denver, Salt Lake, then Dallas. In Atlanta, we were running late from a radio interview before the concert and there was bumper-to-bumper traffic on the highway heading toward the arena. The Atlanta police escorted our seven-car motorcade on the shoulder, bypassing the traffic. At the arena, Gotti, Alchemist, Twin, and I were outside smoking haze in a patio area when forty dudes with CTE (Corporate Thugz Entertainment) and Snowman T-shirts and blue bandannas bogarted their way through the back entrance smoking cigarettes and weed and swigging on big gallons of liquor.

Who the fuck is these niggas? Gotti, Al, Twin, and I wondered. Seeing fifteen Snowman tees, it clicked that it was Young Jeezy and his crew. Young Jeezy walked through the gate in shades and a blue rag covering his face under his hat. I realized that Young Jeezy and his team were claiming Crip. That was new to me—Atlanta Crips. I didn't know if 50 had invited them, but they were cool with Young Buck and the way they bogarted their way inside reminded me of Mobb Deep.

Thirty minutes later, 50 flew onstage with the loud explosion and once again it was on. After 50's set, Buck came out chest-naked, lit blunt in hand, doing his usual Buck Marley set—a marijuana tribute—with Spider Loc. Buck suddenly stopped and called Young Jeezy onstage. Hav, Shaka, Man-Man, and I watched from the side-stage TV monitor waiting for our turn to perform. Jeezy performed a few songs and Buck brought his set to a close. Jeezy and his team bounced and Buck walked over to the side-stage wardrobe where 50, Yayo, and Banks were getting ready to hit the stage. 50 grabbed Buck by the arm crazy tight and screamed at him. "You ever pull some shit like that again, I'm gonna send your dumb ass home! What the fuck is wrong with you?" Buck just kept quiet.

Buck hadn't even asked 50 if Jeezy could perform and Jeezy did more songs than he was supposed to do, when he really wasn't supposed to do anything at all. Jeezy played Young Buck. That was the first time I saw Young Buck do some dumb shit. After the show, some G-Unit members were arguing with Young Buck and his Nashville crew. A fight almost broke out, and it was tense for the next couple of shows.

After about twenty-five shows on Eminem's Anger Management tour, we arrived at the last venue—Detroit's Tiger Stadium. It was the perfect way for Eminem to end his tour: in his hometown. For the first time on the whole tour I told Alchemist I wanted to kick it with Shady. In Shady's dressing room, Em's hype man Proof from D12 sat smoking a strange-looking red cigarette. "You wanna try one of these?" he asked, offering one of the strange-smelling smokes. "They're Japanese cigarettes." I figured, *What the hell. I'll take a toke.* It was the most horrible flavor in the history of tobacco, like a rolled-up shit turd. That was my first and last time kicking it with Proof. He was murdered in a Detroit club the following year. He was a cool dude.

Inside Al's bus, which was notches above the luxury of Mobb Deep's bus, Atlanta rapper Lil Scrappy and his homeboy were smoking heavy. Scrappy's homeboy had sickle-cell too, so we talked about it for a while. In between the parked tour buses, crunk rapper Lil Jon was cooking chicken on a barbecue grill. Lil Jon and Scrappy opened the show every night, then Ciara, then 50, then Shady.

Lil Jon cracked open a tall can of beer and guzzled half of it. He put a whole chicken on the grill with seasoning. Lil Jon looked over at us and said, "After you drink some of the beer, you stuff the beer can up the chicken's ass and prop the chicken upright so that it's sitting on the beer can. Then you let it cook and let the beer steam get all inside the chicken for flavor. You have to let it marinate." Lil Jon cracked open another beer and in a proper tone, as if hosting a cooking show, said, "I usually use this time to have me another beer whilst we wait."

Wow, a crunk cooking lesson. We walked away shaking our heads. Lil Jon offered us some chicken and that was our cue to bounce. *I'd rather not.*

For this particular show at Tiger Stadium, everybody's stage entrance was different from all the other shows. 50: "Ya'll know the Infamous Mobb Deep, right?"

Crowd: *"Yeahhhh!"*

50: "Well, check this out!"

Havoc and I came out from both sides of the stage and started "Quiet Storm." It was crazy! Tiger Stadium looked gigantic. I had flashbacks from when Pops kidnapped me and we lived in Detroit. We used to go to Tigers games and now I was performing there.

One minute into Hav's verse, he suddenly disappeared from my peripheral vision and I didn't hear him rapping anymore. *"Oooh!"* the crowd said at the same time like something bad just happened. I looked to my right and saw Havoc holding on for his life inside the elevator hole onstage that 50 had risen out of during his entrance. The stage production crew had left it open by mistake. A stagehand ran out to try to help him but Hav lifted himself out real quick, mic still in hand. "I'm all right!" he said, and we kept performing. I knew Hav was embarrassed but he snapped right back.

After Detroit, we went back home to New York and Shady added one last show at Madison Square Garden. The Garden show was special for us the way that Tiger Stadium was for Shady. While we were onstage performing "Shook Ones," I looked to the left of the front row and saw Nicole Kidman going crazy with her hands in the air dancing to our music. I was shocked. She was with the men's-magazine model Vida Guerra. That was the highlight of the concert.

During the short break before I went back on tour, KiKi found a new townhouse development in New Jersey for $780,000. Our last house was almost

$300,000 less. But since we made the G-Unit deal, I figured it would be safe to buy the spot and pay it off quickly with tour money.

At the tail end of August 2005 we flew to London to start the Massacre European tour. It was time for my son Shaka to start school again, so he had to stay home. 40 Glocc and Twin came along. In London, a tour bus met us at the Ritz-Carlton. We had to share our bus with M.O.P for this leg of the tour.

Get Rich or Die Tryin' was premiering in London the night we arrived, so we got spiffy for the red carpet. Hundreds of paparazzi cameras and fans lined up as we made our entrance. 50 pulled me to the side before we left the hotel. "When you see cameras, make sure you're right next to me. I want Mobb Deep to benefit from all this promotion," he said. So that's what I did. Mase was with us overseas too. On the red carpet, Mase ran past everybody to stand next to 50 for the paparazzi pictures and interviews. It wasn't my style to knock people out of the way and fight to stand next to 50 for a picture like a male groupie. I'll just catch the next picture.

After the movie that night, one of 50's super-rich friends, Amir, threw a party at his mansion in downtown London. "Wait until you see Amir's crib in London. This nigga is stupid rich," 50 had been telling me throughout the tour. "These rappers out here think they've got money, these niggas ain't got shit."

Amir had a hundred of the baddest broads in London at his spot for the party, nonstop glasses of champagne, and free drinks all night. Jim Sheridan, the director of *Get Rich or Die Tryin'*, came to the after-party with us. He's Irish, and when I told him I was part Irish, he talked to me a lot after that. We were having so much fun I found myself doing the sandwich dance with some chick and Jim Sheridan. The whole time, 50 kept it strictly professional, standing in a casual suit, holding the same champagne glass for hours, chatting with everybody who approached him. It was impressive to see him not lose his focus amongst all that foolishness. After a while, 50 called me outside to the front of the house, where he and Amir were standing.

"I wanna show you something," he said. Amir pressed a hidden button and the whole cobblestone entrance to his house started going down like an elevator, revealing an underground garage with twenty exotic cars. After thirty spilled drinks and eighty broken champagne glasses, the party was over and we went back to the Ritz. Following London, we went to Germany, Scotland, Ireland, France, and Italy. Same shit every night—movie premiere, concert, after-party.

As I was packing my bag to head to Italy, my uncle Lenny called. My grandmother had just died. Bernice Johnson, the original H.N.I.C. She was ninety-two.

The last time I saw her was in 2002 or 2003 when I took my kids to visit her for Christmas at her new house in Cold Spring Harbor, Huntington, Long Island. She had Alzheimer's disease and it seemed as if she didn't recognize the kids or me. It was weird. She still looked healthy and happy, though.

Ever since I was thirteen years old, I had been running the streets hard trying to pursue a music career. From ages six to fifteen, my grandmother sat me down and taught me how she built her business from nothing into something tremendous. But after my grandmother's business grew big, problems started to surface. She was used to doing everything herself and being the H.N.I.C., but her business became so successful that it was too overwhelming for her to run on her own. Grandmoms hired a handful of her closest girlfriends in key positions, but most of them tried to take advantage of her and manipulate situations for their own benefit. That taught me to never hire friends. She started making bad business decisions. A few family members stepped in to help get things back in order, and even though their intentions were good, that was another error—family could be worse than friends in that situation. She needed to hire qualified professionals. Dwindling clients; constant changes in music, fashion, and dance trends; plus IRS problems—at the end of the day, what was left was an untended business in serious debt.

My mother and a couple of other ladies who grew up in my grandmother's dance school, like Kerri Edge and Ashanti's mother Tina, wanted me to step in and gain control of the business when I was around twenty-four back in 1998. But I was busy building a career and life of my own. My uncle

Lenny came to live with her in 1989 to help her with everything. I was so caught up in my own world back then, I figured Uncle Lenny knew what he was doing. Grandmoms was diagnosed with Alzheimer's disease around 1995 and Uncle Lenny took care of her along with my grandmother's close friend and dance student Wesley. "T'Chaka, your grandmother told me that all of her money, homes, and her building are going to you when she passes away," my moms told me. "I don't want anybody to try to swindle all of your inheritance. You need to hire an inheritance lawyer and make sure you're getting what is rightfully yours."

But when I would go visit, Lenny seemed like he was doing an excellent job. He took care of Grandmoms extremely well. Lenny told me that he was concentrating on saving the three homes and that he would make sure they were left for me to own later in life. I really didn't care about inheritance. I just loved my grandmother. To me, that was my grandmoms's life, not mine. I'd get my own. I had to focus on my career and if I inherited any of my grandmother's things, that would be a blessing that I would cherish and pass on to my children.

When Grandmoms died, I was hurt but I knew she lived a full life. I wasn't concerned at all about what she left behind for me, if there was anything at all. I let Uncle Lenny handle that stuff and I never mentioned it to him. I don't know what ended up happening with her estate. I left it in the hands of the Most High.

That day, we flew in 50's G-5 to Italy: plush leather, marble, and gold trimming.

As soon as we got to the Ritz-Carlton in Rome, I called Mobb Deep's Italian engineer Steve Sola in New York to tell him we were in his hometown and ask him where we could get authentic chicken parmigiana. "Anywhere!" he said. "It's Italy!" But most of the restaurants we tried looked at us with disgust and acted as if they didn't want to serve us because we were black.

50's hotel room was connected to ours, and we left the doors open to walk in and out of each other's rooms. You could see the Coliseum from our window. 50 was eating a huge bowl of shrimp and spaghetti. He must have seen me scoping it because he offered me a bowl. That shrimp spaghetti was good as hell. 50 and I had a long talk after we ate about how stupid a lot of fans were for believing Jay-Z when he tried to discredit me. "If the fans who side with Jay knew you personally, they would love you," 50 said. "But fans only go off what they hear. Jay-Z just manipulated the fans' perception of you, but they don't know the real. Perception is powerful."

That next night, Alchemist and I got our hands on some strong hash and weed. We were making fun of rappers who didn't say anything meaningful in music, so I started freestyling my own version of a meaningless verse about how they called hash "shit" in France. *"To makes me a hit, I smokes me a block a shit, then I gets in the zone of Al Capone."* I was high as hell, repeating the rhyme over and over, adding more to it. Alchemist was cracking up. But that stupid freestyle ended up being a real song "That Go," with Keak da Sneak, a rapper from the Bay Area.

50 was on some military shit with his crew, the way I had been in the house in Long Island when my boys thought I was crazy. I knew what it took to succeed and was around a bunch of knuckleheads who didn't share my vision. I saw a lot of my character in 50. His moves were calculated and his mind was sharp. He inspired me to snap back into position, but it wasn't easy now that I'd been blinded by the limelight and luxurious lifestyle. I was overindulgent with drugs, alcohol, jewelry, cars, women, publicity. The Evil Bastard inside me was turning into a real monster.

What the fuck are you doing? I'd ask myself. *Stop it, man.* But it was hard to snap out of it. 50 would tell me, "All you need to do is get your health and body in shape and you'll be unstoppable."

Havoc started swimming in liquor like a tequila worm. Even worse, Hav seemed like he wasn't enthusiastic about the music industry anymore. It was just a job. Alchemist and the rest of us would constantly try to cheer him up and remind him that he was the best in the business, but he was soon back to acting depressed, destroying every hotel minibar, leaving behind six hundred-dollar bills for 50 at checkout. We gave him the nickname Mr. Minibar because he would drink all the liquor in his room, then come to my room and scheme on my minibar liquor. At first I'd think, *Wow, Hav came to kick it with me.* Five minutes later he would discreetly make his way to my minibar, then leave the room. He did that to everybody on the tour, including 50.

Havoc and I were both fucking up in our own ways.

· · ·

Our last stop on the international run of the Massacre tour was in a super-rich, tiny sovereign state called Monaco at the south of France. Before Monaco we stopped at a hotel on the water in Marseille, where you can see Morocco, Africa, right across the ocean. *I would love to bring KiKi to this spot*, I thought.

An hour away in Monaco, we stayed at the Ritz-Carlton and shot the "Window Shopper" video outside by the shops, restaurants, and casino. After the shoot, Alchemist, 40 Glocc, Twin, and I went to the casino to play craps. They wouldn't let you in without a button-down shirt and you couldn't get excited and shout out when you won. The whole casino is quiet like a fuckin' library. *"Shhh . . . people are gambling."* Way too bourgeois for me. We got out of there quick.

It was back to America. We did about fifteen more shows in the United States and a bunch of movie premieres, then it was finally over. It felt good to sit the fuck down and relax for a split second.

Havoc and I swapped cars every so often. Hav had a lot of fly cars— a black-on-black 4.6 Range, a black-on-black G-Wagen Benz truck, a yellow-and-black Lamborghini, a white GT3 Porsche, a silver 750 BMW, and a black Cadillac truck. Hav let me borrow the Lamborghini one day, and oh my God, that's the fastest car I ever drove besides my Turbo.

While we were finishing our *Blood Money* album, I got cool with another one of the jewelers who came around trying to get cool with 50. "I'll say your name in my first single and video if you give me $150,000 worth of jewels for $30,000," I offered. And he agreed. I had at least $250,000 worth of diamond jewelry at that time that I only paid like $80,000 for. Being around 50, Banks, and Yayo made me feel like I had to step my shine up. And I did.

Slowly I started to realize that jewelry was played out, and I wanted to start a new trend of not wearing it at all. "Yo, I ain't rockin' chains no more," I told 50 and Yayo one day. But they disagreed: "P, everybody knows you for your forty-inch chain. You started that. You can't switch up now because the kids are gonna think you're broke if you ain't got no chain on." They insisted so I agreed.

But I felt a drastic change coming and I knew that I was going to start a new trend—no jewelry at all. For the time being, I kept the jewels on and wore the rapper costume.

Uncle Lenny set up a big funeral service celebrating my grandmother at La-Guardia High School in Manhattan, aka the High School of Performing Arts. My mother and I went together. The place was jam-packed with old friends, family, familiar faces, and faces I couldn't remember, plus strangers. My man Roger; Craig's mother, Aunt Cheryl; JM's grandparents; Ashanti and her mom Tina; Kerri Edge and her sisters and mother; Ben Vereen and so many others.

People performed dance routines and Ben Vereen spoke, along with other close family friends. They wanted me to speak but I wasn't in the mood. I just wanted to enjoy my grandmother's celebration with my moms. After the service, I got tired of everybody at the reception coming up and saying, "Aww, I remember when you were a little boy," and "I remember when you were born," so I went outside to smoke a cigarette with Kerri, Aunt Cheryl, and Roger, who doesn't smoke. Then Tina and Ashanti walked out with bodyguards as if they were concerned about their safety. It looked strange. They said hi and bye and bounced. Maybe they felt some kind of way about the Irv Gotti and Jay-Z photo situation. *That's definitely how Jay-Z got that picture*, I thought. Maybe they felt some kind of way because I was down with 50 Cent and G-Unit now. 50 had been dissing Ja and Ashanti. Oh well, whatever.

Thinking about all the lives and people my grandmother inspired was amazing. Bernice Johnson helped show countless people, especially black women, how to become successful in whatever they wanted to do in life. She's responsible for Mobb Deep learning how to produce beats. I got the name H.N.I.C. from her. She's the reason I never suffered from stage fright after that Diana Ross incident in Central Park. I love and miss you, Grandmoms.

Blood Money was finished in less than two months. 50 was excited. For some reason, a lot of people seemed to think that 50 created the album for us, saying things like "That album is too G-Unit" or "There's too much 50 influence in that album." But Mobb Deep controlled all the decision making and production, and I designed the album-cover concept—us at a table filled with piles of cash, like we just robbed a bank. Our first single, "Put 'Em in Their Place," was placed in the movie *Stomp the Yard*.

Magazines and radio personalities were printing articles and making comments saying, "*Blood Money* sales stalled at three hundred thousand copies. Seems like Mobb Deep lost their fan base." But the album went gold, five hundred thousand copies sold. People in the streets were saying, "Mobb Deep fell off," "Prodigy is sucking 50 Cent," "Jay-Z destroyed Mobb Deep's career," and "Prodigy hasn't been the same since Summer Jam." But all that girly-mouthed talk was hollow.

One of the songs we recorded for *Blood Money*, "Pearly Gates," ended up being the most controversial. The subject matter deals with growing up in a criminal environment and participating in its illegal activities while at the same time struggling with the moral and spiritual consequences of those choices. Will we go to Hell for our actions? Or is there indeed a heaven for us if we pray for forgiveness? As a youth, I had conflicting views about religion and God mainly because of my struggle with sickle-cell pain. I used to think, *If God is real, then why does God allow me to suffer so much?*

My verse on "Pearly Gates" was my way of venting frustration about what I believed to be a corrupt system of organized religion. At that time, I had come to the conclusion that all the good people of this world, especially my black people, had been made to take part in religious rituals and pray to a God that's not ours. A song is only about three minutes and having only one of those minutes to get your point across in a verse isn't easy. So I must admit that I did a terrible job trying to articulate my point on that track. I offended fans and turned a lot of people off with my choice of words in the unreleased version of the song. The legal department at Interscope Records actually refused to release the album unless I changed some of the lyrics. They told me I couldn't use the words *God* or *Jesus*. I was outraged at first. That's a violation of my Constitutional rights! But instead of making a big deal of it, I went ahead and changed it.

G-Unit set up a *Blood Money* album-release party at the Roxy in downtown Manhattan. 40 Glocc, Alchemist, Twin, Nyce, Nyce's homeboy WOP, Noyd, Fly, this new rapper from Jersey named Sam Scarfo, Gotti, Godfather, Chinky, and a bunch of others met up at the G-Unit office a few hours before the event. Around midnight, we hopped into our cars. About fifteen cars full of people followed us from the office to the spot. The line to get inside stretched the entire block.

A driver was at the wheel of my Yukon Denali with 40 Glocc, Nyce, Sam Scarfo, WOP, and me riding in my truck; Havoc also had a driver, and his Range Rover had himself, Fly, Gotti, Alchemist, and Twin. Havoc and I hired this dude Jay to do security that night. NYPD had the club block completely barricaded. As soon as we pulled up to the corner and double-parked, I noticed three black dudes, about thirty years old, standing on the corner looking suspicious. I sized them up quickly from head to toe, their inexpensive outfits and cheap track sneakers. I immediately knew they were undercover cops, the D's as we called them, detectives.

Growing up in the streets of New York, we learned how to spot the D's easy, examining the clothes, sneakers, attitude, waist, wrists, and neck of a person to judge if they were D's or not. Cheap clothes, a bulge at the waist or back pocket of the pants, and cheap sneakers or rubber-soled shoes were all dead giveaways. The wrists were important because if a person had a sweatband or headband wrapped around their wrists, that's a gun-squad detective. They wore that as a secret sign to let other cops know they're working undercover. It's usually purple or green, but they switch because of people like me who learned these things. The neck was vital because the D's wore silver dog-tag-style chains with their badges tucked under their shirts and only pulled them out when making an arrest or a stop. So if we saw that chain or if they had on a turtleneck or mock-neck shirt, that's a sign. We were used to their elusive ways.

The characters on the corner were definitely undercover cops. Our security guy Jay walked from the club to our trucks and told us that the club was ready for us to walk in, so we hopped out and headed in. We all walked through the back entrance of the Roxy, were searched, then went upstairs to VIP. We ordered shots of Hennessy, bottles of Moët, smoked weed, and kicked it with our guests. DJ On Point, who would fill in for Alchemist when Al was on tour with Eminem, brought us our mics and we walked toward the stage.

We performed a couple classics before getting into *Blood Money*. During "Put 'Em in Their Place," a few Queensbridge dudes climbed onto the side of the stage. I heard commotion behind me and felt people bumping into my back while I was performing. 40 Glocc and Nyce were arguing with Draws, my man from QB who always put a smile on my face when I saw him, so I gave him a pound and signaled for 40 and Nyce to fall back. Drunken Draws danced behind us, waving his hands in the air. It became Mobb Deep featuring Draws live at the Roxy. Ha!

One of Draws's Queensbridge dudes was standing next to him wearing a long gold chain with a medallion. He took off his chain and tried putting it around Havoc's neck while Hav was rapping his verse on "Put 'Em in Their Place," but the chain got caught on Havoc's sunglasses and tangled on the microphone. 40 Glocc, Gotti, and Nyce told him to stop but the dude kept trying to put his chain on Hav's neck. After his third attempt, 40 Glocc punched the dude in his mouth, then stomped him into the ground. Everybody started pushing and shoving to get out of the way, and we had to end the show. Our security, Jay, grabbed Havoc and me and swept us out of the commotion, our boys following.

After pulling off in our vehicles, about six blocks away from the club, my driver informed me that an unmarked detective car had its police lights on behind us. We pulled over on the West Side Highway around Twenty-third Street. A young black undercover cop approached the passenger side where I was sitting. It was one of the three dudes from the corner who I thought were the D's before we went into the Roxy. I rolled down the window.

"Albert Johnson?" he said.

"Yes, what's the problem?"

"Step out of the car, please."

Now I was nervous. First off, the police never walked up to your car and just said your name. That was strange. Secondly, the undercover looked like he was younger than me. *These ain't cops, these are some dudes acting like cops,* I thought. *This is a setup. A robbery.*

A blue-and-white police squad car pulled up and a sergeant or captain stepped out. "Is everything all right?" he asked. The young black undercover pulled out his badge chain. "Yes, sir," he replied. "We've got it under control." This calmed me down. He seemed like a real cop.

"What's the problem?" I got out of the truck and asked.

"Turn around and put your hands behind your back," he said. "I'll tell you in a minute." He handcuffed me then told my driver, "Okay, you can go." They didn't search my truck or harass the other passengers inside. They didn't even read me my rights. This wasn't normal at all. My boys asked, "What's going on? Where are you taking him?"

"To the Midtown precinct," the cop replied, walking me to the un-marked car where his two partners were waiting.

"What am I being arrested for?" I asked the cop beside me in the backseat.

"You'll find out soon," he said.

I calmed myself down with a few deep breaths and snapped into my hustler's mentality. *Think wise,* I told myself. *Don't get aggravated. Just be cool and get what you can outta these dudes. They look like some cool black cops. They're probably rap fans. Start manipulating.*

There was a brief moment of silence as I gathered my thoughts. "Whose idea was it to arrest me after the show?" I asked. "'Cause I saw you guys before we went in." Another moment of silence.

"It was my idea," the cop driving responded. "I didn't want the fans to start rioting if you didn't perform."

Now just reel 'em in. "That was cool. Good lookin', man," I said. "At least I got to enjoy our party."

The driver replied, "No problem. How was the show? And who was fighting?"

"It was good. I don't know who was fighting," I said. "It happened behind us onstage while we were performing."

The driver relaxed and started talking. "Well, get used to seeing us around. We've been assigned to Mobb Deep and G-Unit," he said. *Wow. So this is the Hip Hop Task Force that I've heard so much about.*

"Yeah, I thought I recognized you guys. I've seen ya'll around a few times," I said. I was lying. I'd never seen those fools.

"Yeah, we were at that Lloyd Banks party a while ago," the driver said. "There were a lot of hot women at that one. We've been following you all for a couple months."

Another unmarked car followed them. The other car, with three white undercovers, pulled up alongside us. I looked down at my chest and remembered I had on about $250,000 worth of chains, bracelets, and rings. I wasn't about to let it all go into some grimy police-property room, so I asked the driver, "Listen, do you mind if I use your cell phone to call my manager and have him meet us somewhere on our way to the precinct? I don't wanna go through the system with all this jewelry on."

They looked at all the diamonds I had on. "Go ahead and let him do it. Pass me your cell phone," the one sitting next to me told the driver. I gave him Gotti's number. "Hello, is this Gotti? This is Detective [Can't Remember]. We're taking your man Prodigy to the Midtown precinct and he wants to give you his jewelry. Meet us on the corner of Thirty-fifth Street and Ninth Avenue, okay? Cool. Thanks."

While we were running red lights through traffic, we got pulled over by a blue-and-white squad car. "These idiots are pulling us over!" the driver said. "You see, Prodigy, they're just doing this because we're black. Don't they see our police lights flashing in their face?" I couldn't believe it. Cops were getting pulled over for driving recklessly! This was some classic shit. "Driver! Turn the car off!" a cop in the squad car said over the loudspeaker.

The other unmarked car that was following us, with the white D's in it, was now in front of us. One of the white cops got out of the unmarked car and pulled his badge chain out of his shirt to let them know they were all cops. When the squad-car police realized they'd pulled over black detectives, they apologized, and we went on our way. I was still wondering why the hell I was being arrested. I kept asking but they wouldn't say. It almost seemed like they didn't know. All they said was, "We've got a warrant for your arrest. You'll find out when you get booked and processed."

Gotti was waiting on the corner of Thirty-fifth Street and Ninth Avenue. The D's took all my jewelry off for me, opened the car trunk, spread my jewelry on a towel, and took pictures of it. They told Gotti that they needed to take his picture. I guess they wanted these pictures for their Mobb Deep/G-Unit Hip Hop Task Force file. They wanted to know about everyone around us. But the pictures of the jewelry seemed strange. *What could they use that for?*

"We're doing this so that we are not responsible for anything if something turns up missing when you get out," one of them said.

I told Gotti to contact KiKi and have her call my lawyer. Then they took me into the precinct—fingerprints, mug shots, waiting for hours in a cell before being transported to central booking, the Tombs. The only thing good about the Tombs after sitting in a precinct for hours was that they brought bologna-and-cheese sandwiches and milk to the bullpen holding cells.

On my way through the metal detectors in the hallway, I saw Mike Lighty, Chris Lighty's little brother, waiting on a line to be searched for another bullpen. We said what's up to each other and kept it moving. Mike said that he'd been arrested for fighting somebody and I told him I didn't know what I was in for yet.

The three wooden benches in the bullpen were full of sleeping inmates so I put my jacket on the floor to lie down. The floor was dirty as hell, but when you're tired and locked up you start not caring about dirt. I fell asleep on the hard grimy floor and as soon as somebody got off the bench, I took his spot. The whole place smelled like piss. The toilet didn't have a seat, just a rim covered with dry piss and spit.

A few hours later, the pen was filled to capacity with hardly any standing room. You started to lose time in there. The waiting process, usually about twenty-four hours, seemed like forever if you didn't sleep. So mostly I slept.

At around ten A.M. the next morning, a black detective shouted my name, cuffed me, and led me toward the courtroom to see the judge with my file in his hand. "Officer, can you please tell me what I'm being charged for?" I asked.

"They didn't tell you yet?" he said.

"No, I've been trying to find out all night," I said. He looked at my papers as we were walking. "Did you ever get a ticket for talking on a cell phone while driving?"

"You gotta be shitting me," I said. "That's what this is all about?"

"Yep," he said.

One afternoon I was driving my Porsche through the city talking on the phone. The seat-belt cops hid behind trucks and vans next to traffic lights looking for drivers and passengers without seat belts on. They caught me on the phone. I'd forgotten to pay that ticket, and they issued a bench warrant. But they never came looking for you; they usually waited until you got stopped again, and when they ran your name through the system, they'd see that you had a warrant. The Hip Hop Task Force must have been investigating my criminal history and used the warrant as an excuse to get me. The task force is known for racial profiling. Even though the D's who arrested me were black, they were only following orders from their white superiors. They actually came looking for me like I was America's Most Wanted for talking on a cell phone while driving!

Do they have a Country-Western-Music Task Force? And why not? Those redneck shit kickers are probably some of the biggest gunrunners and coke dealers around. You think not? Why, because they're white? The world's so racist it's a shame.

The judge released me with time served—no fine, no bail, case closed. I walked more than thirty-five blocks from the Tombs, down by Wall Street, to Alchemist's crib and took a two-hour nap on his couch. I woke up, washed up, and bounced because we were leaving for a U.S. tour that night.

The *Blood Money* tour was an amazing time. Ever since seeing Naughty by Nature's stage set at an Apollo concert in the early nineties, I wanted to do something similar but better. *What if we had a stage set built like the projects,* I imagined. Back when we were planning the *Amerikaz Nightmare* tour, I met a guy Snow who built stage sets and wanted twenty thousand dollars to create my vision. Jive didn't want to give us the budget so it didn't happen. But 50 loved the idea and we hired two guys from the G-Unit crew to assemble and pack away the set, which took about an hour on each end. Every night we came out of the front door of the project building at the beginning of the show.

One of our first stops on the tour was an appearance at a small store in Baltimore with people lined up around the block waiting for an autograph. Dudes who looked like they hadn't changed their clothes in years and kids looking like they didn't have a dollar to their name were on line to buy our CD. Meanwhile, I had on tons of jewelry. For the first time in our career, I felt guilty. It was time to truly make a change in how I carried myself and spent my money. Prodigy and Mobb Deep represented the hood; we represented poverty. I felt as though I was rubbing my money and fame in their faces.

Baltimore was one of the most poverty-stricken, drug-and-crime-infested hoods on the map, running neck and neck with D.C., Detroit, and Louisiana. Touring the world all those years had given me the opportunity to witness poverty all over the planet. England, France, Russia, India, all the way back to the U.S.—poverty created criminal thinking and actions. I was seeing things with new eyes.

Speaking with kids at a juvenile detention center in Atlanta was one of the highlights of the tour. There were ten-year-olds locked up for murder and all kinds of wild shit. It felt good to share our experiences with them. The detention center awarded Havoc and me with a plaque showing their appreciation.

In Los Angeles, we had a show at the House of Blues on Sunset and stayed at a hotel directly across the street. Earlier that day, accompanied by our G-Unit radio rep Nelson and our Interscope radio rep Adam Favors, we did a show at Power 106 with DJ Felli Fel. Felli asked us how it felt to be on G-Unit with 50 Cent. "It's great, man. 50 is the best," I responded. "For our signing bonus he bought us Porsches and gave us twenty percent of the Game's publishing. So every time Game makes a hit record, that's a new house for us. So I wish Game nothing but success, 'cause he's making us rich." You should have seen the look on Felli Fel, Nelson, and Adam's faces! Felli Fel changed the subject real quick.

"I hope you've got an army and navy outside waiting for us," Nelson said after the interview. Adam Favors started making all kinds of phone calls in a panic. It was funny. We didn't have to call armies and navies. Trust, we had it covered.

I was relaxing and writing rhymes in my hotel room before getting ready for the concert when 40 Glocc knocked on the door. "Yo, the Game is outside in front of the hotel with some basketball dude," he said. "We got the drop on him, he doesn't even know we're here. What do you wanna do?" 40 pulled out a .45-caliber pistol and continued. "He saw Nyce with the Mobb Deep/Game Over shirt on and got spooked. My man Maniac walked up to him and offered him a one-on-one fight."

"He's still out there right now?" I asked.

"Yeah, cuz, we spit lungies all over his Bentley," 40 said. "Look over the balcony, cuz."

"Give me the gun," I said. "Ya'll niggas put the video camera on Game. I'm gonna shoot the gun off the balcony and we'll catch him on camera ducking and running from the shots."

"Cuz, you trippin'. We're on Sunset," 40 said. "You know how fast police will be here?"

"I'm not gonna shoot him, I'm gonna shoot in the air so we can get him on camera scared to death," I said. "The gun will be long gone by the time police get here."

"Nah, cuz, you gonna make this shit hotter than fish grease," 40 said. "Let's just go beat his ass."

"Okay, I'll meet you in Havoc's room in five minutes."

After I got dressed, I went to Hav's room and told him what I wanted to do. "No, you buggin', P," Havoc said. "I'll go down and talk to him. Real men talk things out."

"What? There's nothing to talk about," I said. "Fuck talking."

"Real men talk things out," Hav repeated. I knew what Havoc meant. Of course men can talk, but in this situation, I didn't agree at all. There was nothing to talk about. Game had been running his mouth about G-Unit and Mobb Deep ever since 50 dropped him, and signed us so I wanted to do something about it.

"Guess what, cuz," 40 said. "I just got off the phone with one of my Blood homies and he said Game called him saying, 'Mobb Deep's on Sunset, come over and let's show these niggas how Cali gets down.' My Blood homie said he's in the car with Suge right now and they've been looking for Game for a while now. They're gonna rob Game when they get here."

This was getting good. Meanwhile, Havoc wanted to talk it out. He was being smart and trying to stay out of trouble. Havoc would get busy if his back was to the wall, but he saw that it wasn't that serious. He was right and I was wrong but I didn't see it at the time. I was a natural born troublemaker. It excited me. Sorry if you can't relate. That's just me. That's the same reason why I'm writing this book from a solitary-confinement prison cell in Mid-State Correctional Facility.

Suge Knight and 40's homeboy pulled up in a red GT Bentley. Our niggas had Game surrounded, his car covered in spit. Somebody from the hotel front desk called the police. As soon as the police pulled up, Game got in his spit-riddled Bentley and bounced. Suge did the same. Damn, I wanted to see some action.

The morning after the House of Blues show, we headed to San Diego. R&B singer Keyshia Cole was working on her second album and looking for beats.

Keyshia's people sent Havoc a number to contact her. In the back of the tour bus, Hav was tipsy; I couldn't tell if it was from the night before or that morning. He called the number. "What's up, this is Havoc. I heard you're working on your new album. You know I got that fire for you but to tell you the truth, I don't wanna talk about music right now. I'm tryin' to holler at you. If you want to talk music, then you might as well hang up right now."

Oh no, why did he say that? I asked myself. I couldn't hear what Keyshia said back to him but I could tell from Havoc's response that it wasn't good. "What? You know my man P already? Oh yeah?" Then he looked at me in shock. I was confused at first, thinking, I know her? Damn, did I bag her back in the day? Then it hit me. Keyshia! From the Beverly Center mall! Oh shit. I bagged Keyshia Cole before she became famous.

Hav immediately ruined his opportunity to produce for her. Keyshia hung up on him. "You know her, son? She said she knows you," he said.

"Yeah, I bagged her a couple of years ago in the Beverly Center. I didn't realize it was Keyshia, it was before she blew up," I said. "Damn son, you just fucked that relationship up. You could've sold her some beats." But Hav was too bent and brushed it off. Keyshia, if you're reading this, I apologize for all that nonsense.

After covering most of the U.S., we toured overseas in London and Paris as usual, then made the trek to Australia and New Zealand for the first time with a connecting flight in Tahiti. In a car on the way to the hotel in New Zealand, my vision suddenly went from blurry to black. By the time we got to the hotel, I was totally blind, only seeing bright lights. I had just seen the movie Ray starring Jamie Foxx and thought I'd suddenly lost my sight like Ray Charles did as a kid. I was scared to death.

The hotel called an eye doctor. "Do you have any medical problems?" the doctor asked after examining my eyes. I told him I had sickle-cell anemia. "Okay, I know what's wrong. You have sickle-cell retinitis." He explained that the high altitude of the long airplane flights decreased the oxygen level in my blood, causing blood vessels to burst in my retinas. After using eye drops my vision slowly started coming back five hours later. Man, it felt good to see my ugly-ass niggas again. Ha!

After New Zealand we flew to Japan. As soon as the promoters picked us up from the airport, the first thing Alchemist and I asked was, "Where's the weed at?" The hotel was plush but the rooms were tiny and the beds even tinier. The toilet seats had buttons that made them heat up. Nobody likes a cold toilet seat.

At the show they didn't have the correct equipment for us to perform, so we only did two songs on a mic with a cord. But there were so many good-looking Japanese girls, dime after dime. The after-party at our hotel was the stuff that dreams were made of. Japanese women got right down to business and aimed to please.

We flew to New York and rested during a short break before heading back overseas to Chile, India, Hong Kong, and England one more time. I'd ordered a bulletproof Chevy Suburban from the same company that 50, Yayo, and Banks had gotten theirs from. It was waiting for me when I pulled up to my house.

The truck cost $120,000 and was worth every penny. The windows could stop an AK-47 and the rest of the truck was completely armored with about five inches of steel. It's bombproof and the tires were "run-flat," which meant that if they were shot, the truck could still drive. Now that we were part of G-Unit, I knew that the jealous and envious bullshit would surface more than ever. Look what happened to Tupac, Biggie, Stretch, E-Money Bags, and 50. It's better to prevent a situation than try to cure the outcome.

KiKi and I moved into an exclusive waterfront townhouse in a gated community in Secaucus, New Jersey, five minutes from Manhattan. Giants Stadium was directly across the water and a lot of Giants football players lived in the community. Corey Webster was our next-door neighbor. "You're crazy for moving your woman around all those NFL players," Havoc told me. "I wouldn't do that shit." But it didn't matter if you moved to no-mans'-land—if a person wanted to cheat, they'd find a way.

I got another offer to costar in an independent film. This one was called *Blackout*, starring Zoe Saldana and Jeffrey Wright. Since I was a kid watching the making of Michael Jackson's *Thriller*, I had always been intrigued with the craft of moviemaking. I also started writing this book around the time of that movie offer. KiKi was writing a book about her life and she inspired me to do the same. Sitting in our new townhouse in New Jersey, I'd stay up all night typing on my laptop. I figured it would make for one hell of a read.

After our short break, it was back to the *Blood Money* tour. Our first stop was London. At the after-party, DJ Whoo Kid was talking to this good-looking white girl who kept checking me out. When she sat back down with her girlfriends, I walked over, we kicked it for about twenty minutes, and I got her phone number. She told me she was from Long Island but lived in Los Angeles. Whoo Kid walked over after she left. "Yo, you know who that was?" he said.

"No, why? Who is she?"

"Lindsay Lohan," he said.

"Lindsay who?" I asked. "Who's that?"

"She's an actress, nigga," he said, laughing. "Did you get her number?"

"Yeah, I didn't know who she was." I may have heard her name once or twice, but I really didn't know who she was.

We caught a flight to Chile, our next concert stop, with 40 Glocc, Sam Scarfo, two G-Unit road managers, and DJ On Point. Forty minutes into the flight, I was playing Miami Vice on my son Shaka's PlayStation Portable when the flight got bumpy. 40 Glocc walked into the first-class section where Havoc and I were sitting and said, "Yo, cuz! The plane is on fire, cuz! The engine just blew up!"

My heart almost jumped out of my chest. "Ladies and gentlemen, please remain calm," the captain said over the loudspeaker. "We are going to have to turn back around and make an emergency landing. We lost power in one of our engines." The engine was burning on the right side of the plane. Havoc gripped the armrests. The turbulence made the flight feel like a full-fledged roller-coaster ride. I just kept playing Miami Vice. *I'm definitely not gonna die on an airplane*, I said to myself. *I've got a lot more work to do out in the world and I know that the Most High is actually carrying this plane and will set it down safely at our destination.*

After landing, we rushed to find an airport bar for some drinks to calm our nerves. The concert in Chile was canceled and we flew out the next day to Bombay for our first performance in India. No other American rappers had ever performed in India. Mobb Deep was the first. Ten hours into the eighteen-hour flight, my sickle-cell pain crept up. By the time we landed in Bombay, I was in bad shape.

India's extremely poverty-stricken and we had on all kinds of jewelry, so people looked at us like we were insane. Cows, considered sacred in India, roamed freely in the streets, and the beaches were overpopulated with fully dressed people. The Marriott Hotel was the most modern structure; everything else looked like squalor. After checking into our rooms, 40 Glocc, Sam Scarfo, our security guard House, and I went to the hotel restaurant and ordered curry chicken—everything had curry in it. I was trying not to think about all the pain I was feeling. *Mind over matter. Just relax,* I kept telling myself as House reminisced on club fight stories from the '90s. "P, I remember when TLC had a party at the Roseland Ballroom in Manhattan. I saw you and your boys walk in and ten minutes later ya'll got into a fight and shut the whole party down. You remember that?"

"Oh wow, you were there?" I said. Small world.

After eating, the moment I feared finally approached. I had to go to the hospital. I was fighting tears with severe pain pounding all over my body as I was wheeled into the hospital in a wheelchair. The Indian doctors broke the bad news that pain medication, IV tubing, and saline-solution bags were illegal in India. The doctors seemed very knowledgeable—the only problem was, they had none of the necessary supplies to treat me. A doctor pulled my man Ree from G-Unit to the side and told him, "I know where you can buy all those things he needs. You have to take a train and a taxi two hours and buy these supplies off the black market." The doctor wrote down instructions, like sending Ree on an Indiana Jones mission to find the Lost Ark of the Covenant. I was wheeled on a stretcher into the back room that I thought I would die in.

Slowly I felt the sickle cells accumulating and spreading throughout my body. Then I felt something that I never felt before—the sickle cells moving to my heart. It was time to put in an emergency call to the Most High. *I know you're not gonna let me die like this! You better not let me die like this! Please, don't let me die like this! After all the dangerous shit I've been through, don't let sickle-cell take me out!*

I'd experienced pain so incredible that it made me laugh and laughter so joyous that it made me cry. When you experience the paramount of those feelings, you learn they are actually one and the same. My pain became so great in that rusty old Bombay hospital that I laughed out loud, delirious.

Then something strange happened. All of a sudden it felt like all my dead friends and relatives were in the room with me. I couldn't see them but I sensed their presence—Grandmoms, my grandfather, Pops, the Scarface Twin, Killer Black, Yamit, E-Money Bags. I spoke to all of them out loud, asking for help. I wanted to live. A few minutes later, the pain in my heart was gone. I thanked them and the Most High.

Ree made it back with morphine pills in a Ziploc bag, and then the doctors hooked me up to the black-market IV tubing. I missed the Bombay concert. Havoc, 40 Glocc, and Sam Scarfo performed without me. We booked a flight home the next morning, and I checked into Montefiore Medical Center in the Bronx. Havoc was mad that I didn't make it to our Hong Kong concert, but my body needed to heal. It seemed that all Havoc cared about was the money, because he was really upset with me for refusing to go. When I think about it now, he had the right to be upset; if I'd been taking better care of my health, I wouldn't have missed the concert.

After I healed, I came up with an idea to record a solo mix CD to prepare the world for my next solo album, *H.N.I.C. Pt. 2*. Alchemist and I traded ideas. I came up with the name *Return of the Mac*, as in a person coming back for revenge with a Mac-10 gun.

Al came up with all sorts of samples from black seventies movies because our plan was to give the whole mix CD a retro feel, like the sound track to an old flick. While we were busy recording, Lloyd Banks released his second solo album, *Rotten Apple*. The album was hot but a lot of people hated on it like they hated on *Blood Money*. It was obvious that a lot of people wanted to see G-Unit fail. Maybe we were too arrogant to realize our own creative faults.

CHAPTER 13

RETURN OF THE MAC

Ayo the hood broke my heart into pieces
Thun the streets took my dreams and shattered them
and turned me into a creature
Monster money got me not giving a fuck
All I care about is music and who I gotta cut
with the Mac, UZI, .47 pick a weapon
a million ways to die my .25 will end it

"Bang on 'Em"

Summer of 2006, Brooklyn, New York: I began filming the independent movie *Blackout* out in Flatbush. My role didn't have too many lines, so the director, Jerry LaMothe, told me to improvise. The second day on set, I shot a scene with Jeffrey Wright, who was one of my favorite actors.

After filming wrapped, I connected with one of 50 Cent's video directors, Dan the Man, to shoot a paranoid, psychotic, grimy video for my mix CD song "Mac 10 Handle." Bloody couch and mirror stabbings, hallucinations of Satan and some guy in a Michael Myers mask. No jewelry, no half-naked females, no fashion show. The video was an overnight success on the Internet, with over four hundred thousand views in three days. It was completely against the grain. I wanted to show 50 my work ethic and how I could create a huge buzz on my own. I was trying to spark his interest in signing me as a solo artist and releasing *H.N.I.C. Pt. 2* under the G-Unit brand. But before I stepped to him with the idea, I wanted to show him what I could do.

I always had a complex about my teeth. I didn't smile in pictures or in front of females because I had a slight gap between my two front teeth, and after so many years of smoking cigarettes and weed, my teeth were stained yellow. Plus I had two pointed incisors on either side of my front teeth. I believed those sharp pointed teeth were a trait from my moms's side of the family because many Caucasians had those two sharp pointed fangs.

"One day, when I get enough money, I'm gonna fix my teeth and have a pearly white Hollywood smile," I'd tell KiKi.

"Yes, please," she'd say. "I still love you and all, but damn!"

While Havoc and I were enjoying the success of *The Infamous* in 1995, I found out from Twin and Draws that Nas had a nickname for me that he used behind my back. He and his boys called me Rat Boy because my two front teeth looked like a rat's. It was funny, but deep down it made my complex worse.

So after shooting the "Mac 10 Handle" video, I asked KiKi to find an oral surgeon who could give me a beautiful smile.

KiKi set up an appointment with Dr. Rizzo, whose office was five minutes from our New Jersey townhouse. One thing I was a punk about was going to the dentist—needles in my mouth, drilling, root canals, all that. But one month and twenty thousand dollars later, I looked like a new man, smiling every chance that I got. It was the best twenty thousand I ever spent in my life. To all the fellas who are reading this and all the Rat Boys across the map, fight back! Fix your jibs instead of wasting money on foolishness. And

Nas—thank you. You inspired me once again to be all I could be. Ha! I love ya, boy!

Right after I got my pearly whites, 50 called a meeting at his office for the entire G-Unit roster. When Havoc and I showed up, Olivia was there along with Banks, Yayo, and M.O.P's manager, and Young Buck was on speakerphone. Mase never signed to the label because Puffy was asking for too much money to buy him out of his existing Bad Boy contract. 50 started the meeting. "I called this meeting today because I wanna let ya'll know that I've been spending a lot of money to promote you all on tour and several other expenses and I haven't been seeing a profit on a lot of my investments," 50 said. "Plus, I heard that some of ya'll ain't happy." Then he turned to Olivia. "For starters, I spend all kinds of money for your hairstylist, makeup artist, stylist, studio time, and I don't see you making any hits for a good album." Olivia tried to make excuses but they weren't good enough.

50 then turned to M.O.P's manager. "And as far as M.O.P, I got ya'll up in my house studio for several months and I don't see any work being done. Mobb Deep did over forty songs within a few weeks before we even inked the deal. It's been almost a year and I haven't seen any effort from you guys." M.O.P's manager tried to make excuses but they weren't good enough.

Then he turned to Banks. "And I don't know what your problem is. You've got the work ethic, you make the good songs, but you act like you don't wanna do the promotional work it takes to sell the album correctly. Now, I know you've had some personal issues with your family lately, but I lost my moms, Banks, I know what it feels like to lose a close family member. That didn't stop me from doing what needed to be done."

Banks had recently lost his father and was mourning, so he probably hadn't done a lot of necessary promo. I started to feel uncomfortable listening to the discussion between 50 and Banks. It sounded personal and I felt like it was none of Mobb Deep's business, but 50 obviously wanted us to hear it. "I heard you're upset with your album sales," 50 continued. "Well, I got on songs for all of ya'll albums. I wrote choruses, got in the videos—it's up to ya'll to lyrically perform at your best and do the work it takes to market and promote the projects. I'm not gonna do it all for you. As a matter of fact, I'm not doing any more features on any of ya'll songs or videos because I'm carrying all the weight. Ya'll have to start pulling your own weight. Yo Buck! You there? You heard what I said?"

Buck mumbled through the speakerphone. "Yeah, I'm here. Don't worry, 50, I'm the cleanup man," Buck said. "I got hits on this album. We good."

That was some real disrespectful, cocky shit he just said, I thought to myself. *What, is he trying to say his shit is better than 50 Cent, Mobb Deep, Yayo, and Banks?* Buck used the wrong choice of words as far as I was concerned. Then 50 continued, "Yayo was locked up and his album was on hold until he got out. He missed a lot of big promotion while he was gone but he did what he had to do when he got home."

Yayo cut in and said, "I'm not complaining about album sales, man, I'm good. Whatever needs to be done, I'm doing it."

Then 50 said, "Look at what P just did with his video on the Internet. He shot a video for a mix CD song on his own. He's not waiting for me to help him; he's pushing himself, making himself hot. Niggas need to be doing shit like that."

Then Banks came out of left field and said, "What, is this meeting all about me? Because you seem to be focused on me the most."

"No, it's not all about you," 50 said. "I'm talking to everybody, but you need to start doing your promo work before you start complaining about your album sales. I want everybody in here to look down under the table and tell me what you see."

Everybody looked under the table, confused. "I don't see nobody rocking G-Unit sneakers," 50 said. "I see Gucci, Louis, Fendi, Timberland, but I pay you endorsement checks every month to wear G-Unit."

50 made that endorsement deal with Yayo, Banks, Buck, and maybe Olivia before Mobb Deep came around. We weren't a part of that deal so he wasn't talking to us. "From now on, I'm deading that deal and you won't get your checks anymore," 50 told them. "So ya'll can forget about that."

Wow, I thought. *If 50 gave us that deal, I would've worn G-Unit to sleep at night and in my casket.* Buck mumbled over the phone once more,

"I got this, 50, me and Spider Loc is going hard. I'm the cleanup man, trust me." Buck needed to shut up and listen to what was being said. He needed to hand in a good album instead of talking all that cleanup-man shit.

"This nigga's frontin'," Banks jumped in and said. "He ain't happy. Ain't nobody happy with this label." Banks slammed his fitted hat on the table and sat back in his chair.

"Oh yeah?" 50 looked at Banks and said. "You wanna bounce like Game and start your own label? I got you. I'll call my lawyer and tell him to get you a deal over at Geffen and you can do your own thing from now on." Banks stormed out of the meeting.

A week later, 50 dropped Olivia and M.O.P from the label. I wanted to ask 50 to put *H.N.I.C. Pt. 2* out on G-Unit, but after that meeting, I didn't feel right about asking him. I didn't want to get shot down or put him in an awkward position by having to tell me he wasn't interested in doing my solo album. So I kept it to myself for the time being.

When 50 acknowledged that he liked what I was doing with my mix CD video, it added fuel to my already existing fire. Alchemist and I finished *Return of the Mac* and I planned to release it through DJ Whoo Kid as a street mix CD. But then I got a call from Bob Perry, who'd been missing in action since *Free Agents* and was now working for Koch Records, offering two hundred thousand dollars to buy *Return of the Mac.* I took that paper—two hundred thousand up front in one check—and ran. When I told 50 how much I got from my mix CD, he was like, "Wow, how the hell did you pull that off? That's good."

After I got that money, I shot three more videos for the mix CD—"Stuck to You," "NY Shit," and "7th Heaven" featuring Un Pacino, a rapper from Ocean Village projects in Far Rockaway, Queens, whom I met through Twin. I released the videos one at a time, every few weeks. The buzz was strong for *Return of the Mac* and the press gave rave reviews for the "Mac 10 Handle" video, so Koch was ready to release the mix CD immediately. Alchemist and I did a photo shoot for the CD artwork wearing classic mafia-style suits. I came up with nicknames for Alchemist and myself—Bumpy Johnson and Dutch Schultz, old-time Harlem gangsters who went by the same names.

Harlem rapper Cam'ron had been enjoying a successful run with his group the Diplomats, aka Dipset. They dropped a bunch of hits on Jay-Z's Roc-A-Fella Records and the crew had two rising solo artists, Juelz Santana and Jim Jones. Right before *Return of the Mac* was released, Jim Jones put out a hit single titled "Ballin'." Juelz Santana and Jim Jones were both on Koch Records, so we were labelmates. Alchemist was also signed to Koch.

Return of the Mac was released and sold about fifty thousand units, just what I needed to get my buzz going for *H.N.I.C. Pt. 2*. A month later, I got a call from a dude named Scientific, whom Sam Scarfo introduced me to, telling me about this company Voxonic that wanted to start a record label. Voxonic had a patent for some kind of new voice-translation technology where they could take song lyrics and translate them into any language. He said that they were looking to promote the new technology through a record label but didn't have any experience with the music industry and needed artists and some-body to help run the label. I told Scientific to set up a meeting with the owner so I could find out if it was worth my time.

Later that day, Twin called and said that he, Godfather, and Ty-Nitty were about to shoot a video for a song we did for a European compilation album. Twin said that the company gave him five thousand dollars cash for me to appear in the video and he had the cash on him. KiKi and I bounced to Queensbridge where the video was being shot in front of Havoc's old building. I parked the bulletproof Suburban on Twenty-first and walked over to meet everybody.

On the block, I saw friendly faces that I hadn't seen in years. "What up, thun!" my man Bumpy greeted me. The last time I saw Bump was when he had Worm on the back of his BMX bike and Worm shot his gun in the air trying to scare me. Ha! Bumpy got locked up after that and did like six years.

I shot my scenes real quick because KiKi was waiting for me in the truck. She's not very sociable with people and didn't trust anybody, so she fell back. While Twin, Bumpy, and Godfather walked with me back to my car, we saw Green Eyes walking toward us on Twenty-first. I hadn't seen him since I stopped dealing with Bars'N'Hooks. "P, I need to speak to you real fast," he said. We stepped aside.

"What's the word, man?" I asked.

"Look, the nigga Preme is upset with you because you've been talking about him on your songs," Green Eyes said. "He had some niggas out here looking for you. I already told niggas that they gotta fall back because you my nigga, P, but just stop talking about all that shit in your songs." While Green Eyes was talking, Bumpy and Twin walked over.

"You good, P?" Bumpy asked. "What's up with this nigga right here?"

"Yeah, it's all good," I said. "We good."

"A'ight, just let me know 'cause anybody front on you, thun, and niggas is getting fucked up out here."

Then Twin said, "You good, P? You sure?"

"Yeah, we're just talking. Chill," I said. They backed up.

Green Eyes then said, "You my nigga, P, you know I love you, man. Preme just feel like it's none of your business, so just leave all that shit alone. I'm out, man. I'll see ya'll later on." I gave him a pound and he left.

Green Eyes was referring to "Rotten Apple" on *Return of the Mac*, where I had a line saying, "*If Pac was still alive we'd be on the same team, we got bigger fish to fry than that bitch Supreme.*" I was referring to Tupac's friendship with E-Money Bags and Majesty, and how that would have eventually made us friends. I called Preme a bitch because he had E-Money Bags killed and got 50 shot up. So fuck Supreme. Simply put. You send niggas, I send 'em back in plastic. Send bitches, I send bitches back pregnant. Simply put.

Godfather told me one day that some Supreme Team niggas were walking around the projects asking about me, saying they were going to kill me. But I didn't know what he was talking about and didn't care. Now Green Eyes confirmed it. Oh well, see me when you see me, nigga.

Twin gave me my five thousand dollars and KiKi and I left. My relationship with KiKi was getting a little better. After I caught those cheating messages in her phone, I became real coldhearted. The G-Unit deal only made me worse. She probably thought I was cheating a lot, but 99 percent of the time I was just working on music and kicking it with my boys. I'd rather chase money. I spent long hours in the studio, and came home around five A.M. every day ever since KiKi and I were first together. It was a rare occasion for me to take a break, and a vacation was out of the question. Vacation? What's that?

Working so hard, I was missing out on time with my kids and my woman. I used to bring my son Shaka with me to the studio and office back when he was three years old—until 2002, when I started smoking and bullshitting again. I didn't want him around all that.

Scientific hit me back and told me Voxonic offered to give me a fifty-fifty deal with a four-hundred-thousand-dollar advance and ownership of my masters. Vox also offered an ownership percentage of the company as well as an executive position at the label with a five-thousand-dollar-per-month salary and fully paid living expenses, which was worth an additional five thousand per month. I told 50 about it and he said, "Yo, how the hell do you be making these crazy deals? That's amazing. Take it!"

Looking over a rough contract, Mobb Deep's new lawyer, Evan Friefeld, had the same response as 50. He couldn't believe it. Evan wanted to make minor adjustments to the deal terms before I signed the contract, so he told me he'd contact me when it was ready to be finalized. After my call with Evan, I drove to the studio to see what was up with Havoc. On the drive to Queens, I got an e-mail that surprised me. It was Lindsay Lohan. She asked if I was in New York and said that I should come to a club in Manhattan later that night called Bungalow 8 where she'd be hanging out with a few of her girlfriends. I hit her back and told her that I'd meet her there.

I had twenty dollars in my pocket and zero in my personal account. I called my accountant, Arty Erk, and asked him to transfer five hundred dollars into my ATM account so I could have spending cash for the club. Mobb Deep kept all our real money in a business account that we couldn't touch, so when we wanted money, we made transfers through our accountant. It kept us from spending too much.

Havoc wasn't at the studio, but our engineer Fly was there with Nyce. I told Nyce about Lindsay's invitation and asked him to come along. Eleven P.M. rolled around and we hopped in my bulletproof Suburban and stopped at the gas station to get gas plus some bread from the ATM. But when I checked my account, I still had zero! Sometimes the money transfers don't go through until the next day. *Damn.* I put ten bucks in the bulletproof, enough to get there and back. Now I only had ten bucks and Nyce had twenty. Wow. We were going to an exclusive Manhattan club with thirty bucks to hang out with some million-dollar white chicks. Oh well, at least we were looking good.

There were two black bouncers at the door who I figured might recognize me. "What's up, man, it's Prodigy," I said. The bouncer looked at me like I was retarded.

"Are you on the guest list?" he asked. "It's a private party."

"I should be, check it out. Prodigy from Mobb Deep."

"Nah, I don't see you," the bouncer said after glancing at the list. "Sorry."

"Yo, I'm Prodigy, son. Mobb Deep. It's just two of us." I hated feeling like I had to beg or prove that I belonged in a club.

"Sorry, I can't let you in," he said, looking at me as if he couldn't care less.

"I'm here with Lindsay Lohan," I said. "She's waiting for me."

"Who?"

"Lindsay Lohan," I repeated. "Can you please tell Lindsay that Prodigy is at the door? Thank you." The look on his face was priceless.

Lindsay walked Nyce and me through the packed club to her VIP tables, where she had bottles of Grey Goose and Belvedere. Bungalow 8 looked like some tropical-jungle-type shit inside, a predominantly white crowd sprinkled with blacks and Latinos. I'd been there before with Alchemist. Lindsay's friends were wearing Mardi Gras–looking white masks, drunk and dancing crazily to rap music. Lindsay introduced me to her assistant; we poured drinks and started dancing while Nyce danced with one of the mysterious masked ladies. Another masked lady got behind Nyce and had him in the sandwich—he looked over at me with a Kool-Aid smile. After a handful of songs, Nyce and I walked to the bar so it wouldn't seem like we were drinking all of Lindsay's liquor.

"Prodigy?" a young black bartender looked at me and asked. "Oh shit, my favorite rapper! I love Mobb Deep. What can I get for you?"

"Two shots of Hennessy on ice," I told him, since we were on a tight budget.

"Man, I'm hooking you up with a bottle on the house," the bartender offered. I thanked him for the bottle—he saved us from looking stupid—and walked back to VIP. On the way, I bumped into RZA from the Wu-Tang Clan. We were surprised to see each other. Then I got back to Lindsay.

The ladies poured shots of Hennessy and Nyce started dancing with the same masked female. She lifted her mask to get some air and I saw it was Ashlee Simpson, Jessica Simpson's younger sister. I told Nyce so he'd know he had a celeb on his hands, then Lindsay pulled me back to her. I saw her looking at her BlackBerry after a while and her mood changed. I asked her what was wrong and she said, "This guy I used to mess with is fuckin' stalking me. I think he's in the club."

"Oh yeah? Well, let me know if you see him and we'll fuck him up," I said. "You good with me. I ain't letting nobody bother you if you don't wanna be bothered. Just let me know." After another hour of drinking, dancing, and grinding on each other, we said our good-byes. I don't know if Nyce got Ashlee's number but regardless, we had fun that night.

October 26, 2006, was Alchemist's birthday and Twin, Godfather, Ty-Nitty, my cousin JM, JM's homebody Rome, Alchemist, and I gathered at Al's Manhattan apartment to celebrate with a case of Heinekens, a case of Coronas, and a lot of Kush. Twin was pushing to go out but Alchemist and I wanted to stay in the apartment and make music.

Atlanta rapper Ludacris was having an album-release party for his new singer Shareefa at the Show nightclub near Times Square. "Come on, yo! It's Al's birthday!" Twin said. "Let's go out!" We rolled out three cars deep—Alchemist and me in my bulletproof Suburban, JM and Rome in JM's gold drop-top SL Benz, and Twin, Godfather, and Ty-Nitty in a black Hummer H2. I usually snuck a .22- or .25-caliber handgun into clubs if there were only a few of us, but there were seven of us so I left the pistol in my truck, in the storage box between the driver and passenger seats.

Velvet ropes surrounded the club's front entrance. A black doorman came over. "What's up man, Prodigy and Alchemist plus five," I announced. The doorman said to give him a minute, then he walked inside the club. While waiting, I looked toward the street to my left and saw three plainclothes detectives from the Hip Hop Task Force. I recognized them from the night they arrested me after the *Blood Money* release party at the Roxy. I didn't see the black cops; it was the white ones who looked like military dickheads. I wanted to point them out to Alchemist and Twin so they'd remember their faces. "Don't look now, but over to the left you're gonna see three white dudes by a black car," I said. "That's the Hip Hop Cops."

The doorman came back with a young white woman with a clipboard in hand. "What's up, guys?" she said. "We're working on clearing VIP tables for you now. How many is it? Seven? I've got three tables and there's a one-bottle minimum per table, so you have to buy three bottles, okay?"

"How much are the bottles?" Alchemist asked. "And what if we don't want to drink?"

"You have to buy a bottle in order to get a table, and they cost four hundred dollars apiece," the lady said.

"$1,200?" Alchemist and I said in unison. "To get into a party?" Al and I looked at each other. "I'm ready to bounce, man," Al said. "They're trying to play us."

The lady came back after a few more minutes with another offer. "It's really overcrowded in there and we only have room for you guys in the VIP section," she said. "So I can let you in but you have to buy at least two bottles. That's only eight hundred, come on. I know you've got that."

"Man, fuck this lame party," Al said. "Let's go."

We jumped in our rides and rolled out with my Suburban leading the pack, JM's Benz behind me, and the black Hummer behind him. A few blocks away, I got a call on my cell from JM. "Yo, the D's just pulled me over," he said.

"Word? You're clean, right?" I asked.

"Yeah, we good," he said. "Ain't nothing in here."

"Okay, well, call me back when they let you go," I said. "We're gonna stop to get some food." Alchemist wanted to stop at Pop Burger in the Meatpacking District. I stood outside with Twin, Godfather, and Nitty to smoke a cigarette while Al ordered.

"Yo, the D's cut right in front of me to pull JM over," Twin said. "He doesn't have anything in the car, does he?"

"No, he said he's clean," I said. "They cut in front of you to pull him over? That's strange." Alchemist came out with the food bags and the two of us hopped back into my truck heading toward his apartment. I called JM to see if he was okay.

"We good, son. They're letting us go now," JM said. "Where ya'll at?" I told him to meet us at Al's apartment.

Alchemist and I stopped at a red light directly across the street from his building on Thirtieth Street and Ninth Avenue. While waiting for the light to change, I spotted an empty parking spot diagonally across the street from us in the middle of the block next to Al's building, which was like winning the lotto in Manhattan. So when the light turned green, I made an illegal U-turn up Ninth Avenue and backed into the spot. Just as I was about to parallel park, a yellow cab with a 6Y tag at the top and a red flashing police light on the dashboard pulled in front of my truck. *Damn. The gun squad!* They must have been behind me at the red light, following us for some time.

The squad was only after guns. They didn't care if you had weed, crack, dope, or any drugs as long as they didn't find a gun. I knew I was going to get locked up. *Fuck it*, I thought, *I'll beat this with illegal search.*

Two D's hopped out of the cab, one approaching my side and the other on Alchemist's side. "Turn the vehicle off and put your hands in the air!" I turned off the engine and complied. Another unmarked car pulled up behind us. "Driver! Roll down your window!" Bulletproof windows only rolled down four inches, enough to pay tolls and talk through. I rolled the window down as far as it went.

"The window doesn't come down any further because the truck is bulletproof," I told the cop.

"Unlock the door and step out of the vehicle!"

"I have to take off my seat belt first," I said. I didn't want them to think I was reaching for a weapon. I stepped out of the truck. The cop tried to open the door for me, a shocked look crossing on his face when he felt the weight of the heavy door. Alchemist got out too.

"Do you have any weapons on you or in the car?" the cop asked.

"No," I replied. They frisked us, ordering that we sit on the back bumper as they began searching my truck without permission. Two more plainclothes detectives stepped out of an unmarked black car behind my truck. JM and Rome pulled up in the Benz looking at us, shaking their heads. JM parked and walked up next to us on the sidewalk. I was waiting for the moment the D's would find the gun. *Any second now. . . .* "10-11!" One of them yelled from inside the truck, their code for "We found a gun!"

"Stand up, turn around, and put your hands behind your back," the two D's from the second unmarked car said, slapping on cuffs and searching us again, rougher this time. "Yo, look across the street," JM said. I saw a third unmarked car parked with D's sitting low in the seats, watching. "Those are the D's that just pulled me over a little while ago," JM said.

"Call my lady and tell her to call my lawyer," I told JM. "Call her now, son. Good lookin'."

"Keep it moving!" the D's told JM and Rome. "Walk up the block." They threw Alchemist and me in the yellow cab and brought us to the Midtown South precinct on Thirty-fifth Street between Eighth and Ninth avenues, locking us in separate holding cells for the long hours of waiting.

While sitting in my cell, one of the arresting officers brought my bag of food from Pop Burger and my pack of Newports. "You're not supposed to smoke, but I'm hooking you up," the detective told me. "You didn't get it from me." A celebrity bust is a big deal for police; it might give them a nice promotion. Uniformed officers came to my cell asking for autographs and pictures on their camera phones.

"Yo, Alchemist!" I yelled through the cell bars after about an hour. "Happy birthday!"

"Good lookin'!" Al yelled back from a distance. "You're a funny muthafucker!"

The arresting officers pulled me out of my cell into an interrogation room. "Look, we know the gun belongs to one of you so just tell us. Whose gun is it?"

"I don't know about no gun," I said. "We do music, we don't use guns."

"Listen, we're willing to work with you. We'll forget about the gun and rip up the sheet if you're willing to give us information. Do you know any drug dealers or criminals that you can help us bust? Any information at all." Ha! Those D's were some real clowns. They continued, "To tell you the truth, we just want information on 50 Cent. Does he buy drugs or guns? Maybe you could help us set up a buy and a bust. Will he buy some drugs off you?"

I took a deliberate deep breath and exhaled hard, putting my head in my hands to give them the impression that I was thinking about working with them. "Can I get a cigarette?" I asked. They fumbled in their pockets to find me a smoke. "Between us, maybe you can drop a gun in 50's car and help us get him," one of the officers said. "Maybe some drugs. Does he let you get in any of his cars? You and your friend are gonna get a lot of time, man. We're trying to help you get out of this situation. Nobody will ever find out that you helped us."

Those crooked muthafuckers wanted me to plant a gun in 50's car! I smoked the cigarette fast and asked for another. "So what's it gonna be?" one of the officers said. "I'll rip up the arrest sheet right now and we can act like this gun of yours never happened." He told his partner, "Go grab the sheet." His partner came back with the sheet. "Take it or leave it. What's it gonna be?"

"Nah, if I gotta do time, then so be it," I said, finishing my second cigarette. "I'm not a rat."

Back in my cell, I went to sleep on the hard wood bench wondering if they were putting Alchemist through the same thing. About an hour later, two different detectives took me back to the same room and tried the same bullshit, staring at me with hateful eyes. "You know what, you fucking bastards make all this money while we make crumbs and our white women turn into groupies going to your shows and hotels," one detective said, his tone sounding like he wanted to hang me on a tree branch. "I fucking hate that black rap bullshit."

"I know what you mean, Officer," I said. "It's crazy because not too long ago, we did a concert at Madison Square Garden and I saw Nicole Kidman in the front row going crazy to our music. She loves rap." The officer's face turned bloodred.

"Take this motherfucker back to his cell!" he ordered his partner. "Get him out of my face!"

I lit my last cigarette in my cell and stood on the bench scribbling on the ceiling with my lighter—Mobb Deep, G-Unit, Infamous, H.N.I.C. Pt.

2—taking advantage of the time and free advertising space. An hour or two later, the arresting officers took me upstairs into a conference room where a handful of agents were seated around a table all wearing blue nylon jackets with the letters ATF printed on the back in yellow. "Why don't we just do this, you write a statement and admit the gun is yours so we can send your friend Alan home," one of the agents said, meaning Alchemist, pushing a legal pad and pen toward me. I took the pad and pen and started writing.

I slid the pad over to the ATF agent, who read it and then slammed the pad down and said, "Put him back in the cell!" Ha! The vague statement didn't offer any of the information they were looking for. They took me to a different holding cell with Alchemist. I asked Al if he stuck to the script and he confirmed that he did. I asked if the D's were trying to get him to plant evidence on 50 and he said no, they just wanted him to confess that the gun was mine and not his. But Al kept telling them, "I don't know about any gun."

A transport van brought us to 100 Centre Street, the Tombs. Later that afternoon, the judge let Alchemist, who didn't have a criminal history, out with no bail and hit me with fifty thousand dollars' bail. My lawyer, Irv Cohen, negotiated my bail down to seven thousand and 50 Cent put up the money. At around five P.M., Alchemist and I walked out of central booking and went straight to the G-Unit office so I could tell 50 how the gun squad and ATF were trying to set him up. 50 was already highly aware of how crooked law enforcement could be. "My nigga, be careful about who you let inside your cars, office, house, hotel rooms," I told 50 in the conference room after detailing what happened. "These police niggas are trying to set you up for real."

The D's confiscated my bulletproof truck because of a New York State law that says if you're caught with guns or drugs in a vehicle that's in your name, if convicted, the state keeps your vehicle and auctions it off. I pleaded not guilty and was taking the case to trial, so I had to wait for the outcome of the trial to find out the fate of my truck. So I was back in my Porsche. I rode to a studio in an old warehouse in Bushwick, Brooklyn, to listen to beats by a production duo known as Sid Roams who Twin had been working with.

Voxonic had agreed to my terms in the contract and we were close to finalizing the deal. The owners of Vox—F.D. was in his late sixties and his son R.E. was a few years older than me—had their main office in a ten-million-dollar brownstone that F.D. owned on Sixty-second Street and Lexington Avenue, down the block from my old high school, Art and Design. Voxonic had just inked a deal with Ky-Mani Marley, one of Bob Marley's sons, who starred in the Jamaican underground cult-classic movie *Shottas*. Ky-Mani's album was a month away from being released, so the office was filled with his promotional items. They were planning for him to tour with Van Halen.

The new year, 2007, came around and my trial was set to begin at the end of February. My little cousin JM was in Laurelton, Queens, taking over the streets with purple haze weed. JM knew somebody who had a hundred thousand dollars in counterfeit cash, the best fake money I'd ever seen. "You're making a lot of money with the smoke," I told him. "Don't start fucking around with that fake money. That's a federal charge."

"Nah, I'm not trying to get into that," JM assured me. "My man gave me ten stacks because he owed me a favor."

"Okay," I said. "Don't have the feds coming at you."

The next day, JM's moms, my aunt Janice, called saying that the D's ran up in their house and found five pounds of weed, two guns, and five thousand dollars in fake money and confiscated both of his drop-tops, the SL Benz and Pontiac Solstice. JM's mother's front door was knocked off the hinges, hanging by a few screws, when I went to visit him after he was bailed out. "The feds came to talk to me at the precinct," JM told me. "Because they found the five thousand in funny money. They asked me if I was getting the money from you!"

"What?" I said. "From me?"

"They wanted to know who had the master dye that created the money," JM explained. "They said, 'Who are you getting it from? Your cousin Prodigy out in New Jersey?'"

"How the hell do they know where I live?" I said. "They must have had our phones tapped. No wonder my phone has been ringing funny lately." What I was about to find out through my trial would confirm that my many years of paranoia were for good reason.

My lawyer, Irv Cohen, insisted that I wear a suit to my trial. I didn't own any suits, so I bought an affordable brown suit from the Men's Wearhouse. KiKi and I talked it over and decided not to bring the kids with us to court. I didn't lie to them about what was going on, I just didn't want them sitting through it.

The first day of trial at the Supreme Court at 100 Centre Street, the DA gave my lawyer and me an offer—five years if I pleaded guilty. I was facing a maximum of seven to fifteen years because of my extensive criminal history. My lawyer and I asked for a postponement to have more time to get the case together. The judge granted us three months. The new trial date was set for June.

At my lawyer's office in the Woolworth Building by Ground Zero a few days later, Irv introduced me to an older black gentleman with green eyes named Rodney. Rodney had been in the FBI for many years, the fourteenth black agent allowed into the bureau, and started his own private investigation company after retiring. Rodney and Irv had worked together on several cases. I explained, step-by-step, how my arrest took place, including how the same Hip Hop Task Force arrested me the night of the *Blood Money* party at the Roxy. Both Irv and Rodney seemed to have a hard time believing that such a task force existed.

I started working on *H.N.I.C. Pt. 2* and snapped into full rebel mode. *It's time to go the complete opposite direction of these other rappers,* I decided. *While they chase the luxurious life, I'm gonna focus on the people in the hood and real-life issues. Worldwide.* I decided that my album wouldn't be for radio or TV because rap music was created for us to enjoy in the hood. We didn't go to the mainstream, it came to us. Men lie, women lie, and money allows you to lie even easier, but poverty doesn't lie. And Mobb Deep represents poverty. My plan was to literally rage against the machine.

The first batch of songs I recorded with Sid Roams and Alchemist were "Veterans Memorial Pt. 2," "ABC," "The Life," "Young Veterans," "Test Tube Babies," and "Dirty New Yorker." I wanted to shoot a video for every song. I had a social networking site called HNIC2.com to help promote my album. With all the work I was cramming into every minute of every day, June zoomed around fast and it was about time for trial again.

I met with Irv and Rodney for an update and Rodney shared some interesting information that he'd discovered about the Hip Hop Task Force, which operated in conjunction with similar task forces in a few other states. Rodney had connected with the retired New York City detective who started the task force, Derrick Parker.

Derrick invited Rodney to his house to discuss the history of the task force and my case. Derrick explained how it all started when he was a regular uniformed officer from Mount Vernon with a lot of friends in the music industry including Puff Daddy and Heavy D. Derrick's superiors wanted to start doing music-industry surveillance, allowing him to pick his own team and design the task force, promising a promotion to detective if he agreed. So Derrick agreed.

He realized that all the intel his superiors ordered him to gather was inconsequential and frivolous. What they were doing was illegal, so Derrick opened a treasure-chest box and pulled out an entire file dedicated to Mobb Deep. Rodney flipped through tons of photos of us hanging out in Queensbridge and coming in and out of clubs and studios, cars, and other random locations. Derrick told Rodney that they had been doing surveillance on us since 1993. Derrick went on to tell Rodney that after the investigations of Puff, Nas, Tupac, Wu-Tang, and Mobb Deep, his superiors wanted him to expand the intel, putting further funding into the covert operation to follow more rappers—names, addresses, friends, enemies, families, hangouts, and more. Derrick Parker had enough. He quit and authored a book titled *Notorious C.O.P.*, exposing the wrong that was taking place.

As Rodney explained all this incredible information to Irv and me, my thoughts drifted off for a moment. *This shit reminds me of COINTELPRO and the Black Panthers. I always suspected we were being monitored but this is more serious than I thought.*

Rodney told us Derrick Parker had agreed to testify on the stand at my trial about how the task force uses illegal searches to make gun arrests. Derrick knew this all too well because he created that tactic.

Alchemist was my only witness to the illegal search and also agreed to testify at a hearing to suppress the gun evidence. The D's didn't have my permission or a search warrant to go into the box where the gun was located, so the judge would have to toss the evidence out. To make our case stronger, Rodney was trying to link the D's who arrested us to the Hip Hop Task Force.

Alchemist told the whole story from when the D's followed us from the club to when the other D's in the 6Y yellow cab illegally searched my truck. The DA quickly objected to the "followed us from the club" part and the judge agreed that that part wasn't relevant to the case. The judge only wanted to know about what happened from the moment of my illegal U-turn up until the D's found the gun. My lawyer Irv tried to tell the judge that the entire story was relevant but the judge wasn't trying to hear it. After Alchemist, they called one of the D's, the one who brought the food and cigarettes to my cell that night, to the stand. The judge ruled that the gun evidence could come in at trial.

On September 19, Havoc had an album-release party for the solo album he'd been quietly working on, *The Kush*, at SOB's in downtown Manhattan by the Holland Tunnel. Hot 97 promoted the event. About twenty of us rolled that night, so I wasn't concerned with bringing guns but brought a little knife with a razor for a blade. I loved that little thing—it was small, but it could cause severe damage.

At SOB's, after talking with rapper Jeru the Damaja, who had a few underground hits in the early nineties but had since disappeared from the scene, we went downstairs to the dressing room until DJ Premier announced his new group NYG'z.

"Before NYG'z get onstage, we've got a special guest who just walked in and asked to perform," Premier said. "Saigon! Come up to the stage!" We all looked at each other at the same time and said, *"Saigon?"*

"Fuck that, let's go fuck this nigga up," Havoc said. "Come on." Ten of us stayed in the crowd and ten went up onstage and surrounded Saigon, who was with two of his boys and one bodyguard, from behind. I opened the knife and held it concealed in my jacket pocket. I got a good look at all the video cameras in the crowd and I thought to myself, *Don't do anything that's gonna incriminate you on camera. Remember, you're on trial.*

Saigon was caught up in his performance and didn't realize we were behind him. Havoc, tipsy, was about to pounce on Saigon, but as Hav stepped forward to snuff him, I grabbed Hav. "Chill, son. Not like this," I said. "Let everybody else get him." Then Hav walked up to Saigon while he was rapping and said something in his ear while the music kept playing. Saigon stopped rapping, had a quick conversation with Hav, then they gave each other a pound and hug and I overheard Saigon say, "I love ya'll niggas, man!"

As soon as Saigon put the mic down to walk offstage, our boy Tyson grabbed him by the back of his shirt and pushed him into Un Pacino, Nyce, and Wop by the stage exit. They beat Saigon and kicked him under the DJ table, where he hid for a moment before climbing up to hide behind his bodyguard. Peeking his head out from behind the bodyguard, he saw me standing there looking for him, then he reached out and threw a punch at me. I leaned back and caught the tail end of the punch to the side of my head, knocking my fitted hat off; then he threw another swing with the same hand and missed me. As I was leaning back to avoid that last swing one of his boys tried to clothesline me but hit my left shoulder, knocking me to the ground. Then he jumped off the stage and ran out of the club leaving Saigon for dead. Luckily, I didn't stab myself with the open knife in my pocket. My man Fly chased the kid and beat him up bad outside.

Saigon hid in the corner behind his bodyguard as our crew launched bottles and glasses at him, hitting the wall just inches from his face. My boys had him and his bodyguard trapped in the corner now. Fearing for his life, Saigon's bodyguard gave him a piggyback ride, jumping off the stage wearing Saigon like a backpack. With fifteen of my niggas chasing them, they ran out of the club at top speed.

"You see, that's why black people never have nothing!" Havoc grabbed the mic and shouted. "Can't we all just get along?" Then I grabbed the other mic and shouted, "You see who just got beat up and ran outta here, right!? Ayo, DJ On Point, start the music!" While we performed "Shook Ones," Un Pacino, Nyce, Fly, and the crew were outside chasing Saigon through the streets as he ran into oncoming traffic, dodging speeding cars.

"Drop your jewelry and we'll stop chasing you!" Un Pacino shouted. "Drop your jewelry, nigga!" Saigon took his watch off and tossed it behind him. Saigon and his boys hopped into their car service and peeled off. I watched it all on our cameraman Jordan's footage after the show and told him to post it on YouTube immediately. Jordan wanted to edit out the part where I got punched and knocked down but I told him to just post up the entire thing. I didn't give a damn. Anybody can get hit. Shit, you can punch the president if you get close enough. It's all about what's going to happen to you after you do that dumb shit.

The next night, Havoc had another album-release party at another Manhattan club. My man Baja, a graphic artist, designed a flyer with a silhouette of a man running that read: RUN SAIGON, RUN! I had three thousand double-sided flyers printed at Kinko's to scatter throughout the streets of Manhattan before the party.

Smoking weed and drinking backstage, Tyson told me, "P, put the weed out, hurry up! Hurry up! The D's are coming in the dressing room. They wanna talk to you." Two detectives, one black, one white, walked in. "Where's Prodigy?" the black one asked.

"What's up, man?" I asked, standing up. "Is everything all right?"

"Listen, don't worry," he said. "I don't care if you're smoking back here. I came to talk to you about last night. We know what happened and we don't care if you guys beat people up and fight and all that. We just don't want your guys to start shooting people."

"Shooting? No, we don't get into all that," I said. "We just do music. We're just rappers."

"Yeah, yeah, okay," he said. "Seriously, this guy Saigon, is it over, or what? We don't want anything to happen to him."

"Yeah, we don't got problems with him," I said. "A little fight happened and that's that."

"All right, good luck with your court case," he said. "You guys have a good night." Whoa. It sounded like Saigon was working with the D's.

On November 2, 2007, I turned thirty-three. It was a monumental day for my woman, KiKi, and me because we flew to Los Angeles and decided to finally get married. Neither of us believed in European religions based on the Holy Bible, nor did we believe in their marriage rituals or ceremonies, but we decided to do it, mostly for legal reasons. We stayed at Alchemist's beachfront condo in Venice Beach for a couple of days. I called 40 Glocc and arranged to shoot some videos with a director, Ken X. On November 4, KiKi and I flew to Vegas to get married because it only took thirty minutes to get a marriage license there. We went to the Little White Chapel and performed the ceremony with 40 Glocc and my man African Rob as our witnesses. It felt great to be husband and wife. We'd had a roller-coaster relationship for thirteen years and agreed to leave our mistakes in the past and stay together. KiKi was a strong, loving woman to stay with me through it all, so she deserved all the respect in the world from me. We spent the night at the Wynn Hotel & Casino and popped champagne.

Back in New York, it was time for the jury selection. The DA was a young Italian man and his assistant was an Asian man, both in their early thirties. The jurors who they brought in to select from were 95 percent white, only four blacks, and all four told the judge that they couldn't make a proper decision because they claimed to have had family who were hurt by gun violence. Most of the time when jurors say that to a judge, they're just trying to get out of doing jury duty.

Blacks and Latinos need our own people on juries to help decide the fate of our trials and for the trials to actually be fair. The four black jurors were relieved of their duties, and there were only whites left to select from. Irv and I had to base our selections on which ones we thought would not make a biased decision. I looked in their eyes, listened to them speak, and hoped we chose wisely.

The prosecution called the two detectives who arrested me. After swearing in with his hand on the Bible, the second detective began. His testimony was on point until he said, "And when we approached Mr. Johnson's vehicle, I saw a small nickel-plated gun in his hand. He was trying to put it away in the box so we wouldn't see it." I shot him a look like he was out of his mind. I knew I was going to lose the trial after that testimony.

Irv questioned both detectives about the other unmarked D's that pulled up seconds after them: How did they know to come to the location of my truck? "It was just a coincidence," the arresting D's responded. "They just so happened to be driving past and stopped to help us. We didn't call them." There was no way for us to prove that they were profiling, and I was in a bad position.

If I continued with the trial and left it up to the jury, whose side would they believe—Alchemist's or two New York City detectives', who claimed they saw a gun in my hand? The DA went into the hallway and rolled a TV and a DVD player into the courtroom, perhaps to play my "Mac 10 Handle" and *Infamous Allegiance* DVD for the jury to make me look like a menace to society. There were a lot of guns and violence in those videos.

Maybe it was a scare tactic, but it worked. Along with the lies from the detectives, I knew I couldn't win this one. We took a lunch break and the DA stepped to Irv and offered him a new deal—three and a half years in prison, as opposed to the original five years, but only if I accepted the offer within twenty-four hours.

Staring out at the Hudson River and Giants Stadium that night in my backyard, I contemplated my next move. *Do you want to see your kids when they're in their twenties or in three years?* I asked myself. *Do you want to come back in three short years and still have a career or be gone for so long that your music doesn't matter to the world anymore?* I called my moms, brother, Havoc, 50, and a gang of others to see how they felt about my choices. They all wanted me to fight. I felt like an asshole for not listening to 50 when he told me to put surveillance cameras in my truck. That footage would have proved everything.

I had beaten many cases and avoided prison by the skin of my teeth for many years. *You can't win 'em all,* I told myself. *Take the three and a half years, come out smarter, stronger, and better than ever.*

Then came the hard part. I had to go into the house and explain to my kids what was about to happen. Most parents might hide that from their eleven-year-old son and nine-year-old daughter, but I gave my kids the real, all the time.

I told my son first. "But you're not a bad person," Shaka said, dropping tears. "You just carry a gun for protection. You don't run around hurting people."

"Yeah, but that gun was illegal," I said. "I broke the law by having an illegal gun in my truck. I should have gotten a gun license or a bodyguard, but I didn't. So now I have to pay for my mistakes." Shaka understood clearly but he couldn't hold back the tears. I was proud of him for being strong. "Three years goes by fast, kid. Remember when we were together on tour with 50 and Eminem? Well, in two months that will be three years ago. See how fast that went? It seems like yesterday, doesn't it?" He agreed.

We both went into my bedroom and I explained the same to my daughter, Tasia. Tasia took it well also. I don't even think she cried. Maybe while I wasn't looking. After breaking the news to my little ones, I confirmed my decision with my lawyer Irv and got right down to business. If I was going to prison for three and a half years, I needed to leave enough product in the streets to keep my name alive until I got back. I hadn't even signed the deal with Voxonic yet. R.E. from Voxonic came to the trial the next morning and was supportive.

I walked into court that morning with my wife KiKi, R.E., and Irv. Our plan was to accept the three-and-a-half-year deal by pleading guilty and to ask the judge for another three-month extension on sentencing so I could work on my health, finish my album, and do a promo tour before doing my time. The judge granted the three months.

Time was limited so I started knocking songs and videos out fast, planning the promo tour and filming myself every day and loading up HNIC2 .com with footage until the day I started my sentence. I was racing the clock like a madman.

Jerry LaMothe, the writer and director of *Blackout*, called inviting me to the movie premiere on West Twenty-third Street in Manhattan. I brought KiKi, Draws, Sam Scarfo, and Scientific. The theater was packed with press, celebrities, and movie-industry people. After the premiere, Quincy Jones's son QD3 called asking me to star in a new documentary about rappers and guns that he was filming. Then Alchemist got a call about using a song from *H.N.I.C. Pt. 2* for the popular video game Grand Theft Auto. We decided to give them "Dirty New Yorker." Peter Kuys, the distributor and manufacturer for Voxonic, told me that the MP3 player company Sansa wanted me to promote their new MP3 device in exchange for two hundred thousand dollars in marketing and promotion of *H.N.I.C. Pt. 2*. My head was spinning. My plate was full of things to accomplish in a limited amount of time.

After a quick East Coast promo tour, my last performance before turning myself in was at B.B. King Blues Club in Times Square. KiKi and I arrived early to knock out a bunch of press interviews before the show. Backstage, my guests started arriving: Twin, Godfather, Ty-Nitty, Gotti, Chinky, Tyson, Un Pacino, Mazarati Fox—even Bars'N'Hooks popped up, I hadn't seen them in years—Cormega, Noyd, a bunch of 50's boys from G-Unit. The club was packed. The only people missing were Havoc and my man Fly, who eventually showed up twenty minutes before showtime.

After performing a bunch of *H.N.I.C. Pt. 2* songs, Havoc, drunk and tired of waiting, got on the mic and demanded that we do our Mobb Deep songs. I wasn't planning to do Mobb's songs until after my solo set. But once again I didn't want it to look like Havoc and I weren't on the same page because that's a sign of weakness. So I decided to go with the flow.

The show sequence was a little sloppy, but we still killed it. The entire performance was professionally filmed so I could release it on DVD. It was an emotional night for me, even though I didn't show it on my face. KiKi and I got home and I felt like the world was off my back. I was ready to get the time ahead of me over with so I could come back to my family and the world as a brand-new man.

50 came to my crib that weekend for the first time. We weren't expecting him. The kids were excited to see him. We showed him around our place and he told me not to stress and asked me if I could help him write a screenplay for one of his G-Unit books titled *Ski Mask Way*. *Murda Muzik* was one of 50's favorite hood films and he always complimented me on the way I wrote the story. Then we spoke about how Havoc and I had recently found out that Bob Perry from Koch Records was illegally selling Mobb Deep music on the Internet and in stores. Bob put out an album, *Infamous Archives*, without our permission and we were planning on suing him. 50 agreed to back us and make sure we had a strong case.

The day had come, February 29, 2008, and it was time for my sentencing hearing. KiKi and I woke up early. I planned ahead and found out what I was allowed to wear in Rikers Island. I wore a dark-gray sweat suit, a dark-gray skully, two fresh white T-shirts, two pairs of socks, black shell-toe Adidas, and thermal underwear so I wouldn't be cold. I cut tiny holes in the cuffs and bottom elastic of the sweatshirt, stuffing as many little morphine pills as possible inside the holes just in case I got sick. I wasn't trying to suffer from pain inside a prison cage. KiKi filmed me on the drive to the Manhattan Supreme Court, one last piece of footage for HNIC2.com before I went in.

When we arrived at court, all my boys were waiting out front— Alchemist, Havoc, Un Pacino, Tyson, Gotti, Chinky, Nyce, Fly, R.E., and a few others. Press cameras snapped pictures as we walked toward the courthouse entrance. "Good luck, Prodigy!" a white cameraman yelled out. "Take care of yourself, we'll see you when you get home!"

The crew walked inside and took the elevator to the courtroom on the fourteenth floor. Irv was waiting in the hallway. "You ready, kid?" he asked.

"Yeah, let's get this shit over with," I said. I gave KiKi one last kiss and hug, then walked into the courtroom.

The court clerk called my name. I walked to the defendant table to be sentenced by the judge. The court officers cuffed my wrists and led me to a back room. I turned around to get one last look at my wife KiKi, sadness spread across her face.

October 3, 2009
Mid-State Correctional Facility
Marcy, New York / 9:00 A.M.

Taking an early-morning spin around the pebble-lined yard before my daily workout routine was my favorite thing to do in prison. It was my escape from the trivial inmate conversations and annoying noise and chatter that constantly came out of the COs' walkie-talkies. It was peaceful—dirt and pebbles crunching under my sneakers as I walked at a calm pace, the leaves of tall trees rustling in the wind, birds chirping, and my inner voice reminding me how lucky I was to have had so many chances to get my life together. *You better know that after this, your chances are done. If you don't get out there and stick to the script, the rest of your life will be nothing but pain, sorrow, and regret,* I told myself.

As I strolled around the dusty path, I kept thinking about this book *Evolution of a Revolutionary,* an autobiography of Tupac's mom, Afeni Shakur, written by Jasmine Guy. Afeni said something in that book that made me realize why I kept fucking up even though I was trying to live righteous all those years. She explained that the Black Panther Party, which she had been a part of, had overwhelming power mentally and physically—some of the smartest, toughest brothers and sisters ever. They created an incredible amount of positive change in black communities worldwide, even inspiring other oppressed races to stand up and fight for equality. But the Panthers' lack of spiritual power or God in their movement was a major reason behind their downfall. Afeni didn't say it like that exactly, but that's exactly what she meant, and I could relate 100 percent. I had the mental and physical strength to do a lot of good things in life and had a lot of real good success. But I didn't have the spiritual power of God that it takes to do great things.

Ever since I was a teenager, I'd tell people, "I'm a spiritual person but I don't believe in God." I was too young-minded to realize that that was a hypocritical statement. See, I always looked at things from a scientific point of view, so believing something to be true didn't mean it's actually the truth. But when you know something is true, then you're sure and it's a fact. In other words, I didn't want faith in God, I wanted God in fact. I was looking for God all over the place. In my prayers when I was young, in the hospital when I was in tremendous pain, in books, up in the sky, and in my questions to my father.

"Is there a God?" I asked Pops.

"Yes," he answered.

"How do you know that God is real?"

"I've seen God before," he said.

"If you've seen God, then what did God look like?"

"God looks like water."

"Water?"

"Yeah," Pops said. "God looks like water."

God is everywhere and everything. Once I officially acknowledged that God always has been, and always will be in my life, it gave me the power to handle any situation. It put my anger in check and taught me to approach problems as lessons. Nothing is a challenge to me anymore, just an experience. I don't compete anymore, I just create. There's no such thing as opposition, just nature at work.

H.N.I.C. Pt. 2 was released on April 22, 2008, about two months after I went in. It was a commercial failure, selling just over sixty thousand units. To be honest, I wasn't upset, because the main reason I released the album was for my family to have the advance salary and mortgage-payment money while I was in prison. I was aware that that company wasn't capable of pushing my album to its maximum sales potential without me being able to properly promote it. It had nothing to do with the economy, changing trends in the music industry, or my ability to create quality songs. Vox didn't know what to do without me, so they dropped the ball.

About nine months into my bid, Voxonic was so furious that they had to pay my wife ten thousand dollars a month after I'd gotten locked up that they stopped paying her and answering her calls. Wow. They're the ones who agreed to my terms. But I put that album and company out of my mind and focused on the songs I was creating now.

The only things that really matter in life are the things that need to be taken care of right now. As a matter of fact, these are the most important words of wisdom in this book: Yesterday's gone and tomorrow doesn't count unless you take care of your priorities right now.

50 Cent had come to visit me soon after New Year's 2009. He came alone. The whole prison was talking about his visit. In the visitors' room, the COs had to tell inmates and their visitors to fall back and stop asking for autographs. We spoke for an hour and a half about his film company, Cheetah Vision, and the movie he wrote for his album *Before I Self Destruct*. He said he named the character who's his little brother in the film after my son Shaka. 50 had FedExed Shaka a thousand dollars cash as a Christmas gift. Shaka was thirteen and a full-blown skateboarder who wanted to go pro. So he bought a bunch of skate gear with his gift money.

50 told me he was looking forward to my return so we could get started on the next Mobb Deep album. It was a great visit.

"Johnson!" a CO woke me up at around eleven A.M. on a Saturday just after the 2010 New Year and announced, "Visit."

When I arrived at the visiting building, a big smile spread across my face when I saw Havoc sitting alone, sipping on a cup of coffee. *Wow, finally, he came!*

"Yo, forgive me for not visiting and writing you back like I should," Hav said after a handshake and a hug. "There's no excuse for it, man."

"Listen, I just want to communicate more so we can continue to be successful with Mobb Deep," I said. "I can't lie, I sit in my cell mad as hell at you wondering why you don't want to talk. But no matter how mad I get, I always come to the same conclusion—Mobb Deep is more important than both of our personal feelings toward each other. We still have a business to run."

"Nah, it's not like that," Hav said. "You know I love you like my own brother. I just have a hard time writing letters and there's no excuse why I don't visit more."

"Hav, I know you're mad at me for getting locked up and messing up our money flow and I apologize for that," I said. "You used to tell me all the time to stop carrying guns and getting into trouble."

"Man, I used to be scared getting into a car with you 'cause you always had a gun," Hav said.

"I'm done with all that now. Man, I've written seven albums in here so far. I've been wanting to talk with you about music and our plans."

"Yo, the industry is real different now. Even big-time R&B artists are only selling a few hundred thousand units," Hav said. "It's tough."

"Rap music's still selling millions of copies," I reminded Hav. "Just look at Lil Wayne, Jay-Z, T.I., and Eminem. We just have to make incredible music. Not just 'Oh, that's hard-core,' but 'Yo, that's *incredible.*' We can't allow industry sales to fuck with our confidence. Don't ever forget that Mobb Deep is something special. All we have to do is keep it going. Yo, you should visit Lil Wayne while he's in Rikers. Wayne and I have been writing each other letters recently. That nigga loves us, man. He's a good dude. I saw him in Manhattan before I turned myself in and he told me he wanted beats from you. Even Alchemist got a beat on *The Carter 3*. You should have been on that album."

"A'ight, I'm gonna try to get over there. Did you hear the beat I did on 50's new album?" Hav asked.

"Yeah, that shit is hard. I like it. I heard you got something on Eminem and Kanye's new albums. Don't slow down. You need to do more production for other artists. People love your beats, man." Havoc just wasn't good at networking in the business world. Why a person would want to turn down so much money, opportunity, and great relationships is beyond me. I'll never understand Havoc. He's a mystery. Probably the eighth wonder of the world. But I still love him.

"You know me, P, I don't like being around people," Havoc said. "I don't hang out at the G-Unit office because I'm not good with that networking shit, that's what you do. Do you think 50 wants to release another Mobb Deep album? There's a rumor on the Internet saying he dropped us from the label."

"That's just a rumor. We just have to do our part and create great music like we always do."

"Yo, I haven't drank alcohol in two years," Hav said. "Today actually makes two years."

"Wow, keep it up, man." I was really proud of him. "We gotta be more focused than ever before. You know how many people want to see us fall off? If it's hard for artists to sell units right now, well, that's too bad for them. We're in a class of our own. That attitude brought us this far. The moment that you forget that, you're finished. And then I'm gonna be forced to keep it moving on you. Ha!" Havoc laughed, but he knew I was serious.

"See, that's the motivation I've been missing since you've been away," Hav said. "You got me hype now. I was a little nervous about coming up here for this visit. I couldn't even sleep last night. That's why I'm drinking all of this coffee. I had like three cups already."

"Nigga, this is how we feed our families. The bottom line for me was always our business and our music," I said.

"I know," Hav said.

Another thirty minutes passed and we said our good-byes. I told Hav to make sure he sent me beats and he said he would.

In my cell, I sat on my paper-thin mattress thinking about how far Havoc and I had come, all the songs we wrote and recorded, all those beats, tours, parties, after-parties, groupies, videos, interviews, contracts, labels, lawyers, and offices. All the money we'd made, spent, shared, wasted, and given away to so-called friends. Prison gave me plenty of time to reflect. In the street, I didn't think. I just did.

After Havoc's visit, my spirit was at ease. I thought about how other people could inspire you to feel and do better. Havoc inspired me to allow forgiveness. Nas inspired me to prove people wrong. He told Twin I was corny back when I battled him and I'd forgiven him a few times. Hopefully he could do the same for me. Even Jay-Z was a huge inspiration in my life as far as how he carried himself and conducted business. The problems we all had were just petty street bravado. We are a special breed of black men: New York rappers with a gift. We reach millions of people around the world who talk, dress, and act like us.

I'm sure there will be plenty of newcomers filling our shoes when we have officially played out. I wish everybody wellness, love, peace, and happiness. And I laugh at anybody who thinks there's something soft about that. Ha! You've got a lot of growing up to do. I went through the same thing.

ACKNOWLEDGMENTS

A great number of people inspired me to write this book directly as well as indirectly, from my family and friends to people I look up to who don't even know me. I appreciate them all and hope that they too will find some type of inspiration within these pages, my life, and my music. This body of work, along with other goals I've reached, was accomplished while keeping all of them in mind and with their assistance, though they may not even know it. I want to show my sincere appreciation for those who helped make this book possible, so I must pay my respect forward:

The Creator and life force that most know as God—without the grace and power of God nothing would be; my loving mother for teaching me about love, peace, and happiness and for being patient through my juvenile BS as a young kid; my brother, Greg, for being a true big bro, always taking care of me and making me laugh, even in times when I was in tremendous pain and it hurt to do so; and my niece Kenisha and nephew Kenny; my nana, Ms. Bernie Johnson, who would have proudly displayed this book on her coffee table along with her collection of *Jet* magazines; my father, "Lil' Budd," for teaching me about mental and physical strength and fearlessness; my grandfather "Big Budd" for teaching me about discipline, hard work, and determination through the example with his own successful music career; my grandmother, the no-nonsense Bernice "H.N.I.C." Johnson, who schooled me consistently on business, an entrepreneurial way of thinking, money management, and being proud of my black culture—her name and legacy will live forever; Uncle Lenny and Aunt Connie, both of whom have bailed me out and given me shelter in times of need and that little bit of cushion to absorb my hard falls; Ms. Cookie, my wife's mother, for accepting me into the family.

My friend "the Boss" 50 Cent and his staff at G-Unit for opening up several new doors of opportunity for me and introducing me to Dr. Michael Diamond, who is now my nutritionist. It was Dr. Diamond who made the proper connections for me to become a published author. Thanks to my literary agent, the one and only David Vigliano, as well as Michael Harriott for his help in the early stages, David Peak and Laura Checkoway, my new partner in scribe. Without her expert knowledge, wisdom, and understanding of Mobb Deep, Prodigy, and the unique culture of hip hop, this autobiography would not have been turned in and released to the world on time. This gracious young woman has gone the extra hundred miles because she knows the importance of this story. Laura has taught me a lot about this craft. Also, Laura's team—Abby Addis, Shauna Barbosa, and John Pegg III—for their contributions; John Bocelli, Peter Kuys and wife, Mrs. Jay Kuys; the entire Simon & Schuster/Touchstone staff, publisher Stacy Creamer, editor-in-chief Trish Todd, associate publisher David Falk, marketing manager Meredith Kernan, my publicist Shida Carr, and especially my editor Sulay Hernandez, for realizing the value within my life story and helping this book actually get into readers' hands.

My brother from another mother, the Don from Way Beyond—

Havoc—and all his crimies for choosing me as a friend and partner instead of a larceny victim when we first met. Ha! Otherwise, the world would have never had Mobb Deep. We balance each other out like yin and yang. Our life is a never-ending studio session and as always, we'll make the best out of it. And with thanks to Havoc's mother, Ms. Mercedes: This beautiful woman took me in as a son and put up with our loud noise as we were mastering our art; RIP Ms. Iesha, Steve Rifkind, and Matty C, all I can say is, Wow, I love those guys; Chris Lighty, for all his assistance and his calm, levelheaded approach to business from which I learned a great deal; my West Coast family Alchemist, Ice-T, Neil Diamonds, Evidence, Sid Roams, Block, Big Bad 40, and African Rob. These brothers held me down when I had no one else to turn to. Can't forget Marvis Johnson, Sam Scarfo, Fly, Jake One, Kerri Edge and the Edge Family, Roger Jeffrey and the Jeffrey family, Bones Malone, Chris Blackwell, Cookie Gonzales, Barry Weiss, Lord Nez, T-Dubbs (Tyson), Un Pacino, S.C., and King Benny; my attorneys Irv Cohen, Bob Kalina, Jack Reynolds, Londell McMillan, and Evan Friefeld for their advice, time, and consideration; my accountant Arty Erk for all of the tough love he's given Mobb Deep when it comes to our finances; Dan the Man Melamid, Stretch Armstrong and Bobbito, Peter Oasis, Domingo Neris; Loud staff: Puerto Rican Rob Hernandez, Chef Lowe, Gaby Acevedo and Nelson Taboada, Dan Tanna, Chris Green, Ola Kudu, Schott Free, Buda Lugo, Frank V, O.J. Wedlaw, and the Loud Street Team East to West, Come Chantrel, Judd Gueverra, Kirk Harding, Erika Elliott, Teresa Sanders, Chris Mack, Seth Abrams, Sean C, Liz Hausle, Rich Isaacson, Jon Rifkind, Geo Bivins, Girard Hunt, Jeff Swierk, Geordan Reisner, Noa Ochi, Aikio Tucker, Che Harris, Randy Roberts, Sanchez Stanfield, Brandon Finley, and Shane Mooney; Violator staff: Ice Younossi, Mike Lighty, Laurie Dobbins, and Claudine Joseph; G-Unit staff: Rene Castillo, Jeremy Bettis, Nikki Martin, Alvon Miller, Chris "Broadway" Romero, and Whoo Kid.

All the radio stations across the country and overseas that supported us throughout the years. Special shout to Tim Westwood, Mark Wahlberg, Adrien Brody, Jamie Foxx, Rick Gonzalez, Hassan Johnson, and Nicole Kidman. Thanks for appreciating Mobb Deep's music. The journalists, photographers and video directors who have captured memorable Mobb Deep moments through the years. All the concert promoters around the world.

I wanna give a special thank-you to all the supporters, fanatics, and straight hip hop junkies. Without you, there is no reason to do what I do.

Representation:

Management
Micro Management Group
E-Mail: Info@Micromanagementgroup.com
Phone: (347) 850-4311
Website: www.micromanagementgroup.com

Booking Agent (Shows, Appearances, Speaking Engagements)
Agency Name: A-List Talent Agency
Direct Phone: (646) 235-4302
E-Mail: Ice@A-Listagency.com

ABOUT THE AUTHOR

As one-half of the hip hop phenomenon Mobb Deep, Albert "Prodigy" Johnson sold millions of albums, performed throughout the world, and recorded with the elite of hip hop, R&B, and rock with his signature style of hard-core, reality-based music. Born with the hereditary disease sickle cell anemia, Prodigy battled with pain for his entire life and promoted the importance of a healthy diet, spiritual enrichment, and a positive, productive lifestyle. He lost his battle with sickle cell anemia in 2017.

ABOUT THE EDITOR

Hip hop has taken writer Laura Checkoway around the world. The former senior editor of *Vibe* magazine, she has penned revealing celebrity profiles and investigative features for numerous publications. As a documentary filmmaker, Checkoway continues to share stories that impact, haunt, and last. She lives in Brooklyn, New York.

SCDAA

"Break The Sickle Cycle"®

"Over 100,000 reasons to speak up about Sickle Cell Disease . . ."

There are thousands of people whose lives are affected by the pain and devastation of sickle cell disease. The cycle will continue until a cure is found for this inherited red blood cell disorder, which too few of us know much about.

In the United States today, approximately 100,000 Americans have sickle cell and more than 2,000 babies are born with the disease every year. Globally more than 300,000 babies are born with the disease every year. Sickle cell disease is most common in African Americans and those of Mediterranean, Middle Eastern, and Indian ancestry.

The Sickle Cell Disease Association of American, Inc. (SCDAA), provides universal leadership to create awareness of the impact sickle cell disease has on the health, economic, social, and educational well-being of the individual and their family and provides support through advocacy and programs.

Sickle cell disease is a global health issue!

Please join SCDAA and Prodigy in the "No Pain" Campaign. The "No Pain" Campaign will create national sickle cell disease awareness while raising needed funds for programs, services, and research.

We need you in the fight against this devastating disease. Help us to *Break The Sickle Cycle"!*

Please make your charitable donation online today by logging on to www .sicklecelldisease.org.

For more information about Sickle Cell Disease or to volunteer please contact us at:

Sickle Cell Disease Association of America, Inc. (SCDAA)
231 E. Baltimore Street
Suite 800
Baltimore, MD 21202
(410) 528-1555
(800) 421-8453 Toll Free